Critical Digital Literacies
as Social Praxis

Colin Lankshear and Michele Knobel
General Editors

Vol. 54

The New Literacies and Digital Epistemologies series
is part of the Peter Lang Education list.
Every volume is peer reviewed and meets
the highest quality standards for content and production.

PETER LANG
New York • Washington, D.C./Baltimore • Bern
Frankfurt • Berlin • Brussels • Vienna • Oxford

Critical Digital Literacies as Social Praxis

Intersections and Challenges

EDITED BY
JULIANNA ÁVILA & JESSICA ZACHER PANDYA

PETER LANG
New York • Washington, D.C./Baltimore • Bern
Frankfurt • Berlin • Brussels • Vienna • Oxford

Library of Congress Cataloging-in-Publication Data

Critical digital literacies as social praxis: intersections and challenges /
edited by JuliAnna Ávila, Jessica Zacher Pandya.
p. cm. — (New literacies and digital epistemologies; v. 54)
Includes bibliographical references.
1. Educational technology—Social aspects. 2. Digital communications—
Social aspects. 3. Computer literacy—Social aspects.
I. Ávila, JuliAnna. II. Pandya, Jessica Zacher.
LB1028.3.C755   371.33'4—dc23   2012029664
ISBN 978-1-4331-1694-0 (hardcover)
ISBN 978-1-4331-1693-3 (paperback)
ISBN 978-1-4539-0912-6 (e-book)
ISSN 1523-9543

Bibliographic information published by **Die Deutsche Nationalbibliothek**.
Die Deutsche Nationalbibliothek lists this publication in the "Deutsche
Nationalbibliografie"; detailed bibliographic data is available
on the Internet at http://dnb.d-nb.de/.

The paper in this book meets the guidelines for permanence and durability
of the Committee on Production Guidelines for Book Longevity
of the Council of Library Resources.

© 2013 Peter Lang Publishing, Inc., New York
29 Broadway, 18th floor, New York, NY 10006
www.peterlang.com

Printed in the United States of America

Contents

Part 2. Teacher Education and Critical Digital Literacies

Part 3. Resisting Dominant Narratives

CHAPTER ONE

Traveling, Textual Authority, AND Transformation

An Introduction to Critical Digital Literacies

JuliAnna Ávila & Jessica Zacher Pandya

There is no Frigate like a Book
To take us Lands away,
Nor any Coursers like a Page
Of prancing Poetry—
This Traverse may the poorest take
Without oppress of Toll—
How frugal is the Chariot
That bears a Human soul.

(Dickinson, 1961, pp. 267–268)

Somebody could drop you off in the middle of nowhere—you can't read you don't know where you at—you're going to get lost. That's power—reading and writing, you got to know that . . . it wouldn't be like I would be stranded not knowing how to read so I'm confident. (Micah, a participant in one of our studies)

We begin at an unusual place to embark on a journey into critical digital literacies: with Dickinson's poem. This particular poem contains the well-worn and canonical idea that literacy can "take us [to] Lands away," a romantic notion echoed in a more pragmatic fashion by Micah when he was asked about the purposes of literacy. Technology and digital literacies have made it possible to travel farther and faster than ever before, and we can communicate virtually with fellow travelers in real time; the human soul is now transported in virtual non-linear worlds. Additionally, digital literacies have changed who is considered literate and what counts as text. In this chapter, we use the familiar view of literacy as *traveling* to examine more novel implementations of critical and digital literacies, and to explore ramifications for the development of critical digital literacies curricula across educational contexts.

As educators, we want students to be empowered to travel across both formal and informal learning environments; we also want them to define themselves, and be defined, as proficient and capable. Traveling with both critical and digital tools can make one powerful indeed. How have these particular tools changed what it means to be a literacy traveler, and a critical one at that? To begin to address this question, in subsequent sections, we define what we mean by both *critical* and *digital* as well as highlight some of the recent scholarship in each area. We also underscore select challenges in being a traveler of this sort, in this particular era, as we know that (critical, digital) literacy-as-travel is often constrained and regulated. We will then turn to an exploration of what the intersection of these two has made (and continues to make) possible as we introduce readers to the chapters contained in this volume, each of which holds promise for further elucidating the complexities of this subfield.

CRITICAL DIGITAL LITERACIES: WORKING DEFINITIONS AND THEORETICAL STANDPOINTS

Freire's (2000) work is often cited as an early example of critical literacies praxis—that is, in practice and in evolution. Critical literacies scholars also draw on Marx's theories of power and domination, as well as Foucault's (1975) understanding of the ways individuals discipline themselves (see, for example, Morrell, 2008). The main, underlying goal of critical literacies praxis is twofold: to investigate manifestations of power relations in texts, and to design, and in some cases redesign, texts in ways that serve other, less powerful interests.

We refer to critical literacies in the plural because the skills and practices they entail are multiple and diverse. Critical literacies provide skills and tools to address social and educational inequalities and assist us in continuing to read the world, a world that is increasingly digital. In the current moment, we see critical literacies as engagement with language that requires consumers and designers of texts not only to decode, encode, and make meaning from texts, but also to *interrogate* them (Berghoff, Egawa, Harste, & Hoonan, 2000; Boran & Comber, 2001; Comber & Simpson, 2001; Dozier, Johnston, & Rogers, 2006; Janks, 2010; Lewison, Leland, & Harste, 2008; Misson & Morgan, 2006; Muspratt, Luke, & Freebody, 1997; Stevens & Bean, 2007). Following the four resources model (Freebody & Luke, 2003), we also see critical literacies as those practices and skills that help investigate the ways readers use texts and texts use readers. Such interrogations can lead to disruptions of taken-for-granted realities, with, as Luke (2012) writes, "an explicit aim of the critique and transformation of dominant ideologies, cultures and economies, and institutions and political systems" (p. 5). After one of us discussed critical literacies with an undergraduate class of English Education students, a student asked, "Should we just question everything then?" Because power constantly shifts in digital worlds, when we as educators teach about and engage in critical literacies in classrooms, we run the "risk" of empowering students to do just that.

In a similar vein, we view digital literacies as those practices in which people use technological tools to engage with, respond to, and create both text-based and multimodal forms of literacies. Recent research has highlighted the need for educators to bring digital literacies into our classrooms (Alvermann, 2010; Alvermann, Moon, & Hagood, 1999; Jenkins, Purushotma, Weigel, Clinton, & Robison, 2009; Paris, 2010; Rance-Roney, 2010; Robin, 2008) even though traditional school definitions of literacies may well be at odds with those that include digital dimensions (Collins & Halverson, 2009; Tarasuiuk, 2010). Digital literacies have called into question our understandings of acquisition and development, even as schools continue to hold on to more traditional, and decidedly less digital, definitions. Additionally, we and the authors in this volume acknowledge that critical literacies cannot simply be mapped onto a digital landscape without a careful revision of assumptions, approaches, and practices (Lankshear, Peters, & Knobel, 1996); this is a road that educators and learners should be traveling together, toward, perhaps, an inversion of authority (which we will discuss in more detail in a later section).

Critical digital literacies, then, are those skills and practices that lead to the creation of digital texts that interrogate the world; they also allow and foster the interrogation of digital, multimedia texts. Along with Dockter, Haug, & Lewis (2010), we theorize that critical digital literacies have the potential to reach learners who might be otherwise reluctant to engage in print-based critical literacies work. Critical digital literacies provide opportunities for students to critique the cultural worlds they inhabit (Gainer, 2010) and to expand their understandings of culture (Hull, Stornaiuolo, & Sahni, 2010; Myers & Eberfors, 2010), while also revising their own literacy and academic identities using digital tools (Lankshear, Peters, & Knobel, 1996; O'Brien, 2003). We believe that there is crucial work to be done at these intersections, work that builds upon the extensive bodies of critical and digital literacies research briefly mentioned above. The authors of chapters in this collection define critical digital literacies in a variety of ways; each definition can be situated within our larger, overarching construct of practices that both foster and afford the ability to design critical digital texts. When educators (and researchers) set out to help students become designers of texts, authority and power—who has them, who deserves them, and where they come from—are often called into question. We turn next to a discussion of the potential of such unbalancing in critical digital literacies praxis.

AUTHORITY AND POWER IN AN INCREASINGLY PARTICIPATORY CULTURE

In our brave new participatory world (Jenkins et al., 2009), critical digital literacies should, arguably, appeal to a variety of educators because, at its best, they offer alternative methods of teaching, learning, production, and assessment that have the ability to disrupt traditional banking systems of education (Freire, 2000). Critical digital literacies offer chances for students and teachers to become designers (Kress, 2010), instead of only consumers, of powerful texts (Gounari, 2009; Janks, 2010)—one of its ultimate goals. In their analysis of frameworks used by literacy and technology researchers, Warschauer and Ware (2008) offer Castells' dichotomous future, in which the privileged "interact" alongside the less privileged, who are "interacted" upon (p. 228). This dire possibility goads those who engage in critical digital literacies—like the authors in our volume—to continue their work. Administrators and teachers under accountability pressures are often skittish about allowing what they perceive to be wild and untamable technologies into classrooms (Merchant, 2010) and even, in some cases, after-school programs (Ávila, Underwood, & Woodbridge, 2008). Who, they worry, will monitor access and use and exposure? Who will "protect" students from the potential monsters on an unregulated Internet? Unfortunately, it is these same contexts in which many underserved children find themselves—without access to the tools of participatory cultures. Through critical digital literacies, we can reach out to and help empower traditionally disenfranchised learners.

We also argue that critical literacies educators would do well to integrate the digital dimension into their work to build upon the practices and engagement that our learners already utilize as they participate in digital literacies, where they are positioned as creators and authors. Dyson (2010) asserted that

> Classrooms too should be defined by such a participatory culture where there is not a linguistically proper "us" and an improper "them" to be fixed. Rather, there is a "we" that embodies distinctive linguistic and sociocultural histories that intersect to open a classroom world to the larger society. Such a classroom world requires a particular ideological foundation. (p. 314)

The "particular ideological foundation" that Dyson refers to can be one built on the assumptions and practices of critical digital literacies, which lend themselves to the creation of participatory cultures and equitable spaces where "we" can become literate in increasingly powerful ways, using media and tools that continue to evolve and become more powerful themselves. Certainly, more than traditional school literacies, critical digital literacies contain the potential to blur the boundaries between "us" and "them," especially when the "us" is the authoritative expert facing the novices. So, from the first, engaging with learners in digital activities results in a constant shifting of the position of expert at the apex. Educators and learners often share the roles of experts and teachers, and when students lead, they define participation itself.

We would like to make a subtle distinction between pedagogy and product in this regard. Pedagogically, power relationships between learners and teachers are made fluid in many critical digital literacies contexts—learners frequently outpace teachers, or even arrive knowing more at the outset. For those of us who enjoy working with critical digital literacies, this may be the most fun part of the whole process: giving up our positions as knowledge-holders and bankers to participate, if not as equals, at least as joint seekers of knowledge and joint producers of new media. This reformulation of the learning process as a participatory one is inspiring and attractive precisely because it stands in stark contrast to the mandated and standardized participation that many of us continue to observe in formal learning contexts (cf. Burn, Buckingham, Parry, & Powell, 2010; Rubin, 2011; Zacher Pandya, 2011). The role shifts—and shifts in authority and power—engendered by critical digital literacies praxis lead us to our next related and overlapping standpoint.

THE POTENTIAL FOR TRANSFORMATION

More than 15 years ago, Peters and Lankshear (1995) asserted that a "transition from print-based texts to electronic text forms and practices . . . opens up space for expanded and enhanced practices of critical literacy" (p. 53). However, they also cautioned that educators would have trouble learning about and subsequently integrating these fast-developing digital literacies into curricula in a timely way (ibid.). Our own teacher education students provide anecdotal support of this caveat and have often confessed that they feel they can't keep up with technology, and so they are hesitant to bring it into their classrooms at all. Critical literacies themselves can be intimidating to educators, but to couple them with digital literacies, and ask teachers to figure out how to integrate the whole complex mess in an educational context that values measurable and testable skills (neither of which these are) often leaves us with present and future educators who are reluctant to engage with either the critical or the digital. Part of the wariness comes, we suspect, from the fact that teachers and learners are likely to undergo role transformations while implementing critical digital literacies. The disruption of authority, and the fluidity of the relationship between learners and teachers (or novices and experts), can unnerve those who usually see themselves as "experts" (see also Lankshear, Peters, & Knobel, 1996, p. 166).

We have begun to think about the nature and utility of *criticism* itself in the transformations entailed by critical digital literacies praxis. Foucault defined criticism as "a matter of flushing out [a] thought and trying to change it: to show that things are not as self-evident as one believed, to see that what is accepted as self-evident will no longer be accepted as such (Kritzman, 1998, p. 155). He also argued that "practicing criticism is a matter of making facile gestures difficult," an act that "is absolutely indispensable for any transformation" (ibid.). We like to think about each critical digital literacies context as transformative in a Foucauldian sense—as "a free atmosphere, one constantly agitated by a permanent criticism" (ibid.).

In the spirit of this kind of criticism, we would like to make difficult, and offer up for possible transformation, two facile tropes: (1) the role of the expert in critical digital literacies, and (2) the idea that digital tools are inherently empowering. In regard to the first, we know that learners are often more comfortable and less inhibited when it comes to learning new technologies, and, given the opportunity, they can easily assume the teacher's role. In terms of the second assumption, we know that simply having technology (such as an interactive whiteboard) does not necessarily provide a learning experience that is qualitatively different from one in which the only tools available are pencil and paper. Even though these may be fairly obvious suppositions, we continue to be surprised at how often we see the dichotomous models of teacher/student and technology/no technology remain at the helm in education.

The idea of transformation appears across a range of research on digital literacies (DeGennaro, 2010; Gainer, Valdez-Gainer, & Kinard, 2009; Gee, 2010; Stein, 2004). We would argue, as do the other authors of this volume, that it entails not just *letting* students teach us, or each other, in isolated instances, but encouraging them to forge their own paths to authority—opening up the classroom landscape so that there's room for multiple paths to knowledge (Ávila, 2008; Merchant, 2009). Additionally, in terms of which tools we use when, we suggest that "a permanent criticism" is needed: why this tool and to which ends? What does it both lend and limit in this particular situation? Just as travel can transform us, so too can assuming a stance of permanent criticism when using and creating digital literacies.

ORGANIZING CRITICAL DIGITAL LITERACIES RESEARCH: PLAN OF THE BOOK

This book was born out of our joint desire to explore theoretical standpoints that would help us understand our engagement with, and analysis of, such praxis. Due to this need, we echo Coiro, Knobel, Lankshear, and Leu (2008), who call for new frameworks through which to study "the new literacies of the Internet and other ICT contexts" (p. 12; see also Wohlwend & Lewis, 2011). In our work with youth in different settings on digital projects, one of the most intriguing aspects of working with critical digital literacies is the generative and flexible nature of the inquiry process and potential products associated with them. As researchers trained to engage with the world from a sociocultural perspective, we are interested in complementary approaches that enable us to account for social practices, contexts, and, to paraphrase Geertz (1972), the meaning-perspectives of critical digital literacies participants themselves. The many theoretical standpoints taken in the following chapters—from discourse analysis to multimodal analyses of digital texts—are, we believe, grounded in the social practices of new literacies, although they also afford space for primarily textual analyses of critical digital literacies artifacts (cf. Street, Pahl, & Rowsell, 2009). We invite readers to build on and expand these theoretical framings, and to appreciate, as we do, the ways they overlap, coordinate, and enlighten.

On a more pragmatic note, as Luke (2012) points out, "while Freirian models provide a pedagogical approach and a political stance, an orientation towards 'voice' and ideology, they lack specificity on how teachers and students can engage with the complex structures of texts, both traditional and multimodal" (p. 8). Another of our primary goals in collating this volume has been to offer specificity, including the use of blogs (Nygard), iPods and mobile media (Garcia), videos (Lewis, Doerr-Stevens, Dockter Tierney, & Scharber; Schmier) and digital storytelling (Nixon; Salter; Smith & Hull). These authors have situated themselves at the intersection of the digital and critical, and in their own ways, each explores how the increasing ubiquity of digital literacies has affected our definitions of critical literacies. They also examine how our ever-changing perceptions of critical literacies affect how we define, teach, and engage in digital literacies.

However, we have organized this book's chapters into three sections based neither on the type of media under discussion, nor on the particular theoretical standpoint(s) of the authors, but instead on three key areas we see emerging in the field. They are, first, "Disruptive by Design," a section with three chapters about youth designing their own critical digital literacies in praxis. Our second section, "Teacher Education and Critical Digital Literacies" explores our interest as teacher educators in the many aspects of this particular praxis that draw and, in some cases, discourage teachers. The third section of the book, "Resisting Dominant Narratives," brings together three authors whose work serves as cautionary tales to those engaged in critical digital literacies research and praxis.

Disruptive by design

Though the methodological and theoretical standpoints of authors vary, each takes students' multimedia products—videos (Schmier) and digital stories (Nixon; Smith & Hull) as their object of study. Schmier adds to our knowledge base of critical digital literacies in action within formal learning environments as she describes the process of eighth graders constructing a public service announcement in a journalism and digital media studies class (Chapter 2). While focal students were able to reconstruct their literacy identities in this activity, it was not a process without tension. By exploring instances of student agency, and places where students performed in ways not anticipated by the teacher, Schmier illustrates class work that reaches out into and reflects the larger community that students inhabit.

Nixon's research (Chapter 3) represents a larger project of digital storytelling with urban youth in an after-school program. Her focus in this chapter is on the ways that digital storytelling might help children engage in critical dialogue vis-à-vis race, ethnicity, and gender. She examines the digital stories, videotaped developmental dialogues, and other artifacts of five children, ages six through ten, showing how they often appropriated and challenged gendered and raced images they found in the popular media. Nixon's chapter serves as an account of how children can be helped to acquire critical digital literacies skills while interrogating the media images that saturate their lives.

Next, Smith and Hull write from a cosmopolitan, globalized perspective, foregrounding the ethics of authorship and readership as they explore youths' emerging practices (Chapter 4). They analyze videos made by two American high school students in a course on cosmopolitanism, in which students joined an online site to view the videos of, and correspond with, youth in many other parts of the world. Smith and Hull argue that the students were in the process of developing, and deploying, a "digital ethic of cosmopolitan practice" (p. 4). Their research illustrates that we need to teach intentional authoring in multimodal design so that learners can develop their own senses of who they are in the world in relation to others.

Teacher education and critical digital literacies

While we could have easily categorized each of these chapters in other ways, we find their strengths in the ideas and examples they put forth about teachers engaging in critical digital literacies. Issues of authority and power—which we mentioned above—underlie these authors' discussions of how teachers engage in critical digital literacies: Nygard and Garcia describe blogging and gameplay, in Chapters 5 and 6, respectively; while Lohnes Watulak and Kinzer offer a theoretical framework for critical digital literacies in teacher education in Chapter 7.

To elaborate, Nygard describes the effects of a Norwegian teacher's blogging on her students' development of critical digital literacies (Chapter 5). Using observational data as well as group and individual interviews, Nygard suggests that students felt an increased sense of community, were strongly motivated, and, perhaps most importantly, saw blogging in class as a serious and meaningful technology of thought. Nygard's descriptions offer useful examples for practitioners; however, it is the students' discussions of the importance and utility of this kind of classroom- and school-based blogging that are invigorating.

Garcia details how he, along with his ninth-grade students, utilized iPods to construct a scavenger hunt that positioned them, through critical play, as participants with the power to comment on their school and its position in the community (Chapter 6). Students worked individually and collaboratively as they took critical and digital literacies beyond classroom walls. Crossing both "digital and non-digital contexts," his research exemplifies how educators can utilize digital tools in accessible ways that ask students to draw from their own knowledge of new media while still "doing" school.

Lohnes Watulak and Kinzer (Chapter 7) develop and define a theoretical framework for critical digital literacies in pre-service teacher technology education. They explore ways to use this framework with existing technology standards to develop teachers' critical reflective skills. While the space and genre of pre-service teacher education will be familiar to many readers, we have not yet seen such a detailed attempt to integrate critical digital literacies into it.

Resisting dominant narratives

In this last section, we have collected three chapters whose authors resist dominant critical digital literacies narratives—because, even though it is an emerging field, there are already dominant narratives to resist.

Salter explores the default, deficit constructions of students *and* literacies in alternative school contexts—in this case a high school in Quebec, where she was engaged in a critical digital literacies project—and argues convincingly that these taken-for-granted notions of what students (and teaching) ought to be like in such schools narrow and constrain the possibilities for critical digital literacies (Chapter 8). She urges us to interrogate the frames we bring to these contexts, and to "think big" about the possibilities and potentials of individual alternative schools, students, and teachers.

Lewis, Doerr-Stevens, Dockter Tierney, and Scharber share with readers what occurs when critical digital literacies are "sponsored" in an English class by a public-relations firm, a seemingly contradictory coupling (Chapter 9). Using the lens of relocalization, the authors explore what they see as a "conundrum" central to enacting critical digital literacies in schools: schools are part of a global market economy that circumscribes, to some extent, how learning occurs. Although this complexity can be circumvented with tools like critical digital literacies, the authors remind readers that it is no easy feat and may require students to act agentively in unexpected ways.

In Chapter 10, Santo's work theorizing the nature of hacker literacies will open up new vistas. Concerned with acts of agency in a digital participatory world, Santo introduces readers to what he terms hacker literacies. Through illustration of what some users have done with, and in response to, Facebook, Twitter, and Second Life, he adds nuance to what it means to participate, actions that then change the programs themselves. Santo's research exemplifies that re-mediation in digital spaces means that users become designers, and who designs and creates occurs on a continuum with near-constant negotiation.

Hagood, who has long been concerned with critical (2002) and critical digital literacies praxis (2009), has written the Afterword for this collection. Drawing on current research about teacher and student technology practices, Hagood ultimately challenges practitioners to consciously explore the destabilizing effects of critical digital literacies on classroom relationships, identities, and instruction. Her chapter offers a timely reminder: While all educators are losing control in so many places, current and future Common Core State Standards leave us in control of this aspect of our teaching. It is up to us to make the most of it.

REFERENCES

Alvermann, D. (Ed.). (2010). *Adolescents' online literacies*. New York: Peter Lang.

Alvermann, D., Moon, J., & Hagood, M. (1999). *Popular culture in the classroom: Teaching and researching critical media literacy*. Newark, DE: Routledge.

Alvermann, D. E., & Moore, D. W. (2011). Questioning the separation of in-school and out-of-school contexts for literacy learning: An interview with Donna Alvermann. *Journal of Adolescent & Adult Literacy, 55*(2).

Ávila, J. (2008). A desire line to digital storytelling. *Teachers College Record*. Retrieved from http://www.tcrecord.org. ID Number: 15463.

Ávila, J., Underwood, C., & Woodbridge, S. (2008). "I'm the expert now": Digital storytelling and transforming literacies among displaced children. In D. McInerney & A. D. Liem (Eds.), *Research on sociocultural influences on motivation and learning. Teaching and learning: International best practice* (Vol. 8, pp. 349–376). Charlotte, NC: Information Age Publishing.

Berghoff, B., Egawa, K. A., Harste, J. C., & Hoonan, B. T. (2000). *Beyond reading and writing: Inquiry curriculum, and multiple ways of knowing*. Urbana, IL: National Council of Teachers of English.

Boran, S., & Comber, B. (2001). *Critiquing whole language and classroom inquiry.* Urbana, IL: National Council of Teachers of English.

Burn, A., Buckingham, B., Parry, B., & Powell, M. (2010). Minding the gaps: Teachers' cultures, students' cultures. In D. Alvermann (Ed.), *Adolescents' online literacies* (pp. 183–201). New York: Peter Lang.

Coiro, J., Knobel, M., Lankshear, C., & Leu, D. (2008). Central issues in new literacies and new literacies research. In J. Coiro, M. Knobel, C. Lankshear, & D. Leu (Eds.), *Handbook of research on new literacies* (pp. 1–21). New York: Erlbaum.

Collins, A., & Halverson, R. (2009). *Rethinking education in the age of technology.* New York: Teachers College Press.

Comber, B., & Simpson, A. (2001). *Negotiating critical literacies in classrooms.* Mahwah, NJ: Erlbaum.

DeGennaro, D. (2010). Grounded in theory: Immersing preservice teachers in technology-mediated learning. *Contemporary Issues in Technology and Teacher Education, 10*(3), 338–359.

Dickinson, E. (1961). *Final harvest.* Boston, MA: Back Bay Books.

Dockter, J., Haug, D., & Lewis, C. (2010). Redefining rigor: Critical engagement, digital media, and the new English/language arts. *Journal of Adolescent & Adult Literacy, 53*(5), 418–420.

Dozier, C., Johnston, P., & Rogers, R. (2006). *Critical literacy/critical teaching: Tools for preparing responsive teachers.* New York: Teachers College Press.

Dyson, A. (2010). Afterword. *English Education, 42*(3), 307–319.

Foucault, M. (1975). *Discipline & punish: The birth of the prison* (2nd ed.). New York: Basic Books.

Freebody, P., & Luke, A. (2003). Literacy as engaging with new forms of life: The four roles model. In G. Bull & M. Anstey (Eds.), *The literacy lexicon* (2nd ed., pp. 51–66). Frenchs Forest, Australia: Pearson Education Australia.

Freire, P. (2000). *Pedagogy of the oppressed.* New York: Continuum Press.

Gainer, J. S. (2010). Critical media literacy in middle school: Exploring the politics of representation. *Journal of Adolescent & Adult Literacy, 53*(5), 364–373.

Gainer, J. S., Valdez-Gainer, N., & Kinard, T. (2009). The elementary bubble project: Exploring critical media literacy in a fourth-grade classroom. *The Reading Teacher, 62*(8), 674–683.

Gee, J. P. (2010). *New digital media and learning as an emerging area and "worked examples" as one way forward.* Cambridge, MA: MIT Press.

Geertz, C. (1972). *The interpretation of cultures.* New York: Basic Books.

Gounari, P. (2009). Rethinking critical literacy in the new information age. *Critical Inquiry in Language Studies, 6*(3), 148–175.

Hagood, M. C. (2002). Critical literacy for whom. *Reading Research and Instruction, 41*(3), 247–266.

Hagood, M. (2009). *New literacies practices: Designing literacy learning.* New York: Peter Lang.

Hull, G., Stornaiuolo, A., & Sahni, U. (2010). Cultural citizenship and cosmopolitan practice: Global youth communicate online. *English Education, 42*(4), 331–367.

Janks, H. (2010). *Literacy and power.* London: Routledge.

Jenkins, H., Purushotma, R., Weigel, M., Clinton, K., & Robison, A. (2009). *Confronting the challenges of participatory culture: Media education for the 21st century.* Cambridge, MA: MIT Press.

Kress, G. (2010). *Multimodality: A social semiotic approach to contemporary communication.* New York: Routledge.

Kritzman, L. D. (Ed.). (1998). *Michel Foucault: Politics, philosophy, culture. Interviews and other writings 1977–1984.* New York: Routledge.

Lankshear, C., Peters, M., & Knobel, M. (1996). Critical literacy and pedagogy. In H. Giroux, C. Lankshear, P. McLaren, & M. Peters (Eds.), *Counternarratives: Cultural studies and critical pedagogies in postmodern spaces* (pp. 149–188). New York: Routledge.

Lewison, M., Leland, C., & Harste, J. (2008). *Creating critical classrooms*. New York: Erlbaum.

Luke, A. (2012). Critical literacy: Foundational notes. *Theory Into Practice, 51*, 4–11.

Merchant, G. (2010). View my profile(s). In D. Alvermann (Ed.), *Adolescents' online literacies* (pp. 51–69). New York: Peter Lang.

Merchant, G. (2009). Literacy in virtual worlds. *Journal of Research in Reading, 32*(1), 38–56.

Misson, R., & Morgan, W. (2006). *Critical literacy and the aesthetic: Transforming the English classroom*. Urbana, IL: National Council of Teachers of English.

Morrell, E. (2008). *Critical literacy and urban youth: Pedagogies of access, dissent and liberation*. New York: Routledge.

Muspratt, S., Luke, A., & Freebody, P. (Eds.). (1997). *Constructing critical literacies: Teaching and learning textual practice*. Creskill, NJ: Hampton Press.

Myers, J., & Eberfors, F. (2010). Globalizing English through intercultural critical literacy. *English Education, 42*(2), 148–170.

O'Brien, D. (2003). Juxtaposing traditional and intermedial literacies to redefine the competence of struggling adolescents. *Reading Online, 6*(7). Retrieved from http://www.readingonline.org/newliteracies/lit_index.asp?HREF=obrien2/

Paris, D. (2010). Texting identities: Lessons for classrooms from multiethnic youth space. *English Education, 42*(3), 278–292.

Peters, M., & Lankshear, C. (1995). Critical literacy and digital texts. *Educational Theory, 45*(4), 51–70.

Rance-Roney, J. (2010). Jump-starting language and schema for English-language learners: Teacher-composed digital jumpstarts for academic reading. *Journal of Adolescent & Adult Literacy, 53*(5), 386–397.

Robin, B. R. (2008). Digital storytelling: A powerful technology tool for the 21st-century classroom. *Theory Into Practice, 47*, 220–228.

Rubin, D. (2011). The disheartened teacher: Living in the age of standardisation, high-stakes assessments, and No Child Left Behind (NCLB). *Changing English, 18*(4), 407–416.

Stein, P. (2004). Representation, rights, and resources: Multimodal pedagogies in the language and literacy classroom. In B. Norton & K. Toohey (Eds.), *Critical pedagogies and language learning* (pp. 95–115), *Cambridge applied linguistics series*. Cambridge, England: Cambridge University Press.

Stevens, L. P., & Bean, T. W. (2007). *Critical literacy: Context, research, and practice in the K–12 classroom*. Thousand Oaks, CA: Sage.

Street, B., Pahl, K., & Rowsell, J. (2009). Multimodality and new literacy studies. In C. Jewitt (Ed.), *The Routledge handbook on multimodal analysis*. London: Routledge.

Tarasuiuk, T. J. (2010). Combining traditional and contemporary texts: Moving my English class to the computer lab. *Journal of Adolescent & Adult Literacy, 53*(7), 543–552.

Warschauer, M., & Ware, P. (2008). Learning, change and power: Competing frames of technology and literacy. In J. Coiro, M. Knobel, C. Lankshear, & D. Leu (Eds.), *Handbook of research on new literacies* (pp. 215–240). London: Routledge.

Wohlwend, K., & Lewis, C. (2011). Critical literacy, critical engagement, digital technology: Convergence and embodiment in global spheres. In D. Lapp & D. Fisher, (Eds.), *The handbook of research on teaching English and language arts* (pp. 188–194). New York: Taylor & Francis.

Zacher Pandya, J. (2011). *Overtested: How high-stakes accountability fails English language learners*. New York: Teachers College Press.

PART 1

Disruptive by Design

CHAPTER TWO

Designing Space FOR Student Choice IN A Digital Media Studies Classroom

STEPHANIE ANNE SCHMIER

On the first day of school, Mr. Cardenas, a teacher at East Side Middle School, gave his eighth-grade journalism and digital media studies students a homework assignment to come up with questions that they had about the class. The following day, Rosy was the first to ask her question, which was about what topics they would be able to cover in their role as journalists.

ROSY:	On the documentary, what topics will we be able to cover?
MR. CARDENAS:	A broad range. It just has to be about [our city] in some way.
ROSY:	But are there like boundaries you can't cross?
MR. CARDENAS:	Nudity would not be okay and curse words should be kept to a minimum.
ROSY:	What about how do drugs take a toll on the community?
MR. CARDENAS:	That would be great. That would work for the documentary or the PSA....I probably won't ask you to do a pro-drug message. (field notes, 8/30)

The journalism and digital media studies elective that Mr. Cardenas taught was a different type of classroom environment than most of the classes offered at East Side Middle School, a Title I school labeled as "underperforming" by the state based on student performance on standardized tests. The class was structured in a way that transformed the classroom into an authentic workspace where Mr. Cardenas and his students engaged in both traditional and new-media journalistic practices, designing texts such as the print-based and online newspaper that they titled the *East Side Tribune*, blogs, and podcasts. During sixth period, students were journalists, provided with press passes that afforded them freedom to move around the school to report on issues of interest and importance to the student body, and with access to a few digital still and video cameras that they used to perform their roles as journalists. This freedom came with responsibility, as students were required to make appointments to obtain interviews from their sources, which included faculty and administration as well as fellow students and community members.

The short exchange between Rosy and Mr. Cardenas quoted above exemplifies how Mr. Cardenas and his students negotiated the topics that students covered in the texts they designed for the school newspaper they produced and an end-of-the-year film festival in which they participated. While Mr. Cardenas articulated to his students that the journalism and digital media studies class was a space for them to investigate, discuss, and document issues that they thought to be important to the East Side community, he regularly reminded them that this was a school space, with certain rules and regulations that they all must follow, himself included. For example, though Mr. Cardenas made it clear that students would have choice in the topics that they would investigate and document, discourses circulating within East Side Middle School mediated not only what topics should not be covered (e.g., anything requiring nudity or curse words), but also that texts should espouse a particular point of view in line with acceptable ways of talking and acting at school (e.g., an anti-drug perspective).

As I read the space of the journalism and digital media studies class during the year that I spent with Mr. Cardenas and his students as a participant observer, I became keenly aware of how the multiple discourses circulating within this classroom shaped the identities that were performed and the texts that students produced for the class. For example, the question Rosy posed to Mr. Cardenas in their exchange about whether it would be acceptable to document what she saw as the negative effects that drugs were taking on their local community located her within a working-class discourse, where drugs are seen as contributing to the low level of economic resources available to some of those who live in her community, a position that shaped many of the texts that she produced for the class. East Side Middle School is located in an increasingly gentrified community that is socially and culturally diverse, with newly renovated million-dollar homes on the hill overlooking rows of low-income apartment housing below. Despite the diversity of the community, at the time this study was conducted 90 percent of the students enrolled in East Side Middle School came from lower-income households, whereas students from the Hills predominantly attended one of the private schools in the area, a tension that was evident in the texts that many of the students produced throughout the course.

Observing and documenting the processes through which students designed multimodal projects for the journalism and digital media studies class offered opportunities to learn about the ways they used their bodies, texts, and the school space to tell the stories of their own lives and their community. This was particularly evident in the final group project undertaken by students in the class, the public service announcement (PSA). The PSA was a group assignment in which students wrote and performed their message as actors captured on video, and so provided a lens into how students used language, organized space, and moved their bodies to send a message that articulated their perspective on how individuals can work to improve the community to an audience of their peers.

Thus, the purpose of this chapter is to examine the multimodal literacy performances of Marie and Casey, two students enrolled in Mr. Cardenas' journalism and digital media studies class, as they engaged in the process of creating a video public service announcement on teenage pregnancy and abortion. Drawing on ethnographic data from a yearlong study designed to investigate the digital practices and literate identities of adolescents attending an urban public school, this research blends post-structural theories of subjectivity and positioning (Blackburn, 2002; Davies, 1994) with critical discourse (Gee, 2005) and multimodal (Kress, 2003) analytic tools to explore the students' literacies as multimodal, embodied identity performances. According to Hull and Nelson (2005), multimodal texts such as the video PSA designed by the youth in this study afford a different kind of meaning making than the traditional types of school texts that predominate in public school classrooms. From this perspective, allowing youth who are positioned as "low-literate" based on traditional print-based assessments the opportunity to read and design multimodal texts may serve as a "democratizing force" (p. 253), offering opportunities for these youth to reposition themselves as authors, designers, and composers. However, Janks (2000) noted, "design, without an understanding of how dominant discourses/practices perpetuate themselves runs the risk of an unconscious reproduction of these forms" (p. 178). In other words, merely giving students from traditionally marginalized backgrounds access to digital tools with which to design multimodal texts in the classroom runs the risk of students using these tools to create content that mirrors the mainstream media and school-based discourses that position them as "at-risk" for school failure. Therefore, in what follows I explore how Marie and Casey negotiated school-based discourses and dominant representations of constructs such as race and gender as they produced their own digital, multimodal texts.

THEORETICAL FRAMEWORK

This chapter is grounded in a social practice perspective on literacies that leans on post-structural theories of subjectivity and positionality, blended with critical discourse (Gee, 2005) and multimodal (Kress, 2003) analytic tools. Here, literacies are understood as socially situated and discursively constructed practices that vary in relation to the activity of which it is a part (Barton, 1994; Gee, 1996; Luke & Freebody, 1997). Just as literacies are discursively constructed, so too are individuals' subjectivities constructed through their particular life histories and experiences (Davies, 1994). Bringing Blackburn's (2002) notion of literacies performances to this research allows for literacies to be considered "across locations and over time" (p. 313). Understanding literacies performances in classrooms therefore requires attention not only to activities, but also to the ways individuals are positioned and position themselves as they interact within and across particular practices over time. The research presented in this chapter is thus informed by a view of literacies that acknowledges the shifting nature of individuals' subjectivities as they engage in literate practices across multiple social spaces.

Further, I draw on multimodal theories that shed new light on youths' meaning-making in relation to the texts they produce in school-based settings. Analyzing texts from this perspective links students' social practices with their textual representations (Pahl & Roswell, 2006). Thus, this research draws on Kress' (2003) theory and method of multimodal analysis in order to recognize how the practices of students in this particular middle-school classroom are situated within a much wider communicational landscape. Specifically, Kress' framework requires the consideration not only of how any text is shaped by its material form, but how that form is shaped by the discourses that surround the literacies event(s) in which the text was produced. Such an analytic framework is essential for understanding how the discourses that surround particular literacies events in this study shaped and are shaped by the kinds and types of digital texts that the youth produced throughout the year.

DIGITAL LITERACIES WITHOUT THE CRITICAL

In their study of youth engagement with digital media, Ito et al. (2009) described how networked publics such as online social networking sites have provided space for youth to engage in learning with peers through the production of text, outside the purview of teachers and other adults. Mr. Cardenas' pedagogical approach in the journalism and digital media studies class embraced this perspective of allowing youth space to learn from each other through the production of digital texts without adult intervention in the learning process. A social studies teacher with nine years of experience, Mr. Cardenas began teaching the journalism and digital media studies elective after participating in a workshop at the American Film Institute. Over the three years that he had taught the class, he transformed the workshop curriculum into an entire course, which provided opportunities for his students to design texts that were particularly meaningful to themselves and their communities. In the remainder of this chapter, I describe how Mr. Cardenas' approach played out in the construction of one of the digital texts designed in the class and discuss implications, including how allowing students to design on their own, without an explicit critical literacies curriculum, simultaneously empowered students and re-inscribed their positionality as marginal in their underperforming school.

The Public Service Announcement

On a shortened day in April, two months before the end of the school year, Mr. Cardenas introduced the final project for the journalism and digital media studies class, the PSA. Mr. Cardenas began the unit by engaging the class in a discussion of PSA as a genre, as this was their first time designing a PSA:

MR. CARDENAS:	Today we will be starting on the public service announcements. Do you know what a PSA is?
SABINA:	It prevents you from doing things.
VINCENT:	It informs.
ROSY:	Like DARE. They have bumper stickers and shirts.
MR. CARDENAS:	It has to be a commercial
ROSY:	I didn't know that . . . *It's Your Sex Life.* (*Mr. Cardenas makes air quotes as he repeats the title and writes it on the board*) It's about sex education.
MR. CARDENAS:	Does anyone know Smokey the Bear? It was popular when I was growing up. Since the fires last year in Grant Park there is now a sign with Smokey the Bear at the park entrance warning about forest fires. (field notes, 4/8)

As this discussion continued, students named PSAs they had seen on channels such as MTV with topics that included teenage sex, drug abuse, and childhood obesity. After the class had brainstormed a list of topics, Mr. Cardenas chose students to be the leaders of each PSA group, then assigned students to groups of four. Topic selection took place directly after groups were assigned. Mr. Cardenas instructed students,

"Now that you are seated around the room, the leader will be the facilitator of the groups. In ten minutes, decide on the category [for the PSA]."

Marie and Casey, two focal students in this research, were assigned to the same group. Marie, who had immigrated to the United States with her family at age nine from Nigeria, was recognized by Mr. Cardenas as a leader in the journalism and digital media studies class despite the fact that she was failing in some of her core-content classes. As such, Marie was chosen to lead her group. Casey, a white working-class student, was recognized by her teachers and classmates as a successful student both in the journalism class and in her core classes and worked as a co-leader alongside Marie throughout the project.

I was particularly drawn to Marie and Casey's group because of the intense passion with which they engaged in initial planning conversations around their topic. Their group, which also included a girl named Annie and a boy named Joe, chose one of the topics that came up in the class discussion, teenage sex. However, they chose to focus on an aspect not brought up by Mr. Cardenas: abortion. During the ten-minute discussion, the group agreed that their PSA would portray an anti-abortion message. Casey clearly stated her view by telling the group, "Abortion sucks." She shared later in an interview that the selection of their anti-abortion message was partly due to the fact that both Annie's and Casey's mothers had given birth as teens and had each made the decision not to have an abortion. Casey described that she believed her mother had made a good decision because otherwise her sister would not have been born (interview with Casey, 6/11).

From the beginning of the project Mr. Cardenas appeared uncomfortable with the group's topic choice of abortion, but I never observed him asking them to reconsider their choice. I noted his concern with the way they were approaching their topic during their first-day conversation as they discussed including a scene where the pregnant girl's unborn baby would come to her in a dream and haunt her. Mr. Cardenas listened to the group's idea for the scene and his only feedback was "Harsh" (field notes, 4/8). This was the first of many times that Mr. Cardenas would look at me during a conversation with this particular group and ask what I thought. Most often I would try to engage them in a critical conversation to help them think about the message they were sending in their PSA. Their responses always supported their initial design choices, and so Mr. Cardenas allowed them to produce the text that they had originally pitched to him.

Lights, camera, action

As the assigned leader of her group, Marie took responsibility for writing, drawing, and coloring the group's storyboard as they talked through the scenes they would film.

They began referring to their project as the Abortions PSA, which eventually became the title of their video. During the first few class sessions of the project, which lasted six weeks, Marie constantly added, deleted, and modified scenes as the group created their narrative through discussion, including using speech bubbles to illustrate the dialogue. Once their storyboard was completed and approved by Mr. Cardenas, the group chose their roles for the project. Annie agreed to play the pregnant girl and Joe agreed to play her boyfriend. Marie and Casey decided to stay behind the camera, with Marie taking up the role of director and Casey agreeing to be the cameraperson. The group then recruited a few other students from the class to fill the remaining acting roles, including the clinic worker who would counsel the pregnant girl on her available options. They found another student in the class, Marla, to play the unborn baby in the dream sequence that they had first discussed on the day the project was assigned, in which the main character's unborn baby comes to her in a dream and pleads for her life, which influences the pregnant teen not to have an abortion.

After completing their script and gaining approval from Mr. Cardenas, the students used their assigned class camera to film scenes at various locations around campus, including a hallway transformed into a free clinic through the placement of signs on doors that read "ultrasounds" and "checkups" and a rarely used teachers' lounge turned into a medical lab for the dream sequence using beakers, food coloring, and other materials gathered from their science classroom. Once filming was complete, Marie and Casey worked together at Casey's assigned class computer each day to import and edit the film. Though there were four members in their group, Marie and Casey took over full responsibility for post-production, editing their PSA project while the other two group members moved on to other projects, as Mr. Cardenas encouraged students to work on various projects as needs arose. Marie and Casey organized the clips in sequence and added transitions and text slides in iMovie as suggested by Mr. Cardenas.

The completed PSA began with a text slide that read, "In the next 24 hours 2,795 teen girls will get pregnant" followed by a scene of a teenage girl in a bathroom reading a positive pregnancy text. The pregnant teen then went to a free clinic for advice but left without knowing what she would do. When she returned home she fell asleep and dreamt of her baby as an adult. Her baby was in a medical lab and told her mother that she could have cured cancer had she not been killed before she was born. When the pregnant teen awoke from the dream, she answered her cell phone and shared with the caller that she would keep her baby. The final scene ended with the narrator reciting the slogan "Abort your thoughts, not a human being" followed by the grown-up baby thanking her mother for loving her enough not to kill her. Finally, the video contained credits and a montage of outtakes and bloopers (see Appendix A for a full transcript of the Abortions PSA).

Both Marie and Casey shared in interviews that they were happy with the final version of the video that they submitted for the end-of-year film festival, although they were frustrated that Mr. Cardenas would not allow them to include a scene of the pregnant teen sneaking out of a room with a boy looking upset about what she had just done, as he felt that this would be inappropriate for school (interview with Casey, 6/11; interview with Marie, 6/24). Casey told me that she was surprised when the video was selected to screen at the festival because of the topic. However, the video was cut from the film-festival program days before the event, with the students being told that the film would not show due to time constraints. The film-festival program was full, however both Marie and Casey shared that they believed that time constraints were not the only reason the video was not screened for the community.

Performing discursive space through design choice

As I watched the Abortions PSA group's filming and editing sessions, I noticed the care and attention to detail with which they set up every scene. Each design choice was discussed and negotiated among the group members as they performed their multiple roles of filmmaker, actor, set designer, student, and friend. The group regularly spent almost the entire class session setting up the scenes and would only need a few takes at the end of class to capture their work on video. Details, including the design of the pregnancy test and signs for the free clinic, location where each shot would be filmed, and the way in which the actors would move their bodies and speak their lines, were all discussed by group members in detail, with Marie leading the discussion and making the final design choice as director. Further, each time a mistake was made the group would note whether that "take" would be included in the bloopers at the end of the piece.

Watching the film, I noted how the filmmakers drew upon multiple modes in making choices about how to design their text, using written words, images, and spoken language in deliberate ways. For example, for the dream sequence the group decided to have the pregnant teen walk in to the room silently and fall asleep, followed by a text slide that articulated that the she was having a dream (see Table 1).

As I read the text, I found this design choice by the filmmakers to be significant in that the pregnant girl does not say anything and is shown as passive and thus as having no agency, while the grown-up child in the dream is active, a characteristic that is also conveyed through the addition of spoken language in this scene, giving the child voice. The spoken-language choices, such as the use of the word "killed," invoke a pro-life discourse, establishing the filmmakers' perspective that a fetus is a life. In this view, the pregnant girl is not only killing her unborn baby, but all those who will suffer and die from cancer (whom she will not be able to cure) as well.

Table 1. Scenes from the Abortions PSA

Time	Screenshot	Image	Action/Movement/ Sound	Spoken Language
1:28		The girl in a white uniform shirt and dark pants sleeps on two chairs.	The girl walks into a room, rubs her head and lies down to take a nap.	
1:36		White words on a black background in all capital letters aligned on the bottom left of the screen: "While asleep, Angie has a dream."	Writing appears in the frame for 3 seconds.	
1:39		The grown-up child mixing chemical solutions behind a table.	The grown-up child pours colored liquids into containers as if she is experimenting to make medicine. When she finishes talking, the screen fades to white.	Grown-up child: You see, Mom, I could have cured cancer. I could have saved the world. But you killed me.

DESIGNING SPACES FOR THE CONSTRUCTION OF NEW NARRATIVE IN SCHOOL

Producing hybrid discourses

Producing hybrid discourse based within the Foucauldian (1980) conceptualization of power as producing discourses and as something that circulates, I drew upon multimodal discourse analytic tools as a way to illuminate the powerful discourses circulating within the Abortion PSA throughout the production process. A close examination of the PSA project offers insights into the ways that the space of the journalism and digital media studies class afforded opportunities for production of hybrid discourses, allowing participants to perform the space as students who successfully completed their assignments while simultaneously designing texts that were meaningful and important to them.

For example, Casey and Marie positioned themselves as within the discourse of school and performed the role of "good student" as they followed Mr. Cardenas' instructions, stayed on task, and completed each assignment (e.g., topic choice, storyboard, script) as directed without having to compromise the controversial topic that the group chose for their text. Their text matched closely with the purpose of the type of PSA students were asked to create, specifically to inform the audience about actions they could take for the good of the community, thus positioning the audience, which in this case consisted of students and parents, as responsible for alleviating problems in their community. Often PSAs employ scare tactics to lure audience members in and get them to take the issue seriously, such as showing graphic car accidents to prevent drunk driving or a picture of a fried egg to show what drugs might be doing to users' brains. The Abortions PSA filmmakers included such a scare tactic with the dream sequence. That is, they designed a haunting scene meant to portray the seriousness and finality of abortion in order to capture the audience's attention in a way that might leave them open to listening to their message that abortion is not the right choice for a pregnant teen to make when faced with this difficult decision.

Further, Mr. Cardenas told students that a PSA should have a slogan associated with the campaign, such as "Say No to Drugs," or "Only You Can Prevent Wildfires," both of which place ownership for solving the problem they address with the audience. The filmmakers of the Abortions PSA took up Mr. Cardenas' call to include a slogan in their video. Interestingly, this requirement to include a slogan led the filmmakers to add the tag line, "Abort your thoughts, not a human being," creating a tension in the narrative they designed that focused on the pregnant teen's thoughtful decision-making process and the slogan, which suggests that pregnant teens should not think through their options because the right choice is always to follow through with the pregnancy. In this way, the Abortions PSA slogan limits the agency of pregnant teens to make decisions that are best for them. Teens in the audience are told that if they get pregnant, they should not think about the consequences of a decision to follow through with a pregnancy, despite the enormous implications of such a choice. This illustrates how a focus on teaching standard genres such as PSAs with canned slogans shaped the Abortions PSA by deemphasizing the decision-making process that the filmmakers highlighted in the beginning of the piece, thus positioning pregnant teens as agency-less.

This same type of power circulating within school shaped the content of the Abortions PSA that led to the final narrative the group constructed based within Mr. Cardenas' concern over the appropriateness of their content for a school audience and possible push back from the principal or parents about content related to sexual activity. For example, Mr. Cardenas did not allow the filmmakers to include a scene they had filmed showing how the girl became pregnant by being alone in a room with a boy, even though they sought to show that the girl regretted her action. In fact, the filmmakers went further in the other direction and ensured that the scene did not include any physical contact between the two actors at all so as to make it acceptable for a school audience. Despite these design choices, Mr. Cardenas told participants that any mention of sexual activity among the teen actors would be inappropriate, and so the Abortions PSA left out any mention of how the girl became pregnant, which could have served as a preventive message and as such would have addressed one of the main goals of the assignment.

Reproducing dominant discourses

Analyzing the discourses used in designing the narrative of the Abortions PSA brought to the fore how students took up dominant representations of adolescence and working-class girls that pervaded both the school space and mainstream media at the time of this study. Specifically, the discourse of adolescence and the tension inherent in this discourse is evident throughout the Abortions PSA text. Adolescence is commonly viewed as a biological stage that all youth must go through in the same extended way in order for them to develop into adults (Lesko, 2001). This stage is characterized by a lack of ability to make mature decisions due to "raging hormones" (p. 3). However, Lesko articulated how teenage motherhood creates a tension in this discourse of adolescence in that teen mothers grow up "all at once" and are not afforded the extended time needed to develop into mature adults. The Abortions PSA captured this tension in that different modes convey different and even conflicting ideas across scenes. For example, there is tension between the written statement "After having a dream about her child grown up, she knows what she has to do," portraying the pregnant girl as sure of her decision and thus invoking a discourse of adult responsibility, and the image in the previous scene where the girl is shown holding her head in her hands as if still grappling with her choice, thus resisting this early move from teenager to adulthood (see Figure 1).

Further, the discourse of adolescence is reproduced in the last 90 seconds of this four-minute PSA, which features outtakes and bloopers from the students' filming. Bloopers and outtakes are a part of a comedy genre and are often shown at the end of full-length films as well as situation comedies. However, this text is not a comedy and as such the bloopers serve more as an opportunity to laugh after having dealt with a very serious subject. This suggests the filmmakers' own tension in their view of the topic and in their identities as not children and not yet adults, and the juxtaposition of the serious subject matter with the bloopers serves as a way of working through this tension. In this way, the Abortions PSA text is heteroglossic

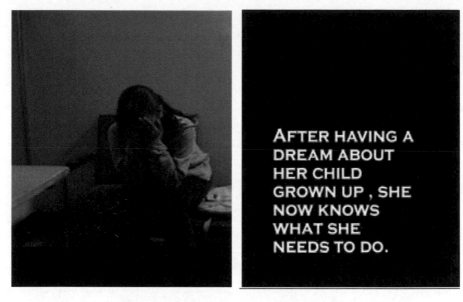

AFTER HAVING A
DREAM ABOUT
HER CHILD
GROWN UP , SHE
NOW KNOWS
WHAT SHE
NEEDS TO DO.

Figure 1. Scenes from the Abortions PSA.

(Bakhtin, 1981), featuring both a professional PSA pro-life discourse where one mistake has dire consequences, and a playful teenage discourse where they laugh at their own mistakes in the bloopers. Thus, we see the filmmakers enacting both a responsible adult discourse where a pregnant woman needs to make the right choice to keep her baby, and a playful teenage discourse where mistakes serve as an opportunity to learn. Since this is one mistake that cannot be undone according to the filmmakers, the teen mother moves from teenager to adult the second she reads the positive pregnancy test, thus reproducing the growing-up-all-at-once discourse of adolescent motherhood (Lesko, 2001).

Similar to the way in which the Abortions PSA takes up adolescence as a discourse, the text that Casey and Marie designed reproduces dominant constructions of girls as well. Davies (1993) argued that gender is taken up by an individual as one's own in ways that are not visible, and thus students can import sexist narratives that reproduce and confirm the oppressive world in which they live. The PSA designers take up such a gendered discourse in their positioning of women as solely responsible for unplanned pregnancies. This is evident in their decision to exclude the father of the conceived child beyond the first scene they had planned and were unable to include, which was meant to show the pregnant girl walking out of the room looking upset, while the boy was not given any lines or directions; thus positioning him as needing only to be present for the act that got the girl pregnant but not for the consequences. Further, there are no other male characters in the piece, thus positioning unplanned pregnancy as a female problem and the choice of whether to terminate or follow through with the pregnancy as solely the mother's decision as well. In this way, they absolve men from the responsibility for childcare and rearing. Since the pregnant mother's decision to keep her baby has consequences for her future success in school, absolving the boy means that he can continue his education and be successful in ways that the girl cannot.

Finally, the Abortions PSA seemed to be shaped by dominant representations of social class, though class was never specifically mentioned in the piece. It was evident to me, however, in the scene of the pregnant teen visiting a free clinic for advice on what she should do. In the scene, there is a disaffected clinic worker who communicates the type of limited substandard care available to those who can't afford to purchase quality healthcare. The clinic worker describes the pregnant girl's options, mentioning the option of keeping the baby first, subtly communicating that this is the right choice. This scene also pushes back against common conceptions of free clinics as places solely for abortions through an image showing that ultrasounds and checkups are provided, things that pregnant woman who cannot afford medical insurance would be able to receive at a free clinic.

The clinic scene is reminiscent of a similar scene in the movie *Juno* (Drake & Reitman, 2007), a popular film at the time, about a teenager who gets pregnant and decides to go through with her pregnancy. The main character Juno was from a working-class family and decided to give her baby up for adoption to a family that appeared to be upper-middle class where her baby could have access to resources that she was not in a position to provide. Juno's social class position in the film is quite similar to the position of the students in this study. Both the narrative of the film and the narrative of the Abortions PSA perpetuated the notion that poor and working-class teens are more likely to become teen parents than their wealthier peers, just as their parents had, thus positioning them as responsible for failing to move up the socioeconomic ladder.

Further, PSA as a genre assumes a singular public good, often rooted in middle-class values. For example, there are several PSAs that portray literacy problems as resulting from a failure of parents reading books to their children. Interestingly, the public good portrayed in the Abortions PSA is that a decision against abortion saves a life, a position that crosses social class lines.

Troubling the empowerment of students through digital media

Hull and Nelson (2005) posited the inclusion of digital multimodality in schools may provide space for diverse views and values to be incorporated into the design of our changing world in ways that the predominance of linguistic texts have tended to shut down. Their multimodal analysis of a digital multimodal story began to uncover some of the meanings and powerful semiotic potential that such forms of design may offer. Engaging in multimodal discourse analysis of the Abortions PSA highlighted ways in which the affordances of the digital, multimodal PSA video assignment did in fact allow Marie and Casey to position themselves as authors, designers, and filmmakers in powerful ways. Further, the youth constructed a persuasive and complex narrative, which is particularly significant in this school, where a singular focus on standardized test scores as the sole measure of students' literacies skills position a majority of students at East Side Middle School, including Marie, as in need of remediation due to a perception that they lack the ability to write persuasive essays. Finally, a close examination of the Abortions PSA videotext highlighted how the filmmakers simultaneously took up and resisted school-based and mass-media discourses that position them as at-risk for school failure. For example, the two filmmakers articulated the importance of their main character being an honor student because they wanted to show that even good students, as they considered themselves to be, make poor decisions that can lead to serious consequences for their success in school and later in life.

While the filmmakers resisted the positioning of teen pregnancy as something that doesn't happen to well-behaved students like themselves, they readily took up the mythologized (Barthes, 1972) view of celebrity and teenage pregnancy prominent in the media, and referenced popular films such as *Juno*, which features a lead character who decides not to have an abortion and still successfully stays in school and maintains her relationship with her boyfriend. In particular, the Abortions PSA video ends with the teen mother happily sharing the news with her friend over a cell phone that she will keep her baby. This decision came after receiving little support or guidance from the free clinic that she visited in order to get help. The filmmakers do not, however, address the consequences of this decision in terms of how it will affect this teenager's life, and merely portray her as a heroine for making the right decision not to have an abortion.

As Janks (2000) argued, merely giving students access to tools with which to design texts without an opportunity to deconstruct dominant discourses can lead to their unconscious reproduction. The ways in which the filmmakers performed the space of the journalism and digital media studies classroom seem to imply that this is the case for the youth in this study, who are often positioned at school as at risk for failure due to their cultural and socioeconomic backgrounds. For this particular assignment, as was the case with other projects throughout the year, the students did not have the opportunity to critique other PSAs or films with similar content, which may have facilitated their ability to think critically about the narrative that they chose to construct. Further, while both Mr. Cardenas and I were at times uncomfortable with some aspects of the narrative of the Abortions PSA, especially the failure of the filmmakers to address the serious consequences and implications of the decision that this young woman made, the power dynamics circulating in the classroom made it difficult for us to articulate our concerns to the students in a way that helped them to think critically about their choices. Despite repeated attempts by Mr. Cardenas, discussions quickly shut down as he struggled to find the "right" language to articulate his perspective to students without imposing his own ethical and political views, which he feared might inhibit their creative process or dissuade them from telling a story that was important and meaningful for them. Mr. Cardenas' struggle here resonates with descriptions of teachers new to the implementation of critical literacies described by Lewison, Flint, and Sluys (2002), specifically in the difficulty he encountered when faced with addressing politically charged issues and questions. From this view, Mr. Cardenas might have benefited from having a group of peers with whom he could discuss the issues that were arising in the class and how he might work through them with his students.

As such, this research points to a critical need for the type of multiliteracies pedagogy advocated by the New London Group (1996), wherein students and teachers engaged in multimodal design create communities of learners who critically inquire into the historical, cultural, and social nature of particular systems and practices in order to transform knowledge for their own purposes. By implementing such a pedagogy in a digital media studies program such as the classroom under investigation in this study, students might be afforded significant opportunities to critique dominant and marginalizing discourses in order to reconstruct new narratives and position themselves as authors and designers of their own social futures (New London Group, 1996).

CRITICAL LITERACIES IN THE MULTIMODAL CLASSROOM

The Abortions PSA exemplified what I observed throughout the year I spent with Mr. Cardenas and his students, specifically the multiple ways in which students drew upon the affordances of the multimodal space of the classroom to design a variety of texts, many of which spoke back to some of the restrictive and regulatory discourses of gender, social class, and adolescence that circulated across the multiple social spaces of their lives. However, some of the texts participants designed, including the Abortions PSA, also used language that reproduced some of the powerful gendered and classed discourses against which they often spoke both in and out of the classroom. The experiences of the youth in Mr. Cardenas' classroom and the texts they designed underscore the importance of engaging students in critical literacies work in multimodal classrooms. Through the process of engaging in critical conversations, youth can become more conscious of some of the powerful discourses circulating in the spaces in which they consume and design texts, thus limiting the potential for the unconscious perpetuation of dominant and restrictive discourses.

Critical literacies stem from a politicized understanding of language, literacy, and texts (Jones, 2006), and focuses on teaching students to understand and negotiate relationships between language and power (Janks, 2000). Janks identified four interdependent components necessary for critical literacies work in multimodal classrooms: domination, access, diversity, and design. In reference to domination, learners are taught critical language awareness and that all texts are constructed from particular points of view that can maintain and reproduce relations of domination. To do so, learners deconstruct the language in the texts they consume and produce, asking questions about whose perspectives are centered as well as who is being empowered or disempowered through language in texts. What Janks refers to as "access" requires teachers to make available dominant forms of language and literacies for students, while simultaneously providing opportunities for the recognition and legitimization of diverse types of texts, including multimodal forms, which compromises the diversity component of critical literacies pedagogy. Finally, design is an essential component in providing students opportunities to reconstruct the narratives they deconstructed through their critical readings, using a range of modalities to write new narratives and construct new discourses.

Throughout my time in the journalism and digital media studies classroom, I encountered moments when Mr. Cardenas engaged students in some aspects of the type of critical literacies pedagogy that Janks (2000) described. The most prominent aspect of critical literacies pedagogy I observed in the journalism and digital media studies class was access to dominant forms of language and literacies, which included reading and discussing articles in the major local newspaper that the class received each day. Mr. Cardenas regularly used the newspaper as a teaching tool, and students examined the genres and types of language utilized throughout different sections of the paper, using them as models for the articles they wrote for the *East Side Tribune*.

Students were also regularly exposed to dominant forms of texts on the Internet, including videos designed by students and professionals. When watching videos that he had chosen as models of exemplary work, Mr. Cardenas would spend time pointing out the features of the texts that contributed to the filmmakers' effectiveness in portraying their messages, such as strategic use of slow motion, background music, or subtitles. Students often modeled their own texts after the examples that Mr. Cardenas provided, while other times they chose to design their texts in their own ways. By allowing students to make their own design choices using a variety of modes, Mr. Cardenas engaged students in the diversity aspect of critical literacies pedagogy that Janks (2000) depicted.

However, I also witnessed what I perceived as missed opportunities for critical conversations to take place throughout my time in the journalism and digital media studies class. For example, though students spent time throughout the course reading articles in the local newspaper, the focus was usually on the structure and genre as opposed to analyzing and critiquing the power, language, and perspectives of the pieces. Also, though students did view each other's texts in order to provide feedback, the focus of these peer interactions was usually on aesthetics. Finally, though students were at times encouraged to design texts around issues of social justice, they were rarely prompted to deconstruct or evaluate the power, positioning, and perspectives on display in the texts designed in the class. As such, I read some of the texts that students designed for the class as reproducing dominant discourses in the way Janks (2000) illustrated. For example, most of the PSA projects reified representations of urban youth as more likely to become drug addicts, school dropouts, and teen parents.

As the description above illustrates, the lack of critical conversations in the journalism and digital media studies class was a powerful silence, of which I was a part. By this I mean that I had opportunities to share my thoughts about incorporating critical literacies pedagogy into the journalism and digital media studies classroom, but did not offer my suggestions to Mr. Cardenas despite his invitations to recommend ideas that could improve the instructional experience for students in his classroom. I made the choice not to offer suggestions because it was not part of my role as a researcher, creating a tension that permeated my work throughout the year.

Janks' (2000) paradigm for critical literacies work speaks to the incorporation of the type of multiliteracies pedagogy advocated by the New London Group. In multimodal classrooms such as the journalism and digital media studies class, incorporating critical literacies work can support teachers and students in designing texts for social action, thus limiting the possibilities that students will reproduce dominant constructions of class and gender as the filmmakers did in the PSA projects. However, it is important to note that this work is difficult and not a matter-of-fact process.

The story of the Abortions PSA shows how providing students access to dominant forms of language and literacies, recognizing and legitimizing diverse forms of literacies and texts, and providing opportunities for students to design texts around topics important in their communities, allowed for the youth in this study, who have in the past been positioned as low-literate based on their social, linguistic, and cultural backgrounds, to reposition themselves as authors, designers, and successful students. It is important to note here some challenges to implementing critical literacies pedagogy into multimodal classrooms that became apparent to me as I read the space of the journalism and digital media studies classroom. First, time is always a factor in schools, especially those with strict curricular mandates and pacing plans. Engaging students in critical conversations around texts takes time, and the benefit of these conversations cannot usually be measured easily by a single item on a test. Instead, teachers will need flexibility in their schedules and to become familiar with ways to analyze critical elements in the texts that students design for their classes. Through this process, teachers will be better prepared to access and support students' facility with deconstructing and reconstructing power, positioning, and perspective in texts. Further, engaging students in conversations around power, positioning, and perspective in the classroom can raise issues that teachers may feel uncomfortable discussing or fear will cause concern from administrators or parents. For example, a critical conversation about the perspectives centered in the Abortions PSA most likely would have brought forth religious and moral ideas that I felt uncomfortable discussing, partly due to my concern over the power I hold in the classroom as an adult, as well as the differences I recognized between some of my thoughts on this issue and those of the filmmakers. Thus, implementing critical literacies pedagogy into multimodal classrooms requires significant professional development to help teachers navigate conversations in ways that open up, as opposed to shut down, diverse perspectives, as well as ways to address concerns that arise from parents and administrators who themselves may be uncomfortable with particular issues and perspectives being discussed in the classroom.

Acknowledgments

The researcher would like to thank the National Academy of Education and the Carnegie Corporation of New York for their generous support of this research.

APPENDIX A
Transcript of the Abortions PSA

Time	Screenshot	Image	Action/Movement/ Sound	Spoken Language
:05		White words centered on a black background in all capital letters: "In the next 24 hours… 2,795 teen girls will get pregnant."	Writing flies in from the top and bottom of the screen.	
:11		A young Latina girl wearing a gray sweatshirt with her hair in a ponytail stands in a school bathroom.	The girl paces back and forth holding a pregnancy test that she has just taken.	
:17		The girl holds a pregnancy test that says EPT on one end and shows a plus sign on the other.	The camera zooms in on the pregnancy test.	
:30		White words centered on a black background in all capital letters "Angie is a 17 year old honors student. She has made a mistake by having unprotected sex…. Because of that one mistake…her whole life will be changed dramatically…"	Writing moves in from the bottom to the top of the screen where it fades.	
:40		The girl with a serious, sad face.	The girl walks outs of the bathroom. The girl's footsteps are audible.	

:42	SHE DOESNT KNOW WHAT TO DO. SO SHE CONSIDERS ABORTION. SHE GOES TO THE FREE CLINIC TO FIND OUT MORE INFORMATION AND SET UP HER APPOINTMENT...	White words on a black background in all-capital letters aligned on the left of the screen "She doesn't know what to do. So she considers abortion. She goes to the free clinic to find out more information and set up her appointment…"	Writing appears in the frame for 10 seconds.	
:52		The girl in a green sweatshirt and pigtails in front of a door with a sign that reads "Free Clinic."	The girl walks up the stairs to the free clinic and opens the door.	
1:13		The girl facing a nurse in front of two doors with signs that read "Ultrasounds" and "Checkups."	The girl walks down the hallway and stops in front of a girl with a clipboard. The camera zooms in on her as she tells the clinic worker she does not know whether she wants to carry out the pregnancy or abort the fetus.	CW: Hello. Welcome to the free clinic. What would you like to do today? Girl: Well, I'm pregnant and I don't know what to do. CW: Would you like to carry out with your pregnancy or abort your fetus? Girl: I don't know.

1:24		White words on a black background in all-capital letters aligned on the bottom left of the screen: "Angie goes home to think about what she should do."	Writing appears in the frame for 4 seconds.	
1:28		The girl in a white uniform shirt and dark pants sleeps on two chairs.	The girl walks into a room, rubs her head and lies down to take a nap.	
1:36		White words on a black background in all-capital letters aligned on the bottom left of the screen: "While asleep, Angie has a dream."	Writing appears in the frame for 3 seconds.	
1:39		The grown-up child mixing chemical solutions behind a table.	The grown-up child pours colored liquids into containers as if she is experimenting to make medicine. When she finishes talking, the screen fades to white.	Grown-up child: You see, Mom, I could have cured cancer. I could have saved the world. But you killed me.
1:49		The girl waking up from her dream.	The girl wakes up, sits up, and puts her head in her hands.	

1:57		White words on a black background in all-capital letters aligned on the bottom left of the screen: "After having a dream about her child grown up, she now knows what she needs to do."	Writing appears in the frame for 5 seconds.	
2:03		The girl on her cell phone wearing a white sweatshirt and black pants outside the clinic.	The girl walks out of the clinic and answers her ringing cell phone.	Girl: Hello. (pause) Hey. (pause). I decided I'm going to keep the baby. (pause) Yes, I'm sure. (pause) Okay, bye.
2:20		A narrator standing in front of the girl hanging up her cell phone.	The narrator pops up and announces the slogan in front of the girl hanging up her cell phone.	"Abort your thoughts, not a human being."
2:22		Grown-up baby's face.	The grown-up baby looks straight at the camera talking to her mother.	Grown-up baby: Thank you, Mommy. You saved me. You do love me.

2:26	Credits	Black background with white writing in all caps in the center of the frame with the names of actors, cameraperson, and director, and also thank you to Mr. Cardenas.	The text fades in and out every 5 seconds.	
2:49		Marie and the three actors pose and Casey's hand with one finger that says "take" and another that reads "!!!!!"	Marie and the three actors pose for the camera. May comes in last then Casey's hand appears.	Marie and the three actors holler. May: For sure
2:54		White words centered on a black background in all-capital letters: "Blooper Time!!!"	Writing appears in the frame for 2 seconds.	
3:00		The girl with her hands in the air laying on chairs.	The girl wakes up and laughs when she realizes the camera is not on, followed by two other scenes where she laughs during a take. Upbeat, bluesy guitar music program plays in the background throughout the remainder of the piece.	Is it on?

3:15		May acting out the last scene with her hands up in the air.	May laughs as she is filming her scene, puts her head in hands and tells Casey to cut.	May: No, cut
3:32		Close up of the girl staring at the camera.	The girl stares at the worker while the camera zooms in on her as the clinic worker recites her lines. The girl has forgotten her lines.	
4:00		The girl on the chairs rubbing her stomach.	The girl wakes up for a nap several times and rubs her stomach. She makes a mistake then laughs.	
4:27		The narrator in front of the clinic	Two more laughing blooper scenes with the girl and May both making mistakes followed by the narrator popping up as she does at the end of the video and reciting the slogan.	Abort your thoughts, not your baby.
4:29		White words centered on a black background in all caps: "PSA: Abortions."	Writing appears in the frame for 2 seconds then fades to black.	

REFERENCES

Bakhtin, M. (1981). *The dialogic imagination.* Austin: University of Texas Press.

Barthes, R. (1972). *Mythologies.* New York: Hill & Wang.

Barton, D. (1994). *Literacy.* Cambridge, MA: Basil Blackwell.

Blackburn, M. V. (2002). Disrupting the (hetero)normative: Exploring literacy performances and identity work with queer youth. *Journal of Adolescent and Adult Literacy, 46*(4), 312–324.

Davies, B. (1993). *Shards of glass: Children reading and writing beyond gendered identities.* Cresskill, NJ: Hampton Press.

Davies, B. (1994). *Poststructuralist theory, gender, and teaching.* Melbourne, Australia: Deakin University Press.

Drake, J. (Producer), & Reitman, J. (Director). (2007). *Juno* [Motion picture]. USA: Fox Searchlight Pictures.

Foucault, M. (1980). *Power/knowledge: Selected interviews and other writings 1972–1977.* New York: Pantheon.

Gee, J. P. (1996). *Social linguistics and literacies: Ideology in discourse* (2nd ed.). New York: Falmer Press.

Gee, J. P. (2005). *An introduction to discourse analysis: Theory and method* (2nd ed.). New York: Routledge.

Hull, G., & Nelson, M. E. (2005). Locating the semiotic power of multimodality. *Written Communication, 22*(2), 224–261.

Ito, M., Baumer, S., Bittanti, M., boyd, d. m., Cody, R., Herr, B., et al. (2009). *Hanging out, messing around, and geeking out: Kids living and learning with new media.* Cambridge, MA: MIT Press.

Janks, H. (2000). Domination, access, diversity, and design: A synthesis for critical literacy education. *Educational Review, 52*(2), 175–186.

Jones, S. (2006). *Girls, social class, and literacy.* Portsmouth, NH: Heinemann.

Kress, G. (2003). *Literacy in the new media age.* New York: Routledge.

Lesko, N. (2001). *Act your age! A cultural construction of adolescence.* New York: Falmer Press.

Lewison, M., Flint, A. S., & Van Sluys, K. (2002). Taking on critical literacy: The journey of newcomers and novices. *Language Arts, 79*(5), 382–392.

Luke, A., & Freebody, P. (1997). Shaping the social practices of reading. In A. L. S. Muspratt & P. Freebody (Ed.), *Constructing critical literacies* (pp. 185–225). Cresskill, NJ: Hampton Press.

New London Group. (1996). A pedagogy of multiliteracies: Designing social futures. *Harvard Educational Review, 66*(1), 60–92.

CHAPTER THREE

Engaging Urban Youth IN Meaningful Dialogue ON Identity THROUGH Digital Storytelling

ALTHEA SCOTT NIXON

INTRODUCTION

This chapter focuses on the digital-storytelling practices of Latino, African American, and Pacific Islander children in an urban, after-school club in Southern California. Specifically, this research shows how digital storytelling, as organized through collaborative, joint activity between children and undergraduate students, can be a critical digital literacies practice to support meaningful dialogue around sensitive issues of identity, race, ethnicity, and gender. Digital storytelling blends image, sound, print, and other communication media in a dynamic, real-time environment (Center for Digital Storytelling, 2011; Lambert, 2010; Lundby, 2009). Children use different media to help them tell a story about an important aspect of their lives. This multimodal practice provides children, who are at a developmental age when issues of identity are salient, the opportunity to be expressive using not just written or oral modalities but also by incorporating multiple media to reflect on questions of who they are and what is important to them.

Researchers have studied identity from several different theoretical perspectives, including consciousness (Dennett, 1991), modernist and postmodern (see Kellner, 1995, for a discussion), psychological (Erikson, 1970; Marcia, 1980) and sociocultural theories (Holland, Lachicotte, Skinner, & Cain, 1998). From a sociocultural perspective on identity, there are different versions of the self-performed (Goffman,

1959), enacted, and lived in moment-to-moment interactions: "Identities are lived in and through activity and so must be conceptualized as they develop in social practice" (Holland et al., 1998, p. 5). Digital storytelling is one such practice in/through which youth can construct identities as they tell their personal stories (Davis, 2004). Children in this study created digital stories about their lives and interests and provided narrative descriptions of themselves as they participated in figured worlds, the socially and culturally constructed worlds in which particular identities are lived: "Figured worlds could also be called figurative, narrativized, or dramatized worlds . . . [where] many of the elements of a world relate to one another in the form of a story or drama, a 'standard plot' against which narratives of unusual events are told" (Holland et al., 1998, p. 53). The figured worlds of these youth included, for example, their lives at school, in their neighborhoods, in society, and online communities. Identities are formed as youth participate in these figured worlds, and their digital stories narrated this process.

There is a long-established research tradition of studying identity through narratives (e.g., Ochs & Capps, 1996, 2001; see also Holstein & Gubrium, 1999; Mischler, 2006; Rymes, 2001; Sfard & Prusak, 2005). Recently, researchers have argued that identity is not only understood through the expression of storytelling, but that identity is the personal narrative: "Lengthy deliberations led us to the decision to *equate identities with stories about persons.* No, no mistake here: We did not say that identities were *finding their expression* in stories—we said they *were* stories" (Sfard & Prusak, 2005, p.14, emphasis in the original). Yet words cannot communicate everything about identity because words do not represent the repertoire of lived experiences in practice (Wenger, 1998).

Studying identity through narratives has limitations if the stories or words are the only focus; however, it is important to understand that narratives include much more than words since "[n]arratives are not usually monomodal, but rather they integrate two or more communicative modes. Visual representation, gesture, facial expression, and physical activity, for example, can be combined with talk, song, or writing to convey a tale" (Ochs & Capps, 1996, p. 20). There are not only speakers and hearers of stories, but also bystanders and addressed and unaddressed recipients of narratives (Goffman, 1981) who use gestures, body position, gaze, and intonation to co-construct stories collaboratively (Goodwin, 1986). In digital storytelling, children use these multiple modalities as they tell stories to each other, but they also incorporate additional modalities with the use of different technologies.

These technologies offer a variety of "mediational means or cultural tools that people employ to construct their identities in the course of different activities and how they are put to use in particular actions" (Penuel & Wertsch, 1995, p. 91). Digital storytelling has the potential to provide youth with opportunities for new sense-making of who they are, using digital stories that incorporate images, text, and sound. This sense-making is not additive; instead, it is qualitatively different: "Multimodality can afford not just a new way to make meaning, but a different kind of meaning" (Hull & Nelson, 2005, p. 225). Through the multimodal sense-making of digital storytelling, youth create new meaning as they are pushed to talk, think, and engage in identity play.

In addition to studying children's identities through the digital stories they tell, identity can be understood through social categories of race and gender. Recent research on identity in the context of new technologies has focused on how these institutional categories of identity are expressed within the domains of technological innovations, such as chat rooms and video games (Tynes, Reynolds, & Greenfield, 2004) or through digital artistic production (Sandoval & Latorre, 2008). The utopian rhetoric of a colorblind Internet challenges the salience of race, class, and gender in this domain; however, although many of the physical cues (i.e., skin color, clothing) children regularly use in the real world are not present in digital worlds, social categories of identity are indeed relevant (Smith & Kollock, 1999). Gender, for example, continues to be important in digital worlds through the use of language that is indexing particular social meanings (Ochs, 1992) and gendered activities (i.e., boys' use of violent video games and girls' use of computer games with friendship themes) (Kafai, 1998). This study shows how the literacy practices of digital storytelling are gendered and raced, as children take up these new technologies.

Only recently have researchers (e.g., Davis, 2004; Hathorn, 2005; Hull & Nelson, 2005; Myers & Beach, 2004) begun to study literacy and identity through storytelling that includes these additional media. In the age of new technologies used by growing numbers of children and adolescents (Lenhart, Madden, & Hitlin, 2005; Rideout, Foehr, & Roberts, 2010), it is important to understand the richness and depth of expression the many tools afford youth and how the literacy practices of digital storytelling encourage or constrain identity expression. I refer to this process as "mediation": a major tenet of Vygotskian sociocultural theories (Vygotsky, 1978) and cultural-historical activity theories (Cole & Engeström, 1993; Cole & Levitin, 2000) of learning and development is the concept of cultural mediation. There are multiple components to this definition, but the basic premise is that individuals interact with the world through the use of cultural artifacts, ranging from basic material constructions like tools to elaborate symbolic constructions like language and online media the children find during digital storytelling.

This interaction with artifacts affects how individuals think about the world and act on the world. Moll (1998) argues that cultural artifacts are used so frequently in our everyday activities and thought processes that it is easy to forget their influence on us. Yet all human activity in the cultural world is mediated by artifacts, and artifacts change how we view the world and develop cognitively (Cole & Derry, 2005). I studied how the tools and media of digital storytelling helped mediate discussions around identity. Also, while the focus of this study is on digital storytelling, it is important not to lose sight of the whole ecology, the contexts in which digital storytelling is embedded, that make possible the potentials of digital storytelling. This study focuses on both the benefits and limitations of digital storytelling on youth identity play within the settings of a media-rich learning environment, and how digital storytelling, as a digital literacy practice, can be a tool for helping children engage in critical dialogue around issues of race, ethnicity, and gender.

Methods

Setting and participants

This study takes place at Las Redes After-School Club, located in Southern California. Las Redes, originally directed by Dr. Kris D. Gutiérrez, is part of a growing network of Fifth Dimension sites in California, across the United States, and internationally (Gutiérrez, Baquedano-López, Álvarez, & Chiu, 1999; Nixon & Gutiérrez, 2007). Researchers at the Laboratory for Comparative Human Cognition started the first Fifth Dimension site in San Diego, California (Cole, 1996), as a design experiment (Brown, 1992; Collins, 1992) based on Vygotskian (1978) perspectives on learning and development and cultural-historical activity theory (Cole & Engeström, 1993; Cole & Levitin, 2000). Guided by these theoretical orientations, elementary school children at Las Redes learn through participation with undergraduate students enrolled in colleges and universities, using goal-directed activity in game playing with different technologies. Digital storytelling is one such technology practice begun at Las Redes with the goal of encouraging meaningful and empowering multimodal literacies praxis for the students.

Las Redes is an imaginary world, called a tertiary artifact (Wartofsky, 1979), where play is one of several leading activities (Griffin & Cole, 1984) for learning and development. At Las Redes, children imagine a world in which they suspend their disbelief of the existence of a wizard "El Maga," who is said to have created the after-school program. The wizard communicates with the children via online letter writing and encourages them to reflect on their learning during game-playing activities. As children play games in the imaginary world of Las Redes, they also suspend their understanding of what experts and novices look like and act like. Children teach undergraduate students, and each other, the rules of the game, how to use new technologies (such as those in digital storytelling), and how to use new strategies in their game playing. In this way, Las Redes is an envisioned space of unconventional learning and untraditional roles.

The demographic background of participants at Las Redes is important, considering that "digital storytelling involves access to a medium which was very recently unavailable to low-income individuals [and] youth" (Davis, 2004, p. 1). The participants at Las Redes included children, ages five to eleven, from a predominantly low-income and working-class community. Approximately 50 children out of slightly more than 1,400 students in the elementary school attended Las Redes after-school club. They were either chosen by the principal or joined the program through word of mouth from family members and friends who had been past participants. Of these 50 children, approximately 20 participated in digital storytelling. A core group of 10 to 12 children participated daily, and the others moved between digital storytelling and other game playing at the after-school program. More girls (almost 60 percent) than boys participated. At the elementary school, 95 percent of the students were Latino/a, 2.5 percent African American, 1 percent Pacific Islander, and 1.5 percent "Other." However, to create greater ethnic and racial diversity at Las Redes, there was a greater representation of African American and Pacific Islander children. At Las Redes, slightly less than 90 percent of the children were Latino/a, approximately 10 percent were African American, and a few of the children were Pacific Islander or Chinese. This study focuses on the core set of children who most regularly participated in digital storytelling, and the digital storytelling work of five children: Maya (a 6-year-old Latina girl), Eva (a 9-year-old Latina girl), Corey (a 10-year-old African American boy), Ryan (a 9-year-old Latino boy), and Teresa (a 10-year-old Pacific Islander girl).

Undergraduate students attended Las Redes as part of their undergraduate Education Studies Minor class assignments. Each academic quarter, approximately 30 undergraduate students worked with the children in helping them create their digital stories. The majority of the undergraduate students were women and each quarter roughly equal numbers of Latino/a, European American, and Asian students participated, with a few African American students. There was a Latina coordinator at Las Redes, who oversaw the general club activities and El Maga's role, and I (an African American woman) was the digital storytelling coordinator at the after-school club. I designed the digital storytelling learning environment and oversaw the collaborations between the undergraduate students and children. As a researcher, I was also a participant-observer who interviewed the children and collected the following data.

Data sources and analysis

To study digital storytelling at Las Redes, there were a variety of data sources. The data analyzed in this chapter include digital stories (a set of two- to three-minute digital stories); video data recorded of the children creating their digital stories and being interviewed; cognitive ethnographies (Hutchins, 1995) the undergraduates wrote about their collaborative, joint activity with the children; and letters the children wrote to and received from the wizard, El Maga. Across the school year, 55 videotapes were collected (each tape holds 60 minutes), 20 digital stories were created, and hundreds of cognitive ethnographies and letters were written; however, this chapter focuses on five children's digital storytelling work and their corresponding videotaped interviews and activities, letters, and cognitive ethnographies specific to those five children.

The data sources included activities that were already a part of the after-school club. For instance, undergraduate students wrote cognitive ethnographies for their class requirements. The cognitive ethnographies showed the undergraduate students' perspectives on digital storytelling. Considering distributed cognition, it is important that studies are "collaborative in that they depend on the knowledge and co-work of practitioners" (Shavelson, Phillips, Towne, & Feuer, 2003, p. 26). This is important because to understand practice, researchers need to include practitioners in their studies (Erikson & Gutierrez, 2002; Feuer, Towne, & Shavelson, 2002; Pellegrino & Goldman, 2002). I addressed this need by including observations made by the undergraduate students who helped implement digital storytelling at Las Redes. Undergraduate students wrote their cognitive ethnographies after each visit to Las Redes (once or twice a week, depending on the number of units they were in enrolled in).

Also, it is a long-established practice that children write letters to El Maga every day. Most often, their letters include what they did that day at Las Redes. El Maga usually responds with questions about what they learned, and why they liked certain things. These letters are written in an online discussion board as well as on paper. This study highlights a salient exchange of letters with El Maga about their digital-story composing, providing a perspective on how children themselves think about the process.

The digital stories children and adolescents created show how the participants expressed their identities through the literacy practices of digital storytelling. Also, because identity is expressed in the stories we tell about ourselves as well as through the activities we engage in, video data captured moment-to-moment interactions throughout the digital storytelling process. For instance, video showed how they collaborated and helped each other or even had conflict or competition in their activities (M. H. Goodwin, 1990, 1998).

To understand participants' decision making, motivations, and rationales for creating the digital stories using particular themes and tools, recordings included a developmental dialogue—a conversation about their meaning-making and new understandings—with them throughout the process. As they were working on their digital stories, I moved around the room with a video camera to sit next to them and talk through their ideas, focusing on the artifacts (such as pictures and music) that they incorporated into their digital stories. I asked them questions about these artifacts (e.g., why they selected the artifacts, what the artifacts meant to them, and how the artifacts tied into their digital stories). The data were collected to answer the following research questions:

1. What are the benefits and limitations of digital storytelling on youth identity play within the settings of a collaborative, media-rich learning environment?
2. How can digital storytelling, as a digital literacy practice, be a tool for helping children to engage in critical dialogue around issues of race, ethnicity, and gender?

To answer these questions, the data were analyzed in an iterative, non-linear process. First, macro-level analyses of identity themes and multimodal literacy practices/tools used across digital stories were conducted. Second, the ways in which conversations around identity, race, ethnicity, and gender unfolded throughout the digital storytelling activity were analyzed, with a focus on multimodality as a method and text within the social organization of and learning of digital storytelling activities. Third, digital storytelling artifacts, such as writings and images, undergraduate students' cognitive ethnographies, and children's letters to El Maga that documented their perspectives on the digital storytelling activities, were coded to show children's identities, interests, voice, and interactions with their co-participants. Lastly, activity logs of the video were created to document students' sense-making processes as they researched—via online websites, multimodal media, and among themselves—their self-selected topics for their digital stories.

THE MULTIMODALITY OF RACE, ETHNICITY, AND GENDER

Examining gender identity through new media practices of digital storytelling

The children at the after-school club examined intertextual, complex understandings of identity through their own and others' practices around media representations. Gender was evident in the types of digital stories girls and boys created. Of the total digital stories selected to analyze, which were representative of the body of digital storytelling work done at Las Redes, 80 percent of the girls wrote about their family and personal life aspirations, and 80 percent of the boys created fictional tales of adventure. This gender difference in digital storytelling themes is consistent with studies of gendered literary socialization and genre of reading preferences of young children (Mohr, 2006). However, it is much too simple to understand gendered practices through digital storytelling themes alone, or in isolation from the ways in which race, ethnicity, and gender were also at work in these narratives. The following is a prototypical example of how images of gender, race, and ethnicity in popular media were appropriated, as well as challenged, by youth and adults at Las Redes, and how this created a site for a cross-age exchange of ideas. This exchange led to a more critical analysis of the social construction of gender in popular media.

While participating at Las Redes, the children introduced me to the popular culture group RBD/Rebelde, whom a few girls wanted to write about in their digital stories. Rebelde is both a musical group and a telenovela or Spanish soap opera. The group originates from México but is televised in the U.S. Many of the girls at Las Redes watched Rebelde at home and at times with their mothers. As one undergraduate co-participant noted,

> A lot of the girls in the class like Rebelde.... At home [Susana's] mother is into it too. In a way Rebelde is a way for Susana to connect what is seen at home with what girls talk about at school. (Amy, field notes)

I documented that the children at Las Redes brought Rebelde stickers, pictures, DVDs, CDs and other collectibles from home. These media became shared artifacts among not just the Latino community at Las Redes, but also among several African Americans. For instance, an undergraduate co-participant documented the popularity of Rebelde among African American girls at Las Redes. He noted,

> I remember once in the beginning of the quarter, Noreen told me that she watched RBD by satellite with subtitles in English. Ever since, I have been very interested to discover why the African American community at Las Redes, specifically the girls Noreen, Charlotte, and Tracey would take interest in an otherwise Mexican pop-culture phenomenon. They all collect stickers. Write letters to El Maga requesting pictures. They know all of the characters' names. They even like to listen to their music despite the language barrier. (David, field notes)

Although the Rebelde media indexed particular ethnic codes about being Latina, these digital-storytelling media and codes were taken up in hybrid ways across ethnic groups. Undergraduates documented non-Latina children incorporating images from the Rebelde website into their digital stories, even though they spoke no Spanish. The children learned with each other and shared their knowledge about Rebelde. These conversations occurred spontaneously in the everyday activities of the children. For instance, an undergraduate described the scene at the school when he arrived at the beginning of site:

> When we walked into the school, I noticed all the parents standing, waiting for their kids by the gate, and as I turned around, there I saw a lot of little kids running, jumping on each other, play fighting, talking about Rebelde (OC: which I still do not know what it's about), and just walking home. (Renato, field notes)

The repeated mention of Rebelde in undergraduate field notes about children's digital stories and discussions in the undergraduate course illustrate the popularity of Rebelde among children, although many adults at the after-school club (myself included) were not initially aware of the fandom. Thus, a valued practice of the children and the adults' curiosity to learn more about what excited the young girls provoked interaction and conversation in which children shared with each other their interests and adults learned more about the cultural worlds of the children. By drawing on children's interests and out-of-school literacy practices, strong relationships between adults and children formed.

Although there were clear affordances in encouraging children to incorporate valued media practices in digital storytelling, such as Rebelde, such media often may promote static or problematic notions of gender identity. Here we begin to see the constraining sides of technology as well.

Gender and sexuality were salient in the media images and songs from Rebelde. The soap opera had a large storyline about high school girls and boys singing in a group, being close friends, and dating each other. The girls were hyper-sexualized in short skirts and shirts, similar to the "naughty schoolgirl" outfits made popular by what Britney Spears wore in her music-video debut. Several children at Las Redes, mostly girls, wanted to find online images of Rebelde and create digital stories about why they loved the group and why Rebelde was important to them.

The children's interests in Rebelde media merged into their digital-storytelling work. One example comes from Maya, a 6-year-old girl at Las Redes, who wrote a simple explanation in a digital story of why she likes Rebelde. She wrote, "Rebelde is pretty because she always paints herself around her eyes. She is also pretty because she is nice to her friends, Mia and Lupita. They are always together so they won't get lost." This narrative shows Maya's understanding of a dual nature of beauty: physical appearance and interpersonal, social behavior. Yet the physical appearance important to young Maya was not what many adult participants at Las Redes valued in the images. Maya didn't write about Rebelde's clothing or dress but focused on her eyeshadow. Similarly, the social behavior of Rebelde, which Maya appreciated, is reflective of Maya's experiences as a young child. Being nice to friends and sticking together so no one will get lost is something that Maya did each day at this site. She stuck by her older brother, who was 9 years old, and at the end of the day waited close by him so that they could walk home from school together. Maya's own experiences served as the interpretive lens for making sense of Rebelde.

Yet, Maya's interests in Rebelde conflicted with the undergraduate students' concerns about Rebelde's attire and the hypersexual images conveyed by the group. Even though the children and undergraduates were usually more aligned in their joint activity, their relationship allowed the undergraduates to point out problematic notions the children held and to write about these concerns in their field notes. As one undergraduate reported,

> I moved on to observe a group of three girls who were working on their project very intently. As I came closer I noticed that they were making their digital story on a Mexican pop music group called Rebelde. When I asked them who those people were, all three girls seemed kind of surprised that I had no idea about this group. Then one of the girls proceeded to explain that they are really popular in Mexico and that all of them are really pretty. She told me that their show comes on Univision and that I should watch them next time. (OC: By observing the scantily clad pictures of the singers I wasn't too sure if they were good examples of role models and someone these kids should be looking up to. But it seemed that their clothing did not bother the kids at all). I thought so because when I asked her what she liked about them so much she told me that she thought they were all really pretty and cool looking. (OC: So I think without even realizing these kids are attracted to the physical appearance of these celebrities. So I don't think it's a good idea to promote such celebrities who instill superficiality in these kids). (Sam, field notes)

We see in this field note a generational gap but also different conceptions of gender at work. For example, the children were surprised at the undergraduate's lack of cultural knowledge about the popular group Rebelde. Also, although the children saw Rebelde as "cool" and "pretty," the undergraduate thought the members of Rebelde were bad role models because of their mode of dress, which encouraged superficiality.

The example of Rebelde made visible that there was not an uncontested object shared by all participants. The staff and undergraduates were in a double bind. On one hand, children were encouraged for drawing on their valued practices and agentive behaviors of choosing their own topics for digital storytelling; but at the same time, adults felt that there were also opportunities for developing critical thought around one's meaning-making practices. Undergraduates, like Sam above, as well as the wizard, wrote about Rebelde. Through letter-writing to the children, El Maga tried to remediate digital-storytelling activity around Rebelde to include social thought on Rebelde's mode of dress and effects of the television media. As El Maga wrote in response to Maya's letter about her digital-storytelling activities,

> How are you? I am doing good. I didn't know that you liked RBD. They are really cool. I don't like all the things about them though. I like their songs and the way they sing. I don't like the way they dress because they don't wear a lot of clothes. I think it's ok not to like something 100%. What do you think? Do you like everything about them? What do you think TV does to us? I think that it hypnotizes us. It makes us forget about a lot of things and it shows us a picture of something that is fake. Then we believe that it is the truth. I like RBD even though I know that some of it is fake. What do you think? Do you think that the girls and boys in RBD are always that happy? I think they are like everyone else and that they get mad, sad, and happy too. Well, I have to go now but please write back soon. Adios. El Maga.

In this letter, El Maga is critical of the way Rebelde members dress while also acknowledging that Rebelde has appealing songs. However, while reflecting on both the strengths and limitations of Rebelde, El Maga neglected to write about both mediating aspects of television media. The response that television "hypnotizes us" and is "fake" shows a one-sided analysis of television media, in general, and the popular television show Rebelde in particular. In doing so, El Maga was able to encourage social critique by asking the children to think about the media they use, but also could at times shut down conversations about the children's digital-storytelling interests by conveying strong opinions that did not encourage critical analysis of the media, multiple perspectives, and joint problem solving.

Encouraging social critique through joint problem solving required a critical analysis of both the enabling and constraining aspects of mediation through Rebelde. There needed to be a balance between discussing with children the limitations of Rebelde, why Rebelde reproduced gendered and sexualized stereotypes, and discussing the strengths of these media in children's lives by listening to the children's voices about why they liked Rebelde.

I had conversations with some of the girls at Las Redes about Rebelde, and through digital storytelling, I learned more about the importance of Rebelde from the children's words. Digital storytelling required children to talk about images, and rich conversations around these images occurred during production time. For instance, a developmental dialogue with Eva, a fourth-grade girl, documents her sense-making around her digital story on Rebelde and why Rebelde is important to her. As illustrated below, unlike the undergraduates—who focused on the outward image of Rebelde, including their mode of dress—Eva never mentioned how the characters dress or their outward, physical appearance in our entire conversation. Instead, she reflected on Rebelde's interpersonal relationships and their singing, music, and dance.

ALTHEA: So tell me a little bit about your digital story.

EVA: Um, I'm doing the digital story about Rebelde. It's my favorite telenovela.

ALTHEA: Why?

EVA: I don't know. It has a lot of cute music. I like some of the characters, how they act and everything.

ALTHEA: Which are your favorite characters?

EVA: My favorite characters are Mia, Roberta, um Diego, and Miguel.

ALTHEA: Why?

EVA: They act good.

ALTHEA: What's good? What do they do?

EVA: A little bit about the novela is some, Mia and Miguel like each other and, but there's a new girl that entered to school, so then she wants to take away Miguel from Mia, and that's a little bit sad.

ALTHEA: Yeah.

EVA: So Roberta used to not like Diego but now they got used to each other and they like each other.

As documented in the interview transcript, Eva shared with me the love interests among the main characters of Rebelde and how two characters in particular are best friends. As a pre-teen, issues of dating and friendships are salient to Eva. Peer affiliation is a leading activity for youth Eva's age (Griffin & Cole, 1984). The social aspect of peer relationships in Rebelde was motivation for Eva to engage in the multimodal literacy practices of digital storytelling. In Eva's words, she "tried to make it like a film" (transcript continued below), and her engagement in story development centered on the social networks of friends in Rebelde. As part of this social network, the friends of Rebelde sing together, and in Eva's words, the show "has a lot of cute music" (line 45). Eva values the musical attributes of Rebelde, as further illustrated in the next part of her conversation with me. The interview highlights Eva's appreciation of Rebelde's singing, dancing, and music. She repeated many times that she likes Rebelde because "they just express their music," and she wanted to "put them singing" in her digital story:

EVA: And so they sing, sing, dance. They just express their music. They express their things. (Starts scrolling through pictures.)

ALTHEA: Awesome. Are they on these pictures?

EVA: Lemme show you. (Scrolls through iMovie project.)

ALTHEA: (Points to an image.) What's that?

EVA: That's Mia. These are all (Points to members of Rebelde individually) This is Miguel, that's Mia, this is Roberta, and this is Diego.

ALTHEA: How did you get the pictures?

EVA: Well, I just went to www.Rebelde.com. You see something like that. (Motions with her hands at the screen.) And then you get the pictures of them. You just search them, you make your folder, and you put them and drag them all in there. (Makes gathering motion with hands.) And that's how I got all of this.

ALTHEA: So what's happening down here? (Points to project timeline.)

EVA:	Well, here. Lemme show you from the beginning. (Drags timeline to the beginning.)
ALTHEA:	What's happening here?
EVA:	(Points to screen.) What I, what I tried to do something here is that I tried, I tried to make it like a film. Like I tried it with Rebelde. And then I put, tried to put all the characters like Mia, Roberta, Diego. And here I put all of them. Here I put the two best friends. (Points to screen.)
ALTHEA:	Um hmm.
EVA:	I put them right here, all of them.
ALTHEA:	Um hmm.
EVA:	I put them singing.
ALTHEA:	Um hmm.
EVA:	I tried to put all types of pictures from them singing.

Eva also likes to sing herself, and as she told me her favorite Rebelde songs, she sang a few lines of music (transcript continued below). When asked if she would like to sing for her digital story, she smiled and said yes. In the days that followed, Eva sat with her best friend at Las Redes (who was making a digital story about *High School Musical*), and together they sang quite loudly and confidently in front of the computer to an audience of anyone who walked past them.

ALTHEA:	Do you like to sing, too?
EVA:	Yeah. (Nods head.) Some of my favorite songs were "Es Así, Así Es," "Un Momento," "Y Soy Rebelde" (Sings the song titles) and those, those are my three favorite songs from the whole thing.
ALTHEA:	Would you like to sing on your digital story?
EVA:	Um. (Nods.)
ALTHEA:	Awesome! You have a good voice. That would sound nice!

The incorporation of cultural media in the digital-storytelling activity gave children like Eva the opportunity to engage in meaningful literacy practices that mixed popular culture with her interests in relationships, music, and dance. These cultural practices might have been censored in formal educational environments (Lewis, 2001; Revilla, Wells, & Holme, 2004), but at Las Redes, while El Maga and some undergraduate students initially wanted to censure Rebelde media, these controversial media were introduced, challenged, and expanded on by the participants. The media and practices of digital storytelling, like all practices, were therefore both enabling and constraining. The media of Rebelde enabled Eva to express her love of music and to consider story structure and character development, as Eva explained, "to make her story into a film." It enabled children to bring their home experiences to the after-school club, and groups of Latina and African American girls came together and created hybrid media practices.

Examining race and ethnicity through new media practices of digital storytelling

The centrality of child-driven interests and teaching and learning opportunities in the digital-storytelling activity created the space where undergraduate students positioned the child as someone with knowledge on important subject matter to be discussed. To further elaborate this pattern of analysis, Corey, an African American fifth-grade boy at Las Redes, had open conversations about race with a Latino undergraduate student, Jesús, who documented this interaction in his field notes. Jesús explained that while Corey was working on the computers creating his digital story, Corey showed him a personal website he designed. On this website, Corey wrote, "I'm African American and proud of it." The technologies and learning contexts of digital storytelling provided the opportunity for Corey to talk with Jesús about why being African American was important to him. Corey shared with Jesús the cultural practices of African ancestors and the relevance of the African American leader Rosa Parks to issues of prejudice. Jesús noted,

> Corey showed me and read to me what he had written on his info link. The very first sentence read "I am African American and proud of it" . . . I [asked] him if he [would] tell me more about his culture. . . . After this I asked him if he knew who from the African American community had recently died. He answered and said that Rosa Parks had died recently adding that she was an inspiration to everyone. I then asked Corey to tell me about why Rosa Parks should be an inspiration and he told me that she had sat where only white people were allowed to sit and refused to get up. I [asked] him if he knew the history that had led up to this and [he] told me that all white people weren't bad but some of them were prejudiced. Having heard Corey use the word prejudice, I asked him if he knew what the word meant and he blew my mind by saying that prejudice was prejudging someone based on the way they look. (By this point I wondered if I was talking to the next Martin Luther King Jr.) (Jesús, field notes)

Digital-storytelling technologies, as in the case of Corey and Jesús' collaboration, provided the tools to promote rich conversations on racial pride, identity, and prejudice. Corey paused from working on his digital story to show Jesús his website. This pause was a rupture in the digital-storytelling activity—a valuable rupture made possible by the flexibility of rules and the centrality of child-directed goals of digital storytelling—and Corey was able to share with Jesús his understanding of these complex issues. Corey took a nuanced stance on prejudice by acknowledging its relationship to the challenges Rosa Parks and other African Americans faced and also by explaining that "all white people weren't bad but some of them were prejudiced." Jesús was impressed by the discussion and promoted this dialogue. In this space, the dialogue with Corey and Jesús was mediated by the technologies and learning contexts of digital storytelling that gave Corey the opportunity to showcase his website and knowledge of African American cultural history and racial prejudice, a conversation that spoke of race and its importance to Corey's identity and sense of pride. Digital-storytelling technologies and the social relations the activity promoted enabled meaningful dialogue around such critical issues.

Digital storytelling resulted in digital literacy practices that supported meaningful discussions of race and ethnicity but also engendered critical dialogue around topics of prejudice and racism. Teresa, a fifth-grade student from the Pacific Islands, sat at a computer to find images to go along with her digital story about her interest in wrestling. She came to the after-school club wearing a t-shirt with images of WWE (World Wrestling Entertainment, Inc.) and her favorite wrestler, John Cena. She wanted to create a digital story about how she and her brother are wrestling fans. While searching for online images for her digital story, Teresa found pictures of WWE professional wrestlers JBL (John "Bradshaw" Layfield) and Rey Mysterio. Teresa worked alongside an undergraduate co-participant, Celia, who came to the after-school club as part of her education minor class to work with children creating digital stories, among other activities. Teresa explained to Celia that she did not like JBL because he was a "racist." In this moment of digital-storytelling activity, Teresa had a conversation with Celia about what racism meant to her and how it related to the popular media of the WWE she valued. As Celia noted,

> Then [Teresa] came across a picture of JBL and Rey Mysterio and she told me that she does not like JBL. I asked her why and she said "He's racist against Mexicans. He does not like Rey Mysterio because he won the championship and he said that Mexicans win everything and that Americans don't win." [JBL reportedly called a SmackDown wrestling crowd a bunch of "fruit pickers" in 2005, and when they responded by calling him names, he answered that he doesn't "speak Mexican" (Wrestle Zone, 2005)]. (OC: I was in shock that she used the word "racist" and I wanted to hear what she thought that word meant. I wanted her to elaborate more on this word.) She said that it means that "Someone is against [a] certain culture and I don't like people that are racist." I asked her what was her reaction when she heard what JBL said, and she said that she was shocked and that he should not have said that, she said that "A match is a match, he shouldn't have thrown in something about race." (Celia, field notes)

As evidenced by Teresa and Celia's interactions, the technology and media practices of digital storytelling supported discussions about race and racism, as did the social relations encouraged by this kind of joint activity of undergraduates working alongside children with a shared goal. Through the technologies made available to the children and the social relations formed between the co-participants at Las Redes, digital storytelling promoted this meaningful discourse to help extend children's understandings of race and racism. Children have experiential knowledge of forms of racism at young ages and recognize this behavior in others (Quintana & McKown, 2008). Digital storytelling drew upon this knowledge, and the conversation between Teresa and Celia documents the importance of participation in meaningful conversations where children can openly discuss their understandings of racism.

Using the technologies of digital storytelling as tools for meaningful discussions, the children at Las Redes shared their experiential knowledge and perspectives on race and racism with the undergraduates, as shown in the examples with Corey and Teresa. Although the children initiated these conversations, it is important not to minimize the roles undergraduate students had in mediating these types of discussions. For instance, one undergraduate, Isabel, shared with a fourth-grade student, Ryan, the cultural origins of the Anime drawings he was using for his digital story. She wrote,

> I told him, "Oh, you chose an Anime character!" He then said: "What is Anime?" (OC: I figured that since he had chosen an Anime character that he would have known what Anime was. To be honest, I was kind of shocked that he liked the character so much to put in his story, but did not know the type of animation that he was looking at. But, I stepped back and realized that I should not assume that he knows something just because I know it and have been exposed to information about it.) Given this, I then explained that Anime was a form of drawing that came from Japan, and gave him examples such as Pokemon and Yu Gi Oh! (OC: I know this because I have a 9-year-old brother who is into those shows.) In order to not confuse him, I told him that Anime was made up in Japan, but that anyone could draw it whether they were Japanese or not. And then he said, "Oh, so, like you learn from the Japan or the Chinese, I mean Japanese, to do this and then you can do it too?" (OC: Here I realized that Ryan learned that just because something comes from one place and is used by certain groups of people, that it does not mean that someone else somewhere else cannot use it also.) (Isabel, field notes)

In sharing with Ryan that Anime originated in Japan, Isabel also explained that anyone could draw it. Ryan immediately drew from this explanation that cultural practices can be shared by different groups of people, regardless of their ethnicity or nationality. This is an understanding that Gutiérrez and Rogoff (2003) argue is oftentimes misunderstood by researchers who equate culture with race or ethnicity. Yet through discussions around his digital-storytelling activity, Ryan gained new knowledge about the meaning of the cultural practices of which he had become part.

CONCLUSION

The tools of digital storytelling, as well as the social relations that this type of activity promoted, provided the space and opportunity for youth to engage in meaningful practices to represent and extend their understandings of complex issues with which they grappled personally and intellectually. There were both affordances and limitations of these media practices for non-dominant youth. Developing a more expansive technological toolkit has both enabling and constraining dimensions that re-inscribe as well as challenge static notions of identity. Through the remediation of their newly acquired media tools, youth engaged in meaningful examinations of gender, race, and ethnicity, topics too often ignored or sidestepped in learning environments (Lewis, 2001; Revilla, Wells, & Holme, 2004).

In the organization of learning in the digital-storytelling activity, the children were the central decision makers in choosing a story around their interests and ideas. This agentive role is important for the process of self-representation. The children constructed texts that represented themselves, their life interests. As with most efforts to introduce student-directed elements into education, there is a tension between the interests of the student and the constraints of the educational environment. Digital storytelling can be a powerful tool for engaging urban youth in discourse about identity, but only if the environment allows them to bring in elements that may initially not be seen as fitting well (e.g., the telenovelas). Many service-learning efforts contain the implicit assumption that university students are going to be teaching K–12 tutees (as do many of the Fifth Dimensions sites around the world), but there is also an assumption that there will be mutual learning by university students; each is a tutor to the other on different aspects of what is to be learned. The traditional hierarchy of adults as teachers and children as students also did not exist in the digital-storytelling learning environment because today's youth are "digital natives" (Prensky, 2001a, 2001b) who bring their own areas of expertise with new-media practices to the activity. Digital youth are resources in this technology-based learning environment, and children worked together through joint activity and collaboration.

The social relations the digital-storytelling activity promoted enabled meaningful dialogue around such critical issues such as race, ethnicity, gender, and power. Using the media of digital storytelling as tools for meaningful discussions, the children shared their experiential knowledge and perspectives on these issues. Children deepened their understandings through this firsthand interaction and discussion around their interests, with adults mediating these types of discussions. Undergraduate students, researchers, and program directors listened to, challenged, and encouraged the children to expand and question their understandings of messages in media.

Images of gender, race, and ethnicity in popular media were appropriated, as well as challenged, by youth and adults at the after-school programs, creating a site for a cross-age exchange of ideas. This exchange led to a more critical analysis of the social construction of gender in popular media. Youth participated in intertextual, complex discussions of race, ethnicity, gender, and power through a critical examination of their own and others' practices around media representations. The tools of digital storytelling, as well as the social relations that this type of activity promoted, provided the space and opportunity for youth to engage in meaningful practices to represent and extend their understandings of complex issues with which they grappled personally and intellectually. A critical examination of gender, race, and ethnicity is oftentimes ignored in public discourse and traditional educational settings (Lewis, 2001; Revilla, Wells, & Holme, 2004), but this practice was promoted and valued at Las Redes and in the digital-storytelling activity.

By making race and the intersections of race, ethnicity, and gender central to the study of digital storytelling, children's practices may challenge the utopian rhetoric of a colorblind Internet, a rhetoric that wrongly states these social categories of identity are no longer relevant in digital worlds (Smith & Kollock, 1999). In doing so, these practices also introduced a conversation that critical race theorists argue is often missing in education research (Ladson-Billings & Tate, 2006). It is important to focus on the consequences of new media and digital literacies on youth identity play within a framework that addresses these critical issues, in order to understand the diversity of participation and representation in digital worlds.

REFERENCES

Brown, A. L. (1992). Design experiments: Theoretical and methodological challenges in creating complex interventions in classroom settings. *The Journal of the Learning Sciences, 2,* 141–178.

Center for Digital Storytelling. (2011). http://www.storycenter.org

Cole, M. (1996). *Cultural psychology.* Cambridge, MA: Belknap Press.

Cole, M., & Derry, J. (2005). We have met technology and it is us. In R. J. Sternberg & D. D. Preiss (Eds.), *Intelligence and technology: The impact of tools on the nature and development of human abilities* (pp. 209–228). Mahwah, NJ: Lawrence Erlbaum.

Cole, M., & Engeström, Y. (1993). A cultural-historical approach to distributed cognition. In G. Salomon (Ed.), *Distributed cognitions: Psychological and educational considerations* (pp. 47–87). New York: Cambridge University Press.

Cole, M., & Levitin, K. (2000). A cultural-historical view of human nature. In N. Roughley (Ed.), *Being human: Anthropological universality and particularity in transdisciplinary perspectives* (pp. 64–80). Berlin: Walter de Gruyter.

Collins, A. (1992). Toward a design science of education. In E. Scanlon & T. O'Shea (Eds.), *New directions in educational technology.* New York: Springer-Verlag.

Davis, A. (2004). Co-authoring identity: Digital storytelling in an urban middle school. *Then*, *1*(1). Retrieved from http://thenjournal.org/feature/61/

Dennett, D.C. (1991) *Consciousness explained*. Boston, MA: Little, Brown.

Erikson, E. H. (1970). Reflections on the dissent of contemporary youth, *International Journal of Psychoanalysis*, *51*, 11–22.

Feuer, M. J., Towne, L., & Shavelson, R. J. (2002). Reply. *Educational Researcher, 31*(8), 28–29.

Erikson, F., & Gutierrez, K. (2002). Culture, rigor, and science in educational research. *Educational Researcher, 31*(8), 21–24.

Goffman, E. (1959). *The presentation of self in everyday life*. New York: Doubleday.

Goffman, E. (1981). *Forms of talk*. Philadelphia: University of Pennsylvania Press.

Goodwin, C. (1986). Audience diversity, participation and interpretation. *Text*, 283–316.

Goodwin, M. H. (1990). *He-said-she-said: Talk as social organization among black children*. Bloomington: Indiana University Press.

Goodwin, M. H. (1998). Games of stance: Conflict and footing in hopscotch. In S. Hoyte & C. T. Adger (Eds.), *Kids' talk: Strategic language use in later childhood* (pp. 23–46). New York: Oxford University Press.

Griffin, P., & Cole, M. (1984). Current activity for the future: The Zo-ped. *New Directions for Child Development, 23*, 45–64.

Gutiérrez, K., Baquedano-López, P., Álvarez, H., & Chiu, M. (1999). A cultural-historical approach to collaboration: Building a culture of collaboration through hybrid language practices. *Theory Into Practice, 38*(2), 87–93.

Gutiérrez, K. D., & Rogoff, B. (2003). Cultural ways of learning: Individual traits or repertoires of practice. *Educational Researcher, 32*, 19–25.

Hathorn, P. (2005). Using digital storytelling as a literacy tool for the inner-city school youth. *Charter Schools Resource Journal, 1*(1). Available: http://www.ehhs.cmich.edu/%7Ednewby/article.htm

Holland, D., Lachicotte, W., Skinner, D., & Cain, C. (1998). *Identity and agency in cultural worlds*. Cambridge, MA: Harvard University Press.

Holstein, J. A., & Gubrium, J. F. (1999). *The self we live by: Narrative identity in a postmodern world*. New York: Oxford University Press.

Hull, G. A., & Nelson, M. E. (2005). Locating the semiotic power of multimodality. *Written Communication, 22*, 224–261.

Hutchins, E. (1995). *Cognition in the wild*. Cambridge, MA: MIT Press.

Kafai, Y. (1998). Video game designs by girls and boys: Variability and consistency of gender differences. In J. Cassell & H. Jenkins (Eds.), *From Barbie to Mortal Combat: Girls and Computer Games* (pp. 90–117). Cambridge, MA: MIT Press.

Kellner, D. (1995). *Media culture: Cultural studies, identity and politics between the modern and the postmodern*. New York: Routledge.

Ladson-Billings, G. J., & Tate, W. (2006). *Education research in the public interest: Social justice, action, and policy*. New York: Teachers College Press.

Lambert, J. (2010). *Digital storytelling cookbook and traveling companion*. Berkeley, CA: Digital Diner Press.

Lenhart, A., Madden, M., & Hitlin, P. (2005). *Teens and technology: Youth are leading the transition to a fully wired and mobile nation*. Washington, DC: Pew Internet & American Life Project.

Lewis, A. E. (2001). There is no "race" in the schoolyard: Color-blind ideology in an (almost) all-white school. *American Educational Research Journal, 38,* 781–811.

Lundby, K. (Ed.). (2009). *Digital storytelling, mediatized stories: Self-representations in new media.* New York: Peter Lang.

Marcia, J. E. (1980) Identity in adolescence. In J. Adelson (Ed.), *Handbook of adolescent psychology.* New York: Wiley.

Mischler, E. (2006). Narrative and identity: The double arrow of time. *Studies in Interactional Sociolinguistics, 23,* 30–47.

Mohr, K. A. J. (2006). Children's choices for recreational reading: A three-part investigation of selection preferences, rationales, and processes. *Journal of Literacy Research, 38,* 81–104.

Moll, L. C. (1998). Turning to the world: Bilingualism, literacy, and the cultural mediation of thinking. *National Reading Conference Yearbook, 47,* 59–75.

Myers, J., & Beach, R. (2004). Constructing critical literacy practices through technology tools and inquiry. *Contemporary Issues in Technology and Teacher Education, 4*(3). Retrieved from http://www.citejournal.org/vol4/iss3/languagearts/article1.cfm

Nixon, A. S., & Gutiérrez, K. D. (2007). Digital literacies for young English learners: Productive pathways toward equity and robust learning. In C. Genishi & A. L. Goodwin (Eds.), *Diversities in early childhood education: Rethinking and doing* (pp. 121–135). New York: Routledge Falmer.

Ochs, E. (1992). Indexing gender. In A. Duranti & C. Goodwin (Eds.), *Rethinking context: language as an interactive phenomenon* (pp. 335–358). Cambridge, UK: Cambridge University Press.

Ochs, E., & Capps, L. (1996). Narrating the self. *Annual Review of Anthropology, 25,* 9–43.

Ochs, E., & Capps, L. (2001). *Living narrative: Creating lives in everyday storytelling.* Cambridge, MA: Harvard University Press.

Pellegrino, J. W., & Goldman, S. R. (2002). Be careful what you wish for—you may get it: Educational research in the spotlight. *Educational Researcher, 31*(8), 15–17.

Penuel, W. R., & Wertsch, J. V. (1995). Vygotsky and identity formation: A sociocultural approach. *Educational Psychologist, 30*(2), 83–92.

Prensky, M. (2001a, September/October). Digital natives, digital immigrants. *On the Horizon, 9*(5), 1–6. Retrieved from http://www.marcprensky.com/writing/Prensky%20-%20Digital%20Natives,%20Digital%20Immigrants%20-%20Part1.pdf

Prensky, M. (2001b, November/December). Digital natives, digital immigrants, part II: Do they really think differently? *On the Horizon, 9*(6), 1–6. Retrieved from http://www.marcprensky.com/writing/Prensky%20-%20Digital%20Natives,%20Digital%20Immigrants%20-%20Part2.pdf

Quintana, S. M., & McKown, C. (Eds.). (2008). *Handbook of race, racism, and the developing child.* Hoboken, NJ: John Wiley and Sons.

Revilla, A. T., Wells, A. S., & Holme, J. J. (2004). "We didn't see color": The salience of color blindness in desegregating schools. In M. Fine, L. Weis, L. P. Pruitt, & A. Burns (Eds.), *Off white: Readings on power, privilege, and resistance* (pp. 284–301). New York: Routledge.

Rideout V. J., Foehr, U. G., & Roberts, D. F. (2010, January). *Generation M²: Media in the lives of 8- to 18-year-olds.* Kaiser Family Foundation. Retrieved from http://www.kff.org/entmedia/upload/8010.pdf

Rymes, B. (2001). *Conversational borderlands: Language and identity in an alternative urban high school.* New York: Teachers College Press.

Sandoval, C., & Latorre, G. (2008). Chicana/o artivism: Judy Baca's digital work with youth of color. In A. Everett (Ed.), *Learning race and ethnicity* (pp. 81–108). Cambridge, MA: MIT Press.

Sfard, A., & Prusak, A. (2005). Telling identities: In search of an analytic tool for investigating learning as a culturally shaped activity. *Educational Researcher, 34*, 14–22.

Shavelson, R. J., Phillips, D. C., Towne, L., & Feuer, M. J. (2003). On the science of education design studies. *Educational Researcher, 32*(1), 25–28.

Smith, M., & Kollock, P. (Eds.). (1999). *Communities in cyberspace.* London: Routledge.

Tynes, B., Reynolds, L., & Greenfield, P. M. (2004). Adolescence, race, and ethnicity on the Internet: A comparison of discourse in monitored vs. unmonitored chat rooms. *Journal of Applied Developmental Psychology, 25,* 667.

Vygotsky, L. (1978). *Mind in society: The development of higher psychological processes* (M. Cole, V. John-Steiner, S. Scribner, & E. Souberman, Eds.). Cambridge, MA: Harvard University Press.

Wartofsky, M. (1979). *Models: Representations and the scientific understanding.* Dordrecht, the Netherlands: Reidel.

Wenger, E. (1998). *Communities of practice: Learning, meaning, and identity.* Cambridge, UK: Cambridge University Press.

Wrestle Zone. (2005, October 30). *JBL's latest racist rant, & backstage news on Warrior DVD.* Retrieved from http://www.wrestlezone.com/news/229295-jbls-latest-racist-rant—backstage-news-on-warrior-dvd

CHAPTER FOUR

Critical Literacies AND Social Media

Fostering Ethical Engagement with Global Youth

ANNA SMITH & GLYNDA HULL

In an era when digital information and communication technologies proliferate, so do opportunities for social interaction and communicative exchanges across localities and nation states (Appadurai, 1996). Via digital means we are now easily able to compose in multiple modes and, with access to the Internet, to do so in response to and in collaboration with international others. Such practices are, in fact, increasingly viewed as central rather than peripheral to literacy (Andrews & Smith, 2011). *Critical* reading implies a reader's active response, as Rosenblatt (1938/1995, 1978/1994) long ago taught us. The interpretation of written language and image resides at the intersection of text, the reader's personal experiences with other texts, and the social world. In a digital age, a reader's response can become manifest *materially* (cf. Coiro & Dobler, 2007). When readers engage with a blog, for instance, they are able, indeed expected, to click on links, add comments, and reblog or remix content. Such response is a customary, expected part of the reading experience. Thus, the reciprocal relationship between reading and writing becomes tighter in the digital sphere, making authorship more obviously tantamount to readership, and vice versa.

New digital configurations of people and ideas have the potential as well to shift social power relations. Previously only those with knowledge of coding languages and access to servers, or even further distant, those with access to publishing companies and their processes, could contribute to and critique the existing bodies of knowledge in a given field. Although inequalities certainly still exist and proliferate (Hargittai & Hinnant, 2008; Schradie, 2011), the capability to be producers and critical consumers of knowledge is now more widely available. Through social media outlets, more people of diverse ages, nationalities, genders, and socioeconomic positions produce news, comment on social issues, and even stage revolutions. These new configurations, in turn, necessitate a new ethic of exchange with distant, unknown, imagined others (Appiah, 2006). Critical reader-writers must orient themselves to take into consideration not just the interpretations they have intended as authors, but also the possible interpretations of audiences previously unimagined and out of reach. Thereby the rhetorical framework of composing not only widens but shifts as compositions wind their way through media and audiences. Writers not only design their meanings via multiple modes (cf. Kress, 2003; New London Group, 1997), but for unknown audiences who have the capacity to respond directly, becoming genuine interlocutors. These new configurations of digital reader-writers and audiences require new critical and creative dispositions toward reading and composing in the digital age.

Hull and Stornaiuolo (2010; Hull, Stornaiuolo, & Sahni, 2010) have suggested that the new ethic of digital literacies is "cosmopolitan" practice—reflexive and hospitable dispositions and habits of mind necessary for ethically motivated rhetorical and semiotic decision making in relation to wide, interactive, and potentially global audiences. In doing so, they drew on research with youth engaged in social interaction and the exchange of arts-based artifacts on a global social network, Space2Cre8. With colleagues and participants from India, South Africa, Norway, Great Britain, and Australia, as well as U.S. sites in California and New York, they described how youthful exchanges on this network are mediated through a developing cosmopolitan ethic—a growing common understanding of how to effectively interact and exchange meanings and artifacts across linguistic, worldview, and geographic boundaries. Such an ethic includes, importantly, sensitivity to the range of possible interpretations and responses to their own and others' postings. As youth begin to compose self-reflexively, revising their profile pages and creating movies and other artifacts to share, and imagining others' possible interpretations of their work, they develop "hospitable" stances in their reading of and composing for their distant audiences. As an important part of this process, youth participate in a collective mentorship method by which they share and appropriate productive practices of critique and commentary as a community.

We find cosmopolitanism, with its emphasis on inclusivity and mutual respect, a generative framework for thinking about the ethics of authorship and readership in a digital and global world. In a nutshell, cosmopolitanism is the idea that one can become, indeed should aspire to be, a citizen of the world, able to embrace local ties and commitments, but also to extend well beyond them, engaging a wider human community, even across divides of seemingly irreconcilable differences. Scholars from a range of disciplines have explored the implications of cosmopolitanism, often in order to respond to conditions associated with globalization and the recognition that ours is an interconnected and interdependent, if conflicted, world. Such implications are far reaching and require, some have argued, a "cosmopolitan turn" in all of the social sciences and humanities (Beck & Sznaider, 2006). In education, cosmopolitanism has been taken up primarily by educational philosophers, who have recently begun to formulate cosmopolitan-minded frameworks to underpin conceptions of teaching and learning appropriate for a global age. Rizvi (2009), for example, explores how we can frame education so as to provide students both a knowledge about global transformations and also an ethical orientation towards them. He thus calls for "cosmopolitan learning" that fosters "a critical global imagination" (p. 265). (See also Hansen, 2010; Papastephanou, 2005.) Our own work, drawing on the concept of hospitality as a crucial cosmopolitan disposition for critical reader-writers in a global and digital age, is one answer to Rizvi's call.

The notion of hospitality has long been part of philosophical thought around cosmopolitanism (e.g., Derrida, 2002; Kant, 1983), for as a phenomenon it brings to the fore the nature of our relationships with guests, outsiders, foreigners, and others (cf. O'Gorman, 2006). For example, according to communications theorist Silverstone (2007), cosmopolitanism requires us "to recognize not just the stranger as other, but the other in oneself" (p. 14). He continues: "Cosmopolitanism implies and requires, therefore, both reflexivity and toleration. In political terms it demands justice and liberty. In social terms, hospitality. And in media terms it requires . . . an obligation to listen, an obligation which . . . is a version of hospitality" (p. 14). As a metaphor for communicating respectfully across difference in a global age, we find the ideal of hospitality to be rich with possibility. An obligation to listen implies a thoughtful openness to possible meanings in a pluralist sense, and an acknowledgment that we can't assume what to expect in terms of others' reactions and intentions. Indeed, we may not always be cognizant of our own intentions and reactions, which makes being open to and adept at critical reflection not only about others' meanings, but also about our own actions and motives, all the more important. To be a hospitable reader, writer, and viewer is thus to tolerate the discomfort that comes with honestly engaging with another around the uncertainties of attempting to understand and to be understood.

In this chapter, we foreground the composing processes and media exchanges of youth in one U.S.–based site on the Space2Cre8 network in relation to their developing digital ethic of cosmopolitan practice. At this New York City site, youth were introduced to the Space2Cre8 social network during a four-week alternative college-preparatory summer academy, which not only fostered cosmopolitan practices via participation on the network, but also offered cosmopolitanism as a philosophical concept at the center of the academy's curriculum. This double emphasis on cosmopolitanism through formal study and discussion in tandem with the practice of cosmopolitan values on the network is unique among the current sites, which typically provide opportunities only for the latter. The compositions that we discuss in this chapter are drawn from two cohorts of 25 youth who attended the program in sequential years. These young people were incoming juniors and seniors from high schools in New York City's Bronx borough. They traveled from the Bronx to New York University for the summer program—in effect, journeying across cultural, geographic, and economic boundaries. The academy was funded externally as a community center–university collaboration set to improve college preparation in terms of traditional school reading, writing, and critical thinking. Students were selected to participate by the community center, and in year two, many participants were acquaintances of the first cohort, as the first-year cohort encouraged their friends to participate during year two. The youth had a variety of interests and future aspirations; several looked forward to futures in film (production and acting), athletics, or criminal justice. They also shared, with many high school students, limited practice composing long-form academic texts. Most reported never having written a full essay independently, and thus, one of the aims of the academy was to demystify academic writing both by providing practice in its traditional forms, as well as by bridging to and from multimodal composing. Anna, co-author of this chapter, served as the director of the program and the instructor of the 21st-century composition course in the summer academy. To devise an alternative approach to college preparation for high school students, she along with the other instructors and researchers at this site designed three college-level courses to be taught by professors and graduate students. These courses mediated students' experiences learning to read and write college texts, while engaging them in a philosophical exploration of college as a cosmopolitan experience—not unlike the participants' current experiences living in the 21st century in an urban center.

In addition to participating in an international digital exploration of cosmopolitan practice, youth at this site studied the concepts of cosmopolitanism through multiple modes of philosophic inquiry. As part of the program, youth read and discussed *Cosmopolitanism: Ethics in a World of Strangers* (Appiah, 2006) in a seminar, while also drawing and analyzing neighborhood maps, blogging about digitally created belief collages, writing college application essays exploring the connection between their personal experiences and their values and beliefs, and designing "cosmopolitan conversation" digital stories (Hull & Nelson, 2005) in their 21st-century composition course. Like youth at other sites around the world, these young people interpreted, critiqued, and posted creative and critical compositions; polled and chatted with one another; and experimented with representations of self through the construction and maintenance of an online profile.

COSMOPOLITAN CONVERSATIONS

This chapter focuses on processes of composing and the circulation of "cosmopolitan conversation" videos through Space2Cre8. In the composition course, the youth initially discussed images from blog posts and profile pictures posted by distant others on Space2Cre8. They considered how they interpreted these images and how to critically read images in blogs and posts. Then Anna provided the youth a series of compositional challenges. As a pedagogical approach to giving assignments, these challenges were designed to build on the youths' existing knowledge and experiences in ways that left compositional and rhetorical choices up to the youth. In the first of these challenges, youth composed their own image-based blog posts on the topic of the seminar course—how our values and beliefs are deeply rooted in our personal experiences—and experimented with a variety of design techniques introduced in the composition course, such as juxtaposition, color, visual metaphor, and foregrounding/backgrounding. They then invited other participants on Space2Cre8 to respond with their own interpretations. Finally, students were given the challenge of composing a digital story with the Space2Cre8 global audience in mind, a movie in which they would explore the intersections of personal values, goals, and experiences (about which they had already blogged) with issues in wider society and the world (which they had been discussing in the seminar course). In this way, youth put into practice the concepts of cosmopolitanism that they had been studying—such as how we engage with strangers whose backgrounds, values, and points of view likely differ from our own.

In their videos, the youth were asked to demonstrate their ability to think deeply about the important issues of our world, to reflect on the perspectives of others, and simultaneously, to consciously maintain or adjust their personal worldview, beliefs, and values. They were also asked to make mindful design choices, planning visual and audio effects to communicate their intended meanings. To begin their compositions, the youth critically viewed and discussed two videos posted on Space2Cre8 by others in the global community. Practicing reflexive and hospitable readings of the videos, they juxtaposed their own interpretations, the possible intentions of the authors, and the possible influence of design elements on both. After responding to the videos and discussing their initial reactions, they reviewed the cosmopolitan conversation video challenge (see Figure 1), and watched the two videos a second time.

First they viewed a video created by Bakhti, a 17 year-old girl from an extra-school site in India, and a frequent contributor to Space2Cre8. Bakhti's video included photographs from her daily life—of family, work, and school—with a voice-over that described aspects from each of these realms, including her father's alcoholism and the lack of a "proper kitchen" in her home (see Hull, Stornaiuolo, & Sahni, 2010). After viewing this video, the New York youth sat silently for a moment and then went on to comment about how they had been struck by her straightforward and honest discussion of her economic status (which required her to work to support for her younger siblings) and familial situation (the death of her mother and neglect by her father). In fact, several participants mentioned how surprised they were that she was open about topics that they would have kept private. One student mentioned that he appreciated Bakhti's revelations, for without them he would have not known how much they had in common, and in this way, she had engaged him by making a connection across boundaries of country and culture. Next, the youth watched a video made by a group of students in Norway in a school-day program. This video showed several images of homeless people, overlaid with a musical track with a sad tone. It concluded with a scrolling message and matching voice-over about why and how people should care for the homeless, to wit, a kind of public-service announcement. The youth mentioned that the music changed how they viewed the pictures, evoking emotional responses that allowed them to picture themselves in similar situations, and though they found the video impactful in this way, they felt the voice-over sounded "scripted," making it also seem a little preachy, or in their words "too much." In these ways, this video reminded them of ones they had previously made in school about social issues, such as drug abuse and dropping out. The participants were finally given the challenge to take on the social issues that matter to them and to a global audience—such as homelessness in the video from Norway—and to do so in a way that was sensitive to their own experiences so they could engage others as powerfully as Bakhti from India had engaged them.

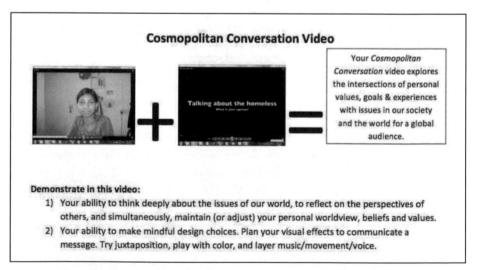

Figure 1. Cosmopolitan Conversation Video Challenge Description.

METHODS OF DATA COLLECTION AND ANALYSIS

In addition to using the results of an automated tracking system that recorded the activity on the social network, we conducted open-ended and focused thematic coding of daily observational field notes (Dyson & Genishi, 2005) to explore how participants took action through talk, enacted identities, and negotiated joint activities. Daily saves of raw media and written compositions were made throughout the month-long academy to capture the sequence of participants' design choices. Documents, which were the result of academy activities, were also collected, such as student-drawn maps of what the youth considered their local neighborhoods before the academy, and reflection on and revision of these maps at the end of the academy. Students filmed commentary regarding these revisions. (See Appendix A for Eva's maps and commentary.) We also conducted and analyzed pre- and post-academy interviews, and we asked the students to capture commentary on their written and designed products via video. We have done verbatim transcripts of these recordings. Reproducing participants' language as accurately as possible, we have not changed their speech or writing to match standard conventions.

As the youth neared completion of their cosmopolitan conversation videos, we conducted composing-process interviews (see Appendix B for this protocol). In these interviews, we asked youth to share their intended audiences, messages, and tone; what design strategies they employed; their composing and collaborative processes; and the reactions they expected from those on Space2Cre8. We also asked them the origin of their initial ideas and feelings for their video; what changes, if any, they considered while composing the film; and what they viewed as the resulting effect of the video. We then watched the video each had created frame by frame, discussing compositional choices. Multimodal transcripts of these interviews were constructed, drawing on Hull and Nelson's (2005) analytic. That is, in a three-column chart, we aligned scene-by-scene the screen shots of the videos in one column; notes about other modes that youth employed in their designs such as sound, transition effects, text, etc., in the second column; and the transcript of the composing interview that referred to the scene in the third column. The transcripts helped us to uncover how students' multimodal compositions conveyed meaning through different semiotic systems such as image, sound, and language.

AUTHORING COSMOPOLITAN PRACTICES

Our analyses shed light on the nature of individuals' engagement with cosmopolitan practices—their semiotic, linguistic, and social choices, intentions, and aspirations with global others as made manifest through a social network, Space2Cre8.

The interactions with and reactions to peers both distant and local influenced the ways in which the youth took up, resisted, and negotiated cosmopolitan practices on- and offline. Reactions to each other's activity online varied, especially initially. One youth, Cody (student names are pseudonyms), did not want to interact with someone he had never met in person. Even when instructors assured him that they personally knew that the youth from the various countries actually existed and were in fact who they said they were, he refrained from engaging, emphatically stating, "They could be anybody." It was only after a Skype video phone call with youth at the London site, for which Cody was asked to be the spokesperson for the New York site, that he watched the videos that youth from the London site had made and posted on Space2Cre8. Then he responded with verbal comments, but not online. In contrast, another participant, Ally, readily interacted with international youth, each day choosing a different country in which to locate youth on the site and to whom she would then post comments. She structured her cosmopolitan conversation video—an illustrated poem—to resemble a video she had seen on Space2Cre8. Students articulated a similarly wide range of influences on how they interacted with and reacted to others. As a result of reading and discussing the texts of the course, youth reported a change in how they approached international and local peers with whom they disagreed, as well as how they approached strangers with whom they imagined they might potentially disagree. Youth also professed that the choices they made in their interactions online and how they interpreted the posts of others were influenced by what they had learned about design elements and multimodal meaning-making.

Drawing on our analyses of youths' engagement with distant others, we call for an ethical turn in digital literacies studies in order to acknowledge and support dimensions of authorship in a global age that require the exercise of empathy and "hospitality" (Silverstone, 2007; cf. Hull & Nelson, 2009). We believe that such a turn is paramount now because of new global formations, opportunities, and challenges, and we hope that it offers a fresh direction for critical literacies studies, engaging the implications of the digital compression of space and time. The youth in our project demonstrated that, not only was authorship for distant audiences central to critical digital literacies, it was key to the development of their own cosmopolitan ethical dispositions. We describe two such youths' composing processes, which were representative of the larger group in terms of how they described the roles that designing and composing played in their growing understandings of cosmopolitanism and the ethical turns they attempted in interacting with local and distant others. First, we examine Tyson's authorship and the role that reading, writing, and video production played for him in developing a cosmopolitan understanding of the concept of "struggle." We then explore Eva's experience of authoring a film that she entitled *Making Conversation*. In her words, this project had an "awesome" impact on how she interacted with others both on- and offline.

Dimensions of authorship in developing critical digital literacies

Tyson, an African American high school junior, was one of several youth whose composing practices illustrate the role that authorship plays in the digital age—particularly the role it plays in developing both conceptual understandings and critical dispositions. Tyson came to the academy well versed in video production. He and several of his peers had taken at least two courses—one in school and the other in an after-school program—on movie making, employing software such as iMovie and FinalCutPro. On the second day of the academy, after viewing posts from each of the participating countries on Space2Cre8, he asked to borrow a video camera for the weekend; he returned not only with footage, but an edited video that he had completed independently. The video was entitled *Tyson's City* and included recordings of major tourist attractions, which he labeled "random footage," and scenes from his neighborhood, including his house, the community fire station, and streets. Over these clips he laid snippets from popular music tracks. He offered to post his video on Space2Cre8 in order to introduce others to the academy.

We share Tyson's early video activities to suggest that, like increasing numbers of youth, he was a fluent composer across multiple platforms and with multiple modes. However, he was not immediately prone to authoring *critically*—that is, intentionally, through a composing process of reflexive, ethically-motivated semiotic choices and revisions to create a multifaceted product for a potentially global audience (cf. Warschauer & Matuchniak, 2010). For instance, other than sharing his initial video the first week of the program, Tyson posted only twice to the site—both times pictures of his favorite rapper, Drake, without commentary or attention to the critical designing challenges he had been given. In fact, he explained that when he began creating his cosmopolitan conversation video, in which he explored the concept of struggle, he was disengaged: "At first, like as I was making it, I wasn't really serious about it. I just wanted to do it just to do it. But then like I started to get more serious. I put more thought into it."

It is this very "seriousness" and "thoughtfulness" that we'd like to explore. Tyson explained several ways that the viewing and compiling of his and others' media shaped and reshaped his understandings and feelings about the concept of struggle. In fact, Tyson initially intended to produce a video about "my money issues." He searched and downloaded several photos on Google Image that showed stacks of money and people with large lottery checks. Having already learned how to compose videos, he initially thought he'd make short shrift of this assignment. It was the process of composing the cosmopolitan conversation video for an international audience that allowed Tyson to revisit his initial idea through iterations of reading, writing, designing, and contemplating. In revisiting his original plan, he further developed both the theme of the video as well as his own engagement in cosmopolitan practices.

The first major shift in Tyson's video came after he viewed Bakhti's video. When Tyson initially watched Bakhti's video, he didn't participate in the discussion surrounding it. However, when challenged to consider a wider audience than those he had previously made films for, namely the international audience on Space2Cre8, he broadened the topic from "money" to "struggle," stating that he knew that everyone could relate to struggle, because he had seen this engagement in relation to Bakhti's video. With this larger concept in mind, for several days Tyson sat still in front of a computer screen at the academy. Occasionally he worked on a different project, photoshopping a picture of a favorite music artist or assisting other youth with technical aspects of their videos. Tyson knew about struggle and wanted to express the struggle he had experienced in his life—and address it in a way companionable to Bakhti's video, too. However, he was unsure about execution.

Tyson seemed thwarted until he remembered the notes he had written while reading the seminar course text, *Cosmopolitanism: Ethics in a World of Strangers* (Appiah, 2006), in preparation for leading a discussion on his assigned chapter. He had been struck by a particular passage in Appiah's text that he felt validated what he knew about struggle: "So, let's start with the sort of core moral ideas increasingly articulated in our concept of basic human rights. People have needs—health, food, shelter, education—that must be met if they are to lead decent lives" (p. 162). Through this quotation, Tyson had found the way to organize his video. He inserted a slide that listed the four basic needs articulated by Appiah and immediately set off composing the rest of his video. Tyson's finalized video included these major sections:

1. Title and topic slides "Struggle in Everyday Life"
2. Introduction of basic needs from Appiah
3. Slides of people struggling with hunger in past times
4. Slides of people struggling currently with homelessness in US, Pakistan, Haiti
5. Slides introducing money as the "main struggle"
6. Transition slide: "People don't just struggle in America"
7. Clip from Bakhti's video with overlay "Let's get Bakhti's point of view"
8. Conclusion and credit slides

Although Tyson created his video quite quickly once he formulated a way to organize it, his conception of "struggle" continued to expand in dimension and nuance over several iterations of reading/viewing and writing/composing, as displayed in Figure 2. (We don't mean to imply that this figure is inclusive of all of the influences on Tyson's processes; rather, it highlights the processes that Tyson mentioned in his interview and those that were discussed in the composition course as noted in field notes.) Figure 2 can be read as composing actions occurring over time from left to right; however, the figure has dashed lines to further emphasize that this is not a causal relationship of one idea leading to another—rather, it was a recursive process for Tyson, one of layering meaning. For instance, Tyson never abandoned his focus on money as a central issue. In fact, he used the same images of money that he found early on, but during the composing process, these photographs took new conceptual shape. Rather than remaining his personal issue, he communicated poverty as historically and globally at the root of each of the basic needs in current society.

The two arrows in Figure 2 are placed where Tyson identified a direct link between composing and reading—when one activity led to another. In these explicit ways, Tyson demonstrated the reciprocal relationship between reading a philosophical text and composing his film. In reading about basic needs, he brought the thinking he had been doing around "struggle" through authoring his video to his reading, and then brought the categories of basic needs from the reading to the organization of his video. Tyson would be the first to say that he had difficulty understanding the course text and that the content he used in composing was one of the few sections of the text that he felt he could grasp. We would also argue that his understanding of the concept of basic needs was far more nuanced after composing than it was when he first became acquainted with it through Appiah's (2006) text.

The concept took on an emotional dimension through Tyson's inquiry. He gave special attention to finding music, the song "Angel" by Sarah McLachlan, to use as background. This song, he remembered, had been deployed in a television commercial about adopting shelter animals. It was the saddest song he could think of, and he made it a point to time his slides to match the phrasing of the song, in order to influence the viewers' interpretation of the images—to feel about the pictures as he did, sad and serious. He saw his video as something to be taken seriously, and he wanted to communicate that he was someone who should be taken seriously as well. When we asked him what he would like people to think and know after seeing the movie, he said, "I may goof around a lot, but I am serious at one point."

After viewing his creation a few times one day at the academy, Tyson asked if he could get a copy of Bakhti's video. He said he needed to show—not just state—that the issues he was addressing were worldwide, and he thought Bakhti's video had done that powerfully. Thereafter he included the portion of Bakhti's video in which she describes her living conditions, which he overlaid with the text: "Let's get Bakhti's point of view. . . ." Tyson believed not only that her video would "sum it up," but he also hoped that Bakhti would receive the message that she was not alone: "She's probably going to think that she's probably not the only one who has those kinds of problems, because it happens all around the world." Tyson saw his video as a visual conversation response and starter. He wanted to put his work in conversation with Bakhti and her work, explaining: "I tried to connect it to somebody that I

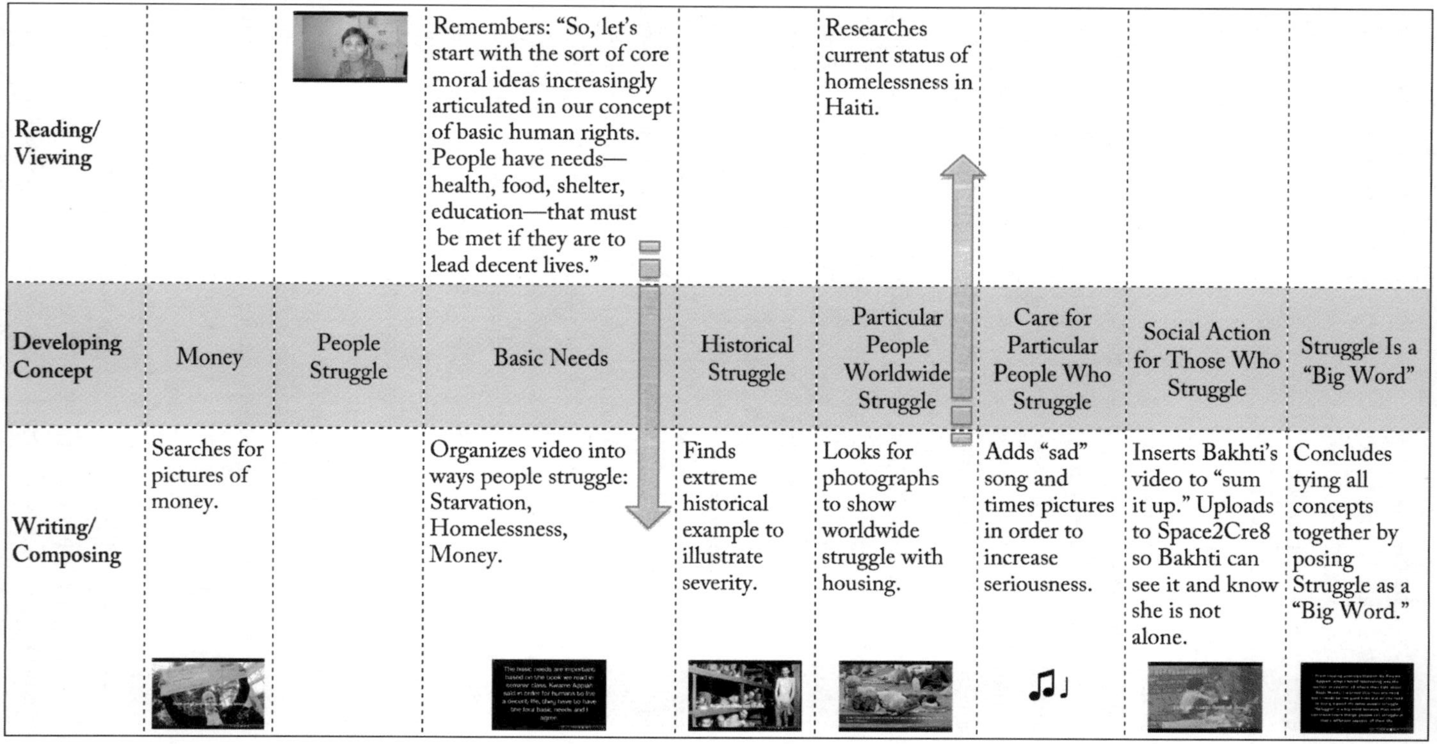

	Money	People Struggle	Basic Needs	Historical Struggle	Particular People Worldwide Struggle	Care for Particular People Who Struggle	Social Action for Those Who Struggle	Struggle Is a "Big Word"
Reading/ Viewing			Remembers: "So, let's start with the sort of core moral ideas increasingly articulated in our concept of basic human rights. People have needs—health, food, shelter, education—that must be met if they are to lead decent lives."		Researches current status of homelessness in Haiti.			
Developing Concept								
Writing/ Composing	Searches for pictures of money.		Organizes video into ways people struggle: Starvation, Homelessness, Money.	Finds extreme historical example to illustrate severity.	Looks for photographs to show worldwide struggle with housing.	Adds "sad" song and times pictures in order to increase seriousness.	Inserts Bakhti's video to "sum it up." Uploads to Space2Cre8 so Bakhti can see it and know she is not alone.	Concludes tying all concepts together by posing Struggle as a "Big Word."

Figure 2. A Learning Map of Tyson's Processes.

could actually talk to because she's on Space2Cre8. She made a video about where she lives at and how they struggle. Like they actually have a house, like a house, but they don't got things like we've got in this country...." He also wanted the video to be in conversation with the author of the course text, indicating that he would like for Appiah to see how his written ideas had been represented in movie form.

In composing his video we see that Tyson was not only applying critical lenses to the text after reading, he was demonstrating the reciprocal processes of critical authorship and readership. He authored a cosmopolitan understanding of struggle—interpreting through composing and layering concepts and media in such a way as to find an entry point into the conversation with others about struggle. In a sense, he authored a "serious" self—as a critical composer who can speak to a range of distant others, from Bakhti in India, for whom he felt much empathy, to Appiah in the U.S., with whom he contemplated having a "serious" conversation about complex philosophical ideas.

Developing cosmopolitan practices through critical authoring

Eva's experiences with composing similarly shaped her understanding of the concepts she studied in the academy. Additionally, like many of the other youth, composing also afforded Eva an opportunity to try on cosmopolitan ethical practices both locally and globally. For Eva, this experience resulted in an "awesome" change in the way she saw and interacted with others in the world.

At the beginning of the academy, Eva, a Latina high school junior, felt ambivalent—at best—about interacting with unknown others. She explained, "Like before when I would get on the train [the New York City subway], I would try to avoid everyone, like, as much as possible, 'cause you know I always thought that people were kind of mean and stuff." Eva didn't avoid interaction only on the train. For the first two weeks of the academy, she sat quietly through all three courses, rarely making a comment. When she interacted with instructors one-on-one, she often shrugged her shoulders rather than speaking. On Space2Cre8, she posted or otherwise interacted only when she was asked to do so.

Like Tyson, Eva began making her cosmopolitan conversation video in response to the videos she had viewed on Space2Cre8, and did so without an articulated aim or outline. Eva explained, "At first it was like, I didn't have any, like, 'this is what I'm going to do,' 'this is what I'm going to do.' It was just—make videos and something will come." She checked out a video camera one weekend to record random footage. On Monday morning as she waited for her train to come, she saw a man playing a guitar in the station. She had seen him almost daily playing music for spare change, as do many musicians along the subway lines, but had usually paid him no attention. This time she remembered the neighborhood map (see Appendix B) she had drawn and labeled with places and people in order to analyze who she considered to be "neighbors" and how she defined "neighborhood." This memory prompted her to realize that although this man did not show up on her map, he was actually part of her daily life. Yet, because she had deemed him different—a white man in a predominately Latino and African American neighborhood—she had ignored him, and if anything, thought he was "weird." Practicing self-reflexivity, she considered the cosmopolitan ideal that as a global society, we can no longer pretend that others don't exist, and she really listened to his performance for the first time and recognized that he was a good musician. She approached the performer with her camera, told him she was doing a class project, and asked him if she could interview him about his life. He agreed, and they talked until her train came. Over the next two days, she had conversations with the owner of the taco truck she frequented. She also talked to a woman she often saw on her train. She then talked to people in the academy whom she realized she had essentially—up to that point—ignored.

After watching the raw video footage she had collected, Eva eventually spliced clips of these conversations together in an order that would show the range of the interests of others around her, as well as the patterns of similarities in their interests—even across what initially might be seen as differences in race, language, age, and gender. In Figure 3, we provide a transcript of the interview snippets that constitute her video.

It wasn't until Eva neared completion of the video that she realized she had been practicing the cosmopolitan ideal of hospitality, especially as exemplified through conversation and dialogue—Appiah's dominant metaphor for a cosmopolitan ethic. That is, she had stopped ignoring her fellow human beings, and she had developed a curiosity about and respect for the diverse interests of others. She explained:

> I didn't notice until yesterday that I'm talking to these people. You don't see it in the video, but they're having a *conversation* with me. I'm not just coming up to them and just like, "Well, what do you do?" I didn't want to do that. I'm not a reporter. I'm talking to these people, which is awesome. These are conversations [pointing to her video clips on the screen]. Real conversations. They're not just questions I go up to ask random people. That's why the title is called *Making Conversation* [shows title screen of the video] because this is conversation. This is what realness is.

This discovery was the most exciting moment of the academy for Eva. She explained the change of mind she had experienced this way:

> Before when you would get on the train and you don't talk to anyone, you don't really learn anything. You don't really experience anything. . . . Even a friend you haven't talked to for a long time—if you actually talk to them, it could be a good experience. It could be a life changer. It's how I changed.

Like Tyson, Eva gained a more sophisticated understanding of a concept, "conversation," as she composed her video. In addition, she concluded her reading of the

Text on screen	What are you passionate about?
Fellow male participant	I'm passionate about skateboarding.
Man in subway	I'm passionate about music.
Fellow female participant and friend	About being independent and making my own money.
Woman on train	My son.
Younger sister	Riding my scooter.
Taco truck server	I love to do a good.
Fellow female participant	I'm passionate about food.
Girl on the train	Music.
Fellow male participant	Basketball.
Text on screen	Why?
Fellow male participant	Because that's something I love to do and won't give up on.
Man in subway	'Cause it brings people together to have a good time, to dance and celebrate.
Fellow female participant and friend	Because you want to have your own stuff and not depend on anybody.
Girl on train	Because I love it. I love the rhythms that people create with it. There's music all over. Even in the train station as we riding. If you listen to the tracks and everything and the wheels there's music all around us.
Woman on train	Because he was never supposed to be born.
Younger sister	Because I like to feel the breeze when I'm riding it down the hill.
Fellow female participant	Because I like experimenting and seeing the different flavors and how my taste buds go crazy.
Text on screen	Has anything gotten in the way of your passion?
Man in subway	A lot of people don't want to have a good time.
Fellow female participant and friend	My grandmother. She's rude. She says rude things out her mouth.
Woman on train	No!
Younger sister	The sidewalk.
Girl on the train	People!
Fellow female participant	I'm passionate about food.
Text on screen	So, what are YOU passionate about?

Figure 3. Transcript of Eva's Cosmopolitan Conversation Video.

seminar course text by daring to differ with its analysis of globalization. She explained how her composition demonstrated the antithesis of the popular idea that the "world is getting smaller" through globalization and technology:

> The world's not getting smaller, it's getting bigger. . . . So when we go up to him [pointing to video] or him, or her and you just talk to them, that brings us closer. You might not notice it, but it does. . .when you cross each other's boundaries. . . . When you actually start to lis-ten to the other person, then it's like, "Oh there's a whole new world that I didn't even know." That's how the world grows [motions smaller and larger].

Eva had realized that engaging with others is not just a cosmopolitan practice, but an orientation towards others, a critical habit of mind, that results in an expansive and inclusive understanding of the world as connections across boundaries are estab-lished and relationships with others previously unknown and distant are developed.

In the crossing of boundaries, Eva grappled with notions of congeniality ver-sus collegiality. When the academy began, she did what she was asked and was kind to others. However, over time she gained a more sophisticated understanding of how to engage with others through cosmopolitan hospitality. She explained, "Like you have your idea and they have their own idea. And you guys both, whether you feel strongly about it or not, you have your ideas and you try to defend your ideas as much as possible." Eva adds texture to the idea of hospitality—that it is more than being open-minded and respectful of others. Rather, for Eva it involves a reflexive and crit-ical accounting of a person's assumptions and ideas in relation to others. In the final weeks of the academy, she not only spoke up, but also started to guide her peers' dis-cussions by posing questions about the content of the courses and challenging oth-ers to explain the opinions they posed. Eva had decided that she would not simply share her video, but use it to begin these same kinds of conversations locally and globally, off- and online:

> Mainly I want to know what people in India are passionate about or people from the Bronx that I've never met. It would be awesome to know, you know? Like when they tell me their passion, I could tell them my passion and we spark up a conversation from there. It would be awesome to have more friends.

After the academy ended, Eva independently posted survey questions about schooling in the differing countries. She had been conducting research for a school report on conditions of schools in urban settings, and felt it wouldn't be enough to just understand what students at her own school felt about their education, but that her understanding could benefit from global knowledge. Explaining what had changed for her during the academy, she noted that not only was she more com-fortable with the group, but she left feeling confident in discussing ideas, feelings, and thoughts with those she would have previously ignored or avoided.

FINAL THOUGHTS

Engagement with media creation at critical points in Eva's and Tyson's creative processes influenced their conceptual explorations of "struggle" and "conversation" in ways that expanded their previously held notions. Their learning was mediated by on- and offline iterations of integrated reading, writing, designing, and discussing. For both Eva and Tyson, critical digital authorship was instrumental to comprehending traditional print texts, as well as reading their social network and interpreting distant youths' artifacts.

Based on the work of Eva, Tyson, and their cohorts, we encourage classroom and out-of-school teachers interested in guiding youth in the development of their critical print and digital literacies to consider the significant role that content creation, or authorship, plays in concept building and learning. In this digital age, traditional content creation, such as book reports, unit projects and essays, cannot be merely digitized and relegated to the end of a unit as capstone demonstrations of content mastery. Rather, as demonstrated by these youth, students' learning is mediated by the active role of authorship within reading, and recursive reading within multimodal designing. As Tyson demonstrated with his use of "sad" music, intentional choice of images paired with words, and a remix of Bakhti's video, teachers can design instruction to challenge the dominant role of static print in literacy instruction. Tyson designed and communicated with each of these modes individually, as well as in concert on the screen. Each of these literacy skills, we would argue, is necessary for navigating learning in the 21st century.

Finally, we would not have learned about the youths' sophisticated and layered meanings, nor their complex designing and concept-building processes, without a "listening" orientation toward the youth (Schultz, 2003), itself a cosmopolitan practice. By this we mean taking a curious, receptive, and responsive stance when engaging with youth and their compositions, listening for patterns in their thinking and feelings with sensitivity to the social, cultural, and communal aspects of their experiences (see also Andrews & Smith, 2011). By creating space and time within the academy for youth to discuss their work and processes in depth with their instructor, Anna, and with the research team in interviews, we learned of their growing confidences and academic risk-taking, which informed our understanding of their learning. Writing conferences are not a new method of instruction, so in addition to tuning their ear for evaluation and instruction within conferences, we suggest that teachers take on the practice of *hospitable* conferencing, engaging in the same cosmopolitan practices discussed in this chapter.

Beyond this, critical digital composition leveraged opportunities for the youth to try on new critical ways of being in the world—both on- and offline. Reading, writing, and engagement with others—distant and near—are tightly woven in the 21st century. The ethical imperatives of digital spaces are not relegated to cyberspace. As Eva recognized and demonstrated in a dramatic shift in her orientation toward unknown others, new configurations of people and ideas online are representative of the same offline, and the ethics of critical engagement in a digital age exists both on- and offline. Eva and Tyson experienced what it means to engage in deep inquiry into concepts, and developed the confidence and the self-reflexive, hospitable literacy practices needed to engage in critical conversation about nuanced concepts with others—even those who seemed very different at the onset.

Curricula and pedagogies built around literacies in this age must be designed for an era characterized by access to and democratization of tools, people, and ideas in digital spaces. The recently released Common Core State Standards Initiative (2010), which was designed for college and career readiness, offers an entire appendix dedicated to defining, describing, and giving examples of "complex" texts, but still only asks of students to write traditional genres of narration and argument—with no nod to complexity of student-produced texts or processes. Not only do we see this as not representative of the writing/composing necessary for college, career, and the 21st century in general, we would argue that youth need experience composing across modes of communication, with others who are distant and unknown, and with similar focus on the composing processes—particularly critical processes—which we have argued have an ethical component around exchange with these distant and unknown others. We do not imagine that online, digital reading and writing should supplant traditional texts; rather, the critical orientations of 21st-century interpretation and composition can be taught in tandem, or in what Leander (2009) described as "parallel pedagogies." Imagine approaching a distant, unknown author, such as Homer, with the same hospitality, openness to other worldviews, experiences, and communication patterns—as well as confidence that these differences can be overcome—that Tyson and Eva developed in only four weeks of focused critical digital engagement. These are the kinds of reading and composing experiences that we believe should be typical in the 21st-century classroom.

Acknowledgments

We gratefully acknowledge the support given for the EXCEL Academy @ NYU by the Teagle Foundation; the NYU Steinhardt School of Culture, Education and Human Development; and the Philosophy Department in the College of Arts and Sciences at New York University; and our community partners at the Children's Aid Society. Many thanks go to fellow members of our EXCEL Academy @ NYU faculty and research team: Joseph McDonald, J. David Velleman, Matt Hall, Tim Fredrick, Dee Anne Anderson, and Laura Davis, as well as members of our wider research group and Kidnet team, including Amy Stornaiuolo and John Scott. We also gratefully acknowledge the support for the wider Kidnet/Space2Cre8 project from the Spencer Foundation. Please see www.space2cre8.com for more information about the project and a demonstration site for the social network itself. Finally, we thank editors Jessica Zacher Pandya and JuliAnna Ávila for their helpful comments on our chapter draft.

APPENDIX A

Eva's Neighborhood Maps and Commentary

Top: Eva's Neighborhood Map before the Academy
Bottom: Eva's Revised Neighborhood Map after the Academy

Transcript of Eva's Revision Commentary

[Eva holds her map to a camera and points to parts of the map as she explains her revisions.]

> I added people. And look, there's a key. These are [referencing the map key] Spanish people; these are Black people; these are Middle Eastern people; Indians and White people. Notice there are <u>no</u> White people, and rarely any. . . Middle Eastern. Notice there are no Indian people living in buildings. They are just working in the stores. Cosmopolitanism has made me real aware of who's around me. Here's [pointing to each building] grocery store, parking lot, grocery store, garage, parking lot, furniture store, apartment building, apartment building. That's basically it, you know. It's a little home for me. That's it. All I added was people.

APPENDIX B

Composing Interview Protocol

At each of the sites on the Space2Cre8 network, youth design multimedia and digital products (see Hull & Stornaiuolo, 2010; Hull, Stornaiuolo, & Sahni, 2010). They share these in various ways across the network. At the beginning of their projects, as they near completion, and/or once the digital products are totally finished, students are interviewed about their composing processes, purposes, and products. These interviews are video recorded digitally, making them a source of data for our ongoing research. Additionally, the interviews serve pedagogical purposes as 21st-century writing conferences as they involve detailed discussion of online, digital, and multimodal literacy practices. Drawing from the protocol below, the conferences engage youth in reflective dialogue focused on the processes through which they are rhetorically framing their compositions for intended and potential audiences both local and global (Andrews & Smith, 2011).

1) Ask participant what his or her digital story/product is about.
2) With participant, view video without stopping.
3) Following the lead of the student, ask a series of questions about the composing processes and rhetorical decisions made by the student, including:
   a. How did you begin to make this? What did you do next?
   b. Where did you get the idea for this story? What inspired you?

    c. Would you say that your movie has a message? If so, what is it?

    d. Who did you have in mind when you made this movie (i.e., audience)? Who would you like to see it? Why? Have they seen it yet? Why/why not?

    e. How do you hope people see you after seeing this movie?

    f. Have you talked to anybody about your movie? Have you made any changes after talking to that person?

    g. Did you work mostly alone or with someone?

    h. Will you post it on Space2Cre8? Why/why not? Did you think about the kids from India, U.S., Norway, South Africa, etc. when making the movie? What do you hope they think about the movie?

    i. How did you make your movie (i.e., the process)? Did you think about any design elements? How did your movie change over the course of making it?

    j. How did your ideas change while making the movie? How did your feelings change as you were making the movie?

4) Watch the digital story again frame by frame, discussing each of the visible composing and semiotic decisions that were made, including:

    a. How did you choose that image (or that scene)?

    b. How did you make the pictures, words, music, etc. match (i.e., work or fit together)?

    c. Why did you put that (picture/music/voice-over) in that spot in the movie?

5) Finally, ask if the youth is satisfied with the product as is, probing for why and asking if he or she would change anything as a result of this conversation.

References

Andrews, R., & Smith, A. (2011). *Developing writers: Teaching and learning in the digital age.* London: University Press.

Appadurai, A. (1996). *Modernity at large: Cultural dimensions of globalization.* Minneapolis: University of Minnesota Press.

Appiah, K.A. (2006). *Cosmopolitanism: Ethics in a world of strangers.* New York: W.W. Norton.

Beck, U., & Sznaider, N. (2006). Unpacking cosmopolitanism for the social sciences: A research agenda. *The British Journal of Sociology, 57*(1), 1–23.

Coiro, J., & Dobler, E. (2007). Exploring the online comprehension strategies used by sixth-grade skilled readers to search for and locate information on the Internet. *Reading Research Quarterly, 42,* 214–257.

Common Core State Standards Initiative. (2010). The standards. Retrieved from www.core-standards.org/the-standards.

Derrida, J. (2002). *On cosmopolitanism and forgiveness* (M. Doole & M. Hughes, Trans.). London: Routledge.

Dyson, A. H., & Genishi, C. (2005). *On the case: Approaches to language and literacy research.* New York: Teachers College Press.

Hansen, D. T. (2010). Cosmopolitanism and education: A view from the ground. *Teachers College Record, 112*(1), 1–30.

Hargittai, E., & Hinnant, A. (2008). Digital inequality: Differences in young adults' use of the Internet. *Communication Research, 35*(5), 602–621.

Hull, G., & Nelson, M. (2005). Locating the semiotic power of multimodality. *Written Communication, 22*(2), 224–62.

Hull, G., & Nelson, M. (2009). Literacy, media, and morality: Making the case for an aesthetic turn. In M. Prinsloo & M. Baynham (Eds.), *The future of literacy studies.* Houndmills, UK: Palgrave Macmillan.

Hull, G., Stornaiuolo, A., & Sahni, U. (2010). Cultural citizenship and cosmopolitan practice: Global youth communicate online. *English Education, 42*(4), 331–367.

Hull, G., & Stornaiuolo, A. (2010). Literate arts in a global world: Reframing social networking as cosmopolitan practice. *Journal of Adolescent and Adult Literacy, 54*(2), 84–96.

Kant, I. (1983). *Perpetual peace and other essays* (T. Humphrey, Trans.). Indianapolis, IN: Hackett.

Kress, G. (2003). *Literacy in the new media age.* London, U.K.: Routledge.

Leander, K. M. (2009). Composing with old and new media: Toward a parallel pedagogy. In V. Carrington & M. Robinson (Eds.), *Digital literacies: Social learning and classroom practices* (pp. 147–164). Los Angeles, CA: Sage.

New London Group. (1997). A pedagogy of multiliteracies: Designing social futures. *Harvard Educational Review, 66,* 60–92.

O'Gorman, K. D. (2006) Jacques Derrida's philosophy of hospitality. *Hospitality Review, 8*(4), 50–57.

Papastephanou, M. (2005). Globalisation, globalism and cosmopolitanism as an educational ideal. *Educational Philosophy and Theory, 37*(4), 533–551.

Rosenblatt, L. (1938). *Literature as exploration.* New York: Appleton-Century; (1995). New York: Modern Language Association.

Rosenblatt, L. (1978). *The reader, the text, the poem: The transactional theory of the literary work.* Carbondale: Southern Illinois University Press; (1994). Carbondale: Southern Illinois University Press.

Rizvi, F. (2009). Toward cosmopolitan learning. *Discourse: Studies in the Cultural Politics of Education, 30*(3), 253–268.

Schradie, J. (2011). The digital production gap: The digital divide and Web 2.0 collide." *Poetics, 39,* 145–168.

Schultz, K. (2003). *Listening: A framework for teaching across differences.* New York: Teachers College Press.

Silverstone, R. (2007). *Media and morality: On the rise of the mediapolis.* Cambridge, UK: Polity.

Warschauer, M., & Matuchniak, T. (2010). New technology and digital worlds: Analyzing evidence of equity in access, use, and outcomes. *Review of Research in Education, 34*(1), 179–225.

PART 2

Teacher Education and Critical Digital Literacies

CHAPTER FIVE

Perforating School

Digital Literacy in an Arts and Crafts Class

ARNE OLAV NYGARD

INTRODUCTION: THE DIGITAL CLASSROOM

In the 2000s, Norwegian school authorities introduced a new curriculum for the entire compulsory education system. Among the changes was an intensified focus on "digital skills" across all disciplines. Partly as a result of this, all high schools in Norway made laptop PCs mandatory, with subsidies to make this feasible for all students. Adding to this, the same authorities, in order to accommodate the needs and demands of the Organisation for Economic Co-operation and Development's "New Millennials" (OECD, 2008), established a system for producing and purchasing digital teaching material, the National Digital Learning Arena (NDLA). This is organized as a website for teachers and students, and its aim is to accommodate all teachers' and students' textbook needs across all disciplines. In other words, during the last five years there has been a massive focus on what can be described as the "digital turn" in how the Norwegian school system organizes knowledge as it attempts to take an active part in this process in order to face the digital future.

In Norway, the schools' focus on digital issues, and especially the introduction of individual student computers, has fueled several debates across a wide spectrum of interests and actors, contributing to the public discourse about the use of computers in the classroom. On the one hand, passionate teachers promote the possibilities of the new medium, both as a way of inspiring students and as a way of enhancing learning, backed up by equally enthusiastic academics and writers making grand claims about the positive effects of digital media and young people's ability to use computers to learn in new and improved ways (Prensky, 2001; Tapscott, 2009). Along the same lines, others argue that the PC and the web have the potential to improve pedagogy and make learning better, more fair, individualized, informalized, and better organized (Selwyn, 2010, p. 12). On top of this, a massive hardware and software industry eagerly promotes the computer as a tool for efficiency and improved pedagogy.

On the other hand, the issue of banning access to websites such as Facebook and YouTube in schools is frequently on the agenda. Teachers regularly step forward with their accounts of loss of control in a classroom of computers, and the widespread use of social media among students is often said to be at the root of this problem. Again, to the rescue come developers of software, with programs that promise to reestablish order and control in the classroom, for example by monitoring students' activities on their PCs or checking class work for copy-pasted text from sources not properly accounted for. Also, arguments about an intellectual decline due to widespread media use are often put forth, with the screen said to promote superficial reading and to disturb concentration, in addition to making it easy to cheat and do homework by means of the copy-paste function (Keen, 2007; Rothenberg, 1997). Furthermore, teachers' unions protest the introduction of digital teaching aids and the lack of teacher influence over how the money for textbooks and teaching aids in general is spent.

In the present chapter, I will give an account of material from a study of a group of Norwegian high school students using computers as a vital part of their everyday classroom activities. As the discussions above reflect, the domain of digital literacy in education is subject to intense discussion. The arguments often range between what Neil Selwyn calls the "booster" and "doomster" traditions of arguments, where technology itself is the agent of either positive or negative change (2010). In this "essentialist" account of technology, interest focuses chiefly on abilities in the medium in itself, without paying attention to the actual settings in which the technologies are used. Similar "essentialist" accounts may be found in traditional views on reading and writing: in what Street (1984) calls the "autonomous model" of literacy, where literacy is seen as a set of skills or cognitive aptitudes, essentially tied to a person's intellectual makeup (p. 1). Indeed, one feature of many of the discussions concerning the new tools for literacy in the classroom is the lack of attention to sociocultural factors and the context in which the technologies are used.

In other words, there is a "distinctively technocratic air" to discussions about contemporary schooling, and critical accounts of actual uses of digital technologies in schools are rarely given (Selwyn, 2010, p. 20). In this study, my aim is to take a critical approach to the various classroom practices involving literacy, taking my theoretical perspectives from the New Literacy Studies (NLS). The NLS understands literacy as various practices that are given meaning in concrete social and cultural contexts. According to Street (1984), studying literacy entails turning away from the idea of literacy as a set of skills or cognitive aptitudes in a person. Instead, Street proposes an "ideological model" of literacy, where literacies are embedded in different ideologies and have consequences only as they act "together with a large number of other social factors, including political and economic conditions, social structure, and local ideologies" (Gee, 2008, p. 80).

AN ETHNOGRAPHIC PERSPECTIVE

Studying literacy as it unfolds, looking at specific literacy events and how they are embedded in contexts, can be done at various levels. One characteristic uniting many researchers of literacy practices is a focus on ethnography as a methodology (Heath & Street, 2008; Street et al., 2009, p. 193; Tapscott, 2009). One dilemma in using ethnography in the field of language and communication is that one may want to adopt ethnographic approaches without necessarily wanting or even needing to become an anthropologist in the traditional sense. According to Street et al. (2009, pp. 193–194), Green and Bloome (1997, p. 183) addressed this dilemma by distinguishing between several different approaches to ethnography. The approach in the present study resembles what Green and Bloome describe as "adopting an ethnographic perspective," which means studying particular aspects of the everyday life and cultural practices of a social group, but not in the extensive manner of the traditional, comprehensive ethnographic study (Green & Bloome, 1997, as cited in Street et al., 2009, p. 193).

I observed and interviewed a group of 12 students in the third year of a non-vocational high school program in a small-town school, Southwest High (all names of persons, schools, and places in the following are fictional), on the west coast of Norway. My initial approach to this research project was open in the sense that I started observing these students without any clearcut research questions, in a way resembling the grounded approach of Glaser and Strauss (1967). I knew one of the teachers at Southwest High, Anne, both as a former colleague and later as a student, having at various points discussed her teaching and how she had discovered the method of using blogs in class. My curiosity was triggered by Anne's ideas of turning the computer into a tool for production and sharing, making the students' classroom activities a matter of participating in public life with ideas, opinions, and criticism via their blogs. As mentioned in the introduction, the recent digital turn in Norwegian schools has been subject to a lot of debate and criticism. Anne gave the impression of having specific ideas about how to overcome what other teachers saw as obstacles to learning due to computer use, such as lack of attention and concentration or misuse of the computer by cheating on tests and copy-pasting homework. In addition, she had a distinct critical approach to her teaching in that she wanted to enable her students to develop their own voices, so to speak, and participate out in the open with their thoughts and ideas.

I observed Anne's class as they used computers and the web extensively as part of their organized schoolwork over a period of three months, from January through March 2010, taking field notes during observation. I also took a few pictures of different literacy events in class, mainly to aid my memory while working with my field notes, and I gathered and used as background material the blog texts that the students had produced during that school year.

In group and individual interviews, I particularly wanted the students to talk about values and attitudes related to uses of literacy and technologies of literacy in the different situations they encountered: in class and during breaks, after school when doing homework or other activities, related to particular hobbies, their personal lives, and so on. I was interested in these students' literacies, given that they are representatives of a generation strongly associated with digital literacy. I also wanted to know how they experienced using social media and blogging as part of their curriculum. I knew of Anne's opinions and ideas on using computers, and I had observed the class at work, but I wanted them to discuss these matters among themselves in order to find out how they evaluated these activities, their opinions on social media use in school versus in their private lives, their thoughts on doing school out in the open versus the more traditional approaches of other teachers in different subjects, and so on.

I decided on group interviews mainly to bring out other aspects than what individual interviews would have yielded, aiming to gain access to the discourse of the group and perhaps also reducing my influence as a literacy researcher; in addition, this also gave me the opportunity to listen in on discussions among the group members (Gentikow, 2005). Even so, I decided based on the group interviews to interview three of the students individually. These were students who stood out from the rest either because of strong opinions on the use of digital tools in class and digital literacy in general or based on other information on which I wanted them to expound.

Southwest High is a school in which I myself had worked as a teacher from 2002 until 2007. I therefore knew the buildings, the different education programs, the school administration, and most of the teachers. This familiarity made it easy for me to establish this particular school as my site of research. As mentioned, I also knew Anne as a former colleague. In addition, I had been teaching students of precisely this age group for approximately 14 years. Although the field notes and interviews are my primary sources, I consider these background data important sources for my research as well. Anderson (2006) describes this approach as "sociological involvement in settings close to [one's] personal li[fe], arenas with which [one] ha[s] a significant degree of self-identification" (p. 375). My background in, and knowledge of, both the school system and the actual school I studied, and thus my ties to a profession that for a good part of my adult life has been linked to my professional and personal identity, fit with the perspectives of what Anderson (ibid.) calls "analytic autoethnography," and my accounts from the classroom and this particular school reflect that stance.

Being primarily interested in the group discourse rather than in individual perspectives, I did not analyze my data with relation to variables such as gender, socioeconomic status, and so on. Although Norway is a financially well-off and relatively egalitarian nation, questions related to inequality and discrimination are far from irrelevant, albeit probably different from how they represent themselves in comparable countries. Still, all the high schools in Norway (with a few exceptions not particularly relevant to this argument) are governmentally funded, as are largely all the students' teaching aids, such as the laptops they use, their textbooks, etc. All the students had similar access to computers and the Internet, attended a public school of good reputation to which they had been admitted on the basis of their grades from junior high school, and showed no particular signs related to their socioeconomic status or background that were of relevance to my study.

The following account will be an attempt to present my material in what Geertz (1973) calls "thick descriptions" to go beyond a mere "I-am-a-camera" description of phenomena and bring out the patterns of specific actions in their contexts (p. 6; see also Heath & Street, 2008, p. 41). I will first describe Southwest High and Anne's path toward the operationalization of her particular ideas about literacy in class. I will then move on to give an account of my analysis of the material from my observations and interviews of the students.

IDENTITY AND DISCOURSE AT A NORWEGIAN HIGH SCHOOL

The group I observed consisted of students in the third year of a non-vocational high school program in a small-town school on the west coast of Norway. All of the students were between 18 and 19 years old at the time of the observations and interviews. Although their education program gives general eligibility for university-level studies, this particular school has its roots in vocational education programs for design, arts and crafts, and in recent years also media and communications. Various school reforms had changed the disciplinary makeup of the school, but there remained a distinct feeling of being a "creative" school, perhaps "the" creative school, among both the staff and the students, distinguishing them markedly from other schools in the district. This sense of identity resembles Gee's notion of membership of a capital "D" Discourse as opposed to small "d" discourses. While small "d" discourses generally refer to matters of language in use, language alone is rarely used to enact activities and identities. In addition to language use and the small "d" discourses, "D"iscourse is made up of socially recognized ways of acting, feeling, using things, symbols, tools, and technologies, and even using your body, clothing, and gestures at the right times and places (Gee, 1999, p. 7; Lankshear, 1999).

The students in this school, then, have traditionally been identified not only by their curricular interests, but also by other discursive features linked in different ways to their aspiring professional identities. In addition to a general occupation with the arts, one such feature is their appearance: clothing and hairdos, identifiable to an extent where students and teachers from other schools, and even parents and other people from the local environment, are often heard referring to "those Southwest High students," acknowledging that there is something typical or particular that links them to this particular school. There has also been a general interest in humanitarian issues among the students, and the school has held annual exhibitions to which friends, parents, and locals have been invited to sell their own art to raise money for a particular institution in a developing country. These things add up to create a school-wide identity.

By the time of my observation period, the school had been through various national reforms and new curricula, and was about to merge with another local school and establish itself as a new and far bigger school with a new name in newly built premises, expanding from 300–400 to 800–900 students. At the time there were mixed feelings about this, and some teachers expressed a distinct fear of losing the school's particular identity. In the early years, the school provided mostly vocational training, educating printers, photographers, illustrators, and the occasional art student, in addition to providing opportunities for supplementary studies to qualify for higher education. At the time of my study, for political reasons, most education programs had become general, non-vocational programs, at the expense of the "creative" subjects, which were allocated less time compared with earlier years. Still, students were able to choose optional classes such as Print and Photography and Visual Arts and Culture, alongside the common core subjects, such as mathematics, foreign languages, history, and Norwegian. Despite the fact that their education had less of an arts-and-crafts profile than earlier programs, the students seemed to have chosen the program out of an interest in visual arts and to a certain extent seemed to have ambitions of making a living from or studying related subjects, such as photography, after high school. This identification with creativity and working with artistic subjects, a strong reason why the students chose Southwest High in the first place, may account for some of the negative attitudes evident in my data toward more traditional academic subjects such as mathematics, Norwegian, and history.

ANNE AND HER WAY INTO BLOGGING: FROM ELECTRIFICATION TO EMPOWERMENT

The person I primarily communicated with during the period of observation was Anne, the students' homeroom teacher and also the teacher of the Print and Photography class. As mentioned earlier, I knew Anne as a former colleague, and at the time we worked together she was curious yet hesitant about using digital technology beyond what her subject and everyday life in school demanded, such as software for manipulating digital images, using the school's learning management system to distribute messages to students, and checking her emails.

When I met Anne a few years later, she enthusiastically explained to me how she had discovered blogging as a way of enabling her students to publish their pictures to a wider audience than just incidental passersby at the school, and how fun this was for her and her students. This immediately caught my interest, because Anne's approach as she explained it stood in stark contrast to the predominantly technocratic perspectives on digital literacy in schools dominating the discourse in the field.

Commonly, in order to legitimize their existence in school settings, digital media are conceived of as a tool for enhancing or increasing efficiency, saving time, or improving pedagogy and learning (Lankshear, 1998, p. 6; Selwyn, 2010, p. 13). Anne, on the contrary, seemed to take as her point of departure an interest in what she perceived as positive effects on her students and the way they approached themselves and their academic work. Although she worded her thoughts differently, she essentially described to me the way she had found literacy practices and tools that enabled and empowered her students to be critically aware users of language and technology in an intelligent manner in the public sphere. This point might seem trivial, but in my opinion it is an important one, representing a shift away from the efforts to make new technologies work under the conditions of the old ones—as it were, attempting to electrify the book and the blackboard—approaches McLuhan (1962) refers to as "the horseless carriage syndrome" (p. 130). In many respects, and perhaps paradoxically, it was in the Print and Photography class, a predominantly visual subject, that these students practiced literacy in an empowering and critical way.

ORGANIZING LEARNING: ANNE'S CLASSROOM ACTIVITIES

Anne's students were part of a larger group of 29. However, it was only in some classes that all of these students were together. In most of the practically oriented classes such as Print and Photography, a maximum of 12 students were together, and the group was reconfigured in other classes, depending on the students' individual choices. During my visit, the students took part in different activities and projects in and out of the school premises, which made a rigid schedule for my observations difficult, if not impossible. In addition, some of the assignments they were given required them to be outside the school premises. My observations are therefore scattered across my scheduled three months, and across the classes available for me to observe.

Since it was Anne's activities linked to her use of blogs as part of the regular school tasks that encouraged my interest, I prioritized this subject during the observational period and when interviewing students. They were also blogging in a different but related class, Visual Culture, which I also observed. For practical reasons, and due to my knowledge of Anne and her specific ideas about blogging in class, however, the bulk of my data is from Anne's classes. Still, through observations across disciplines and comparison of Anne's classes with those of other teachers, a few interesting tendencies emerged.

Learning activities and physical organization of the classroom

First, Anne's teaching had a different physical organization than the classes of other teachers. Whenever the students worked on their computers writing up a blog assignment or with practical exercises (e.g., making a sculpture or taking pictures), they would be wherever it was natural for them to be: at their desks, outdoors, in the photo room, or on the floor. However, whenever Anne wanted to talk to them, either to discuss a practical matter or to present new material, she usually gathered everybody on the other side of the classroom, away from whatever they were working on and, perhaps most importantly, away from their computers. Anne's students were probably no less prone to be distracted than other students with computers in front of them, but they were rarely given the opportunity to drift away. In other classes, such as Norwegian, most activities during a class, typically listening to a lecture, reading a text, and working with exercises from the textbook, took place at students' desks. Attempts were made to regulate the use of computers during lectures, but some students used their PCs for note taking, which made it difficult to control how the PCs were used.

Learning activities, timeframes, and goals

Second, whenever they were given an assignment that demanded prolonged activity at the desk, typically either touching up a picture on the computer or writing a blog post documenting their work, students were given clear goals for their work and equally clear time limits. In addition, they were aware of how and when their work was going to be assessed. Although I observed that they touched base now and then with their social networks online, they rarely drifted away for long stretches of time. This is strikingly different from the kinds of work students did and the kind of engagement I observed in other classes, particularly in theoretical subjects such as Norwegian and history. There students often worked on assignments with no clear goals in regard to when they were supposed to hand in the finished product or even if and how it was going to be assessed.

Blogging and epistemological shifts

This observation relates to the third point, which is to do with the status given the actual product or artifact that the students produced as part of their schoolwork. Anne used the students' individual blogs as hubs for various learning activities in school, largely organizing day-to-day activities according to the status of this blog. Everyone had their own blog linked to the other blogs in class, and Anne's own blog also linked to the students' blogs on a "blogroll," a collection of links to all the blogs. She also frequently linked to her students' blogs from her own blog texts, pointing to and highlighting different students' work and guiding the attention of her own readers toward her students' texts. Most of what the students did during Anne's classes had to be displayed, depicted, summed up, or reflected upon in a blog post; the actual assignment handed in was normally a blog post, either as a blog-only assignment or as reflections tied to real-world products they had made, such as sculptures or installations. The blogs were not hidden behind passwords, but were part of the real-world blogosphere; each student's reflections and arguments were visible, transparent, and open to scrutiny, comments, and criticism from anyone.

The students' response to this way of organizing teaching indicates that these texts had a different status from, for example, the essays that they regularly handed in to other teachers. In terms of organizing and guiding how the class worked, students had to work efficiently in order to meet Anne's deadlines for a given task. Otherwise they risked having to publish substandard work on the web. Given the nature of the blog, this is something most of the students in this class hesitated to do—as one of the students pointed out, "No one wants to be the one who performs badly [on the blog]."

In other words, this way of organizing knowledge—opening up the text for scrutiny, trusting students to contribute to a public discourse in a given subject, and helping students to be confident with these textual practices and tools for literacy—struck me as a notable departure from the literacy practices these students were accustomed to in most other classes. This way of conceiving of what learning is and where it happens suggests an epistemological shift away from the ways of doing school most of them were accustomed to; from the private texts, or as a student expresses it, "the forced texts of [the school subject] Norwegian," destined only for an eventless life in the teacher's drawer, to the exposed and vulnerable contributions to public discourse, open for comments and scrutiny.

Literacy and Blogging from Students' Perspectives

The students' accounts of and reflections on their blogging practices seemed to reveal an awareness of a different kind of literacy activity, or what I saw as a critical digital literacies awakening during my observations of classroom activities. The findings from my interviews with students more or less highlighted the same phenomena across all groups, including in individual interviews, where students spoke about their personal blogs and assessment in greater detail. Their reflections about their blogging activities centered on several topics. I am aware that my material allows a great many approaches, but I have chosen to organize the interviews using the following categories, which are all, in one way or another, related to the students' own accounts of blogging:

I. Community and sharing: related to the network of blogs in this particular class and the way this network is utilized for literacy and learning;

II. Motivational factors: how the activities related to the blogs and the ways these activities are organized motivate the students in different ways; and

III. Organizational factors: how students used the blogs as a way of personally organizing their knowledge.

Community and sharing

One of the consequences of establishing blogs and organizing student work around blogs, with a rigid culture of publishing regularly and on time, was that Anne and her students established a sense of community related to their use of blogs. Whatever they were working on, be it work in progress or finished texts, they published it on their blogs. All students linked to each other's blogs, as well as to the teacher's blog, which again included links to all the students' blogs.

On a positive note, this meant that they could consult each other for inspiration during class while working, to look for ideas or inspiration or to learn something new. Here are some quotes from one of the groups:

STUDENT 1:   You can show the others what you are working on . . .

STUDENT 2:   . . .and then you can look at what the others are doing, which I think is very exciting.

STUDENT 3:   . . .get some ideas.

STUDENT 2:   yes, be inspired by the others.

Student 1 elaborated on this in one of the individual interviews: "I look at the others, how good they are…learn much from it…when you look at the others, you learn new methods, [how to] take pictures, new ideas, and…at least I learn a lot."

On a negative note, the fact that they published openly to the web meant that most of them did not want to publish work that was not up to their standards, since they knew their texts would be read not only by the teacher for assessment, but also by students and other people interested in their blogs. This is one student's take on this: "Everyone sees what we do…the entire school year. And that's rather…personal. If you're not that interested in the subject, you might not get good results…[and in that case] it's not a good thing that everybody can see it…You don't want to be the one person in the class doing badly."

The students also highlighted Anne's blog as an important contributor to their sense of community. Anne kept both a personal and a professional blog, using her professional one as a way of organizing the rhizome of texts in this class. Her professional blog performed several functions in this class: linking to the students' blogs, discussing different matters relating to the subject, linking to interesting articles or inspirational websites, and posting assignments for students. She also had a feature called "Photo of the Week," where she highlighted a photo by one of the students.

The students frequently touched upon Anne's blog in the interviews, giving the impression that they read her blog regularly. One student complained that Anne's blog was updated so often that it was difficult to find what she was looking for at any given moment. However, she also commented that she often consulted Anne's blog in connection with assignments and exercises they were given, because Anne published a lot of useful links, how-to videos, and other material related to the task at hand. Another student commented that she liked to "see who's featured in 'photo of the week'...[Anne] picks one [photo] out, and it's fun to see who's been picked out, because it's often one of the best ones...."

In other words, this group of students had established a community of sharing and inspiration that they themselves thought highly of, according to the interviews and as confirmed by my observations of social interaction in the group. This communal or collective aspect of blogging in particular and social media in general is a much-described and much-discussed phenomenon in the literature on digital media (e.g., Rettberg, 2008, p. 57). In addition, there is a large selection of literature on the profound changes in society associated with changes in the media landscape, referred to in the introduction to this chapter. Nevertheless, I would like to underscore that I hesitate to link the sense of community in this particular classroom to the more or less deterministic discussions of the digital media's role in changing the ways we think and learn. The uses of digital technology in this classroom were largely designed around certain ideas and values tied to literacy and learning, deliberately guided by the teacher, and I have found nothing in my material to indicate that these students were particularly more "digitally native" than, for example, their teacher, Anne. When it comes to their propensity to take up new technologies and new ways of working and thinking, I find it likely that the differences within the group of students in this class were just as large as those within the group of teachers who were teaching them.

Motivational factors

In addition to highlighting the communal aspects of blogging, the students frequently highlighted other characteristics of blogs that motivated them, both related to genre-specific and material factors and to the way their blogging activities were organized. As mentioned earlier, they frequently discussed the external motivation of knowing that they had to publish their work out in the open: "...and they [the teachers] can check immediately if we have done something...and it's the same in 'Visual Culture' [another student confirming], she's checking it constantly, how we're doing on the blog."

One student emphasized how writing for an audience is more exciting than the regular way of writing for the teacher: "...at school, no one else [but the teacher] reads [my texts], so it really doesn't mean all that much." The same student also stated, interestingly, that she had learned a lot from having to explain matters to other people, unlike in many situations where she would just be writing for the teacher.

Several statements contrasted writing on a blog with "regular writing," describing blogging as different because it opened up new ways of expressing themselves. They used terms and expressions such as "more personal," "free," and "shorter" to describe blog writing and mark its distance from the other subjects in school. One student stated, "…when I write on a blog, I feel that I can let my fingers fly.…I write what I think, because that's what I'm supposed to convey."

This sense of distance from other subjects is linked to the language students used when blogging, which they commonly described using expressions such as "not preoccupied with rules and grammar," "less formal," "shorter," and a language that is "oral." The language of ordinary school, academic writing, was described in terms of constraints and rigidity, an obstacle to their thoughts, whereas the blogs allowed a "truer" kind of writing. Students described the language they used in their blogs in the following ways:

STUDENT 1:	…personal…
STUDENT 2:	…oral language, perhaps? That it is more oral…
STUDENT 3:	…yes, much more oral
STUDENT 2:	…more of my own opinions
STUDENT 3:	…yes, I don't review my writing errors as much [on the blog]
INTERVIEWER:	You don't?
STUDENT 2:	Not on the blog, not as much as I do when writing Norwegian essays.
INTERVIEWER:	Even if it is supposed to be published out in the open?
STUDENT 3:	Yes, actually, I still review less…
INTERVIEWER:	…but you still feel that it is…[good enough or sufficient]
STUDENT 3:	Yes, because I feel it's a bit more like oral language, kind of, it's not as structured as in [the school subject] Norwegian, where you have to consider how to build a sentence, [on the blog, I] write what I think.

Their thoughts on writing in this way were linked in many respects to Southwest High's somewhat "creative" identity, as discussed earlier. These particular blogs were perceived as an arena for a different kind of writing than in the general, academic subjects:

STUDENT:	[the blog] is more oral-like…
INTERVIEWER:	Why?
STUDENT:	It is open, for everyone…I don't know…I feel that a blog is supposed to be more personal.
INTERVIEWER:	Even if it is a school blog?
STUDENT:	Even if it is a school blog.

Regarding other subjects in school, another student said, "usually, there are rules for how you are supposed to write, but on the blog, nobody is there to tell you that you're supposed to write just like this, you're supposed to choose freely and the idea is to get other people interested in reading, because that's the idea with blogging, to get other people to read your blog."

Perhaps one of the most important motivational factors was the teacher and her role. The students repeatedly mentioned their teachers, particularly Anne, as an inspiration for their blogging. Apart from the fact that Anne was depicted as a proficient and knowledgeable teacher, they reported that they regularly read her blog. Although I have no direct statements to back this up, I assume from what the students said that they found inspiration in the way she used her blog, and that her digital-text practices functioned as models for their own.

Still, quite a few statements from the interviews related to Anne's overall attitude toward her subject and the way she organized her teaching and prepared for the different activities. The students pointed out that she was always well prepared and organized. Further, the students emphasized that, compared with some of their other classes, Anne's lectures were shorter and almost always followed by some kind of practice: "…and the instant we're done [with the lecture] we are doing it [i.e., some kind of practice linked to the lecture]."

On a side note: Blogs and language

Although not strictly a topic for this chapter, I would like to comment briefly on the students' own descriptions of the language they used in their blogs. As mentioned above, some of the students characterized their blog writing as a departure from the academic language of school into what we typically would recognize as the kind of language used in synchronous communication genres in digital media: texting, online chatting, etc. There is no shortage of criticisms of writing in school where it is permitted to use features such as emoticons, abbreviations, and the kinds of oral attributes that my informants report using. My claim on the basis of this particular study is that there are indications that the writing of blog texts, especially when contextualized and operationalized the way it was done in this class, helps the students establish particular identities as writers. In turn, establishing an identity as a writer using literacy in this way and with these effects might spill over in a positive way to their use of written language in other contexts with other demands. Knowing that you are a good writer in one context may make you believe you can be a good writer in another context, even if being a good writer means different things in each context. Again, although it is important not to be naïve about the effects of establishing writing habits in total opposition to the established norms in school, it is also important to be critical of ideas that the medium might impose bad habits on the user—ideas reminiscent of the "essentialist" accounts discussed earlier. For a linguistic account of these questions, see Crystal (2006).

Organizational factors

One of the patterns emerging from my analysis of my material had to do with the way Anne prepared her classroom activities for ways of organizing knowledge around the blog technology and the effects this had on her students and their learning processes. As mentioned in the previous sections, this enabled the students to share and cooperate in meaningful ways through the network of blogs, and it motivated the students to work differently from what they were allowed to do in other classes and other literacy technologies.

But the students also discussed how the blog approach helped them organize their own personal learning. Barton (2007) outlines eight different features of literacy in different situations and uses in life. Among them is using literacy "as a symbolic system used for representing the world to ourselves. Literacy is part of our thinking. It is part of the technology of thought" (pp. 35–36). As we have seen, the blogs seemed to have significance to the students as their personal tools for organizing knowledge, making sense of the world around them. The blogs were part of their "technology of thought."

This was also true on a concrete, material level. In addition to using the blog as a medium or genre for personal reflection and using the class community of blogs as a source for learning, sharing, inspiration, and motivation, students characterized the blog as a good technology for keeping track of their own progress and ideas. Having everything on a blog was a good way of structuring both their ideas and their work. They had access to everything on the web regardless of their physical whereabouts, and they were able to keep a copy of everything they handed in for assessment, which was otherwise not normally the case: "Everything is in one place and it's easier to…it is nice to be able to reach it from home as well, and…we can keep it, because often, we are not given back the work we do on exams. Now we have [access to it all the time]."

This also meant that they were able to work from other places besides school. Many of their assignments, such as taking photographs of landscapes and structures, could not easily be done in school. Several blog assignments were done outside of school, often directly linked to geographical or physical places of significance to the task they were working on. In this context, the students associated characteristics of the blog medium with different possible ways of organizing their knowledge, and emphasized this as something that worked to their advantage.

CONCLUDING REMARKS

As Erstad (2010) asserts, media issues have increasingly become a defining factor dividing generations, resulting in a public discourse on young people and the conception of them as particularly competent in using digital media (p. 58). Young people are accordingly given labels such as "screen agers" (Rushkoff, 2006) and "digital natives" (Palfrey & Gasser, 2010), and the OECD uses the term "new millennium learners" to indicate that future generations will require different learning strategies, where digital media play an important role (2008). At the core of this is an idea of children and young people as experts in the digital field, the "natives," whereas the teachers are the "immigrants" without real possibilities for learning either the skills or the language to become properly integrated in the digital world (Prensky, 2001, p. 2). This opposition lies at the heart of the discussion on digital technology in schools, and it reflects how many teachers see themselves in relation to digital technologies and learning.

Although my material suggests that digital media play an important role in the lives of these particular teenagers, the interviews also indicate that the picture is more complex than that suggested by the great-divide accounts of generational differences or the impression we get from insider/outsider dichotomies such as "digital natives/digital immigrants."

The myth of the outdistanced teacher

From my study, it is not entirely evident that the teachers are busy keeping up with the students in the digital domain. Although some teachers are reluctant to use computers in class, many of the things the students value about using computers are things they have learned from teachers in school. One of the students reported that a former teacher spurred her into blogging even before she came to Southwest High. As we have seen, students refer to Anne as an inspiration when it comes to digital media use, mentioning how her blog is constantly updated and interesting to follow, but mainly because they find her inspiring as a photographer and a professional with a passion for what she does. What makes this particularly interesting is that it blurs the boundaries between disciplines and technology, or between having discipline-specific knowledge and using digital tools. Anne does not come across as one of those overly tech-savvy teachers eager to put every new gadget into use in the classroom. Her main interest and passion is photography and the visual arts, and the teaching of those disciplines. Still, much of what she does in the classroom revolves around her use of technology, but the technology is deliberately used to expand and enhance her discipline-specific teaching.

Anne emerges in many respects as a trustworthy role model for a certain kind of critical literacies praxis or "Bildung" where the digital tools tie in naturally with the subjects she teaches. She actively participates in the blogosphere, highlighting students' work, sharing links and other material that she finds, setting an example of a kind of digital proficiency beyond the technical aspects of digital media usage that too often dominate discussions of computer use in the classroom. This is interesting in itself, as an indication of what it is possible to achieve with technology in school when it is properly organized and contextualized.

In addition, it is interesting to see these findings in relation to the more academically oriented subjects, in particular Norwegian, and how the students explicitly contrast Anne's practice with the practices in these subjects. Norwegian is a subject that is tied to the notion of "Bildung": the modern ideal of the critically literate and empowered student, who is literate beyond the mere technical aspects of reading and writing. Moreover, the national curriculum gives Norwegian a particular responsibility for this critical literacy education, as the core subject for developing the students' "voice" as writers. In this study, however, critical literacy teaching of the kind normally associated with core subjects such as Norwegian is practiced more or less exclusively in Anne's Print and Photography class.

The myth of the digitally innovative teenager

Much of the writing about "digital natives" postulates today's teenagers as having a particularly active role in digital media, even being innovators of new practices (Erstad, 2010, p. 58; Prensky, 2001). However, when my informants talk about what they do outside of school, what strikes me is how similar they are to those of the generation before them, that is, today's 40-year-olds, when it comes to activities and interests, obviously with a few exceptions. Although digital media play an important role in their lives, many of my informants spend much of their time doing typical after-school activities such as exercising, playing soccer, doing church charity work, or spending time with their families and friends. Also, much of their media usage is characterized by consumption rather than production, such as watching movies on the PC or the television, playing computer games, listening to music, and reading magazines.

Moreover, studies of literacy practices often accentuate the differences between academic or school-based literacy practices and literacy practice "beyond the schoolhouse door" (Hull & Schultz, 2002). Particularly in discussions of digital literacy practices, one gets the impression that creative use of technology is something that happens outside of school and that teachers must look out of school to find innovative and new ways of using technology.

In my material, such assumptions are challenged, suggesting that school plays an important role in presenting digital technology to students. Apart from socializing with their friends on Facebook, much of what can be characterized as production and doing new practices in digital media happened or had its origins in school. As I have touched upon above, some of the students were introduced to social media and blogging by teachers prior to meeting Anne. Others were inspired by Anne's teaching to start their private blogs in addition to the blogs they kept in school. Many of the students reported that they would keep on blogging after they left Southwest High. In these cases, teachers and school contributed not only to introducing social media and new technology, but also to contextualizing these tools and enabling the students to reflect on their digital behavior and to use the digital tools as a means of empowerment rather than just pure entertainment.

Toward new epistemologies?

Naturally, there are limits to how far my material can be generalized. Still, what it at least suggests is that school can play an important role in introducing students to technology, in contextualizing, scaffolding, and practicing critical awareness and constructive, perhaps even disruptive, ways of using tools for digital literacy. In my opinion, teachers can have a unique impact by virtue of the combination of their discipline-specific knowledge and the different digital technologies and tools that can be used to enhance teaching, as Anne's classroom practices demonstrate. It is perhaps here, at the intersection of literacy learning, pedagogy, and technology, that possibilities exist for epistemologically new ways of conceiving of literacy in a digital age.

Technology plays an important role, not alone but as a constantly changing set of socially situated tools for literacy, for making sense of the world and ourselves. Many goals can still be reached with pencil and paper, but as Bolter (2001) declares, the digital media have provided us with entirely new writing spaces: tools and arenas that give us new possibilities for expression and participation in society. As Anne's practices have exemplified, these spaces can be mastered to work to the advantage of students' critical digital literacies in new ways—while they may never tear down the walls of the schools completely, they may at least perforate them.

REFERENCES

Anderson, L. (2006). Analytic autoethnography. *Journal of Contemporary Ethnography, 35*(4), 373–395.

Barton, D. (2007). *Literacy: An introduction to the ecology of written language*. Hoboken, NJ: Wiley-Blackwell.

Bolter, J. D. (2001). *Writing space: Computers, hypertext, and the remediation of print.* New York & London: Taylor & Francis.

Crystal, D. (2006). *Language and the Internet.* Cambridge, UK: Cambridge University Press.

Erstad, O. (2010). Educating the digital generation: Exploring media literacy for the 21st century. *Nordic Journal of Digital Literacy, 5*(1), 56–72.

Gee, J. P. (1999). *An introduction to discourse analysis: Theory & method.* New York & London: Routledge.

Gee, J. P. (2008). *Social linguistics and literacies: Ideology in discourses.* New York & London: Taylor & Francis.

Gentikow, B. (2005). *Hvordan utforsker man medieerfaringer? Kvalitativ metode (How can you explore the media experience?: Qualitative methods).* Kristiansand, Norway: IJ-forlaget.

Geertz, C. (1973). *The interpretation of cultures.* New York: Basic Books.

Glaser, B. G., & Strauss, A. L. (1967). *The discovery of grounded theory: Strategies for qualitative research.* Piscataway, NJ: Transaction Publishers.

Heath, S. B., & Street, B. V. (2008). *On ethnography: Approaches to language and literacy research.* New York: Teachers College Press.

Hull, G. A., & Schultz, K. (2002). *School's out: Bridging out-of-school literacies with classroom practice.* New York: Teachers College Press.

Keen, A. (2007). *The cult of the amateur: How today's Internet is killing our culture.* New York: Doubleday/Currency.

Lankshear, C. (1998). *Critical literacy and new technologies.* Paper presented at American Educational Research Association, San Diego, CA. Retrieved from http://everyday literacies.net/critlitnewtechs.html

Lankshear, C. (1999). Literacy studies in education: Disciplined developments in a post-disciplinary age. In M. Peters (Ed.), *After the disciplines: The emergence of cultural studies.* Westport, CT: Bergin & Garvey. Retrieved from http://everydayliteracies.net/literacystudies.html

McLuhan, M. (1962). *The Gutenberg galaxy: The making of typographic man.* Toronto, Canada: University of Toronto Press.

Organisation for Economic Co-operation and Development (OECD). (2008). New millennium learners: Initial findings on the effects of digital technologies on school-age learners. OECD. Retrieved from http://www.iktogskole.no/wp-content/uploads/2011/01/EDU-CERI-CD200811.pdf

Palfrey, J., & Gasser, U. (2010). *Born digital: Understanding the first generation of digital natives.* New York: Basic Books.

Prensky, M. (2001, October). Digital natives, digital immigrants. *On the Horizon, 9*(5). Retrieved from http://www.marcprensky.com/writing/Prensky%20-%20Digital%20Natives,%20Digital%20Immigrants%20-%20Part1.pdf

Rettberg, J. W. (2008). *Blogging.* Cambridge, UK: Polity.

Rothenberg, D. (1997, August). How the web destroys the quality of students' research papers. *Chronicles of Higher Education, 43*(49), A44. Retrieved from http://www.trhs.weber.k12.ut.us/hatch/my%20local%20web%20files%203/Portfolio/documents/powerpoint/web_research.pdf

Rushkoff, D. (2006). *ScreenAgers: Lessons in chaos from digital kids.* New York: Hampton Press.

Selwyn, N. (2010). *Schools and schooling in the digital age.* London: Taylor & Francis.

Street, B. V. (1984). *Literacy in theory and practice*. Cambridge, UK: Cambridge University Press.
Street, B. V., Pahl, K., & Roswell, J. (2009). Multimodality and New Literacy Studies. In C. Jewitt
   (Ed.), *The Routledge handbook of multimodal analysis* (pp. 191–200). London: Routledge.
Tapscott, D. (2009). *Grown up digital: How the net generation is changing your world*. New York:
   McGraw-Hill Professional.

CHAPTER SIX

Utilizing Mobile Media AND Games TO Develop Critical Inner-City Agents OF Social Change

ANTERO GARCIA

In the spring of 2011, I handed out iPod Touches to the eager and awaiting hands of 17 ninth-grade English Language Arts (ELA) students. The mixed feelings of excitement and apprehension that came with handing out the devices—seen by many of my teaching colleagues as an ill-conceived decision—would act as a harbinger for the constant challenges of balancing hyper-engagement and hyper-distraction in a space focused on developing critical student voices.

Perhaps more than any other recent innovation, mobile media have fundamentally transformed society. Today's mobile media devices—including phones, iPods, and gaming devices—connect the majority of the globe to key networks, economies, and civic opportunities. These ubiquitous devices are often banned from classrooms because they are seen as problematic distractions. As an English teacher with more than seven years of experience in an urban high school, I've seen the ways that mobile media have transformed students' lives. Considering that the vast majority of urban youth of color regularly use mobile media devices like cell phones, I distributed iPods to my students as a way of exploring the ways these devices and the gameplay that occurred with them help students engage critically and transformatively in their schools and communities.

When implemented in the classroom with a strong critical foundation, mobile media can become a tool for powerful learning. They do so by engendering new forms of social participation, which, in turn, shape the social practices and civic identities of young people. In this chapter, I describe the process of critical literacies instruction and transformative gameplay that stem from adapting youth cultural practices and functional components of a participatory media influenced by a "new culture of learning" to engaging pedagogy with urban youth (Thomas & Brown, 2011).

I used a small grant awarded by a local organization to purchase a class set of iPods for this study. Since iPods are significantly cheaper than cell phones, I envisioned that in my class iPods would play the same ubiquitous always-on learning opportunities that day-to-day mobile practices afford students; without the pesky annual contracts and monthly bills, the iPods act identically to iPhones when using a wireless network, minus out-of-the-box phone-call functionality and GPS. Additionally, engagement with mobile computing devices such as iPods also seemed, to me, the most cost-effective way to confront the participation and achievement gap that plagues urban youth across the country.

To engage student in critical use of mobile media devices, I constructed a curriculum that utilized participatory media practices in both digital and non-digital contexts. Pragmatically, this meant guiding students through a scavenger hunt I created for them, asking them to critically interpret their own experiences in and around their school, and teaching them how to use the tools and writing practices required for them to create their own scavenger-hunt clues. This project also meant engaging in alternate reality gameplay that encouraged student role-playing.

Though role-playing may not seem like a necessary component of critical literacies education, it functions in several imperative ways. First, it adds relevance to the curriculum in ways that students are able to understand. By practicing and enacting an activity set that requires critical literacies, students understand these particular applications of critical social and spatial analysis as much more than an abstract concept. Second, role-play bridges the civic development of young people from what is discussed or analyzed from within a classroom to something that is done in conjunction with a larger community. As students traversed, searched for, and found badges in their community, they simultaneously questioned truth statements others have made about the space and critically understood South Central at large as a negotiated space of education and possibility. Finally, these role-playing activities oriented students toward similar identity practices that require participatory media. The way identity is constructed in online space mirrors the activities students engaged in, bridging digital and the non-digital learning experiences. The offline nature of performing physical equivalents of online photo tagging, commenting, and folksonomy—collaborative organizing and "tagging" of information—meant that the transfer of these skills online could occur; by the time this learning unit concluded, with students editing a Wikipedia page collaboratively and curating photographs, students were familiar with these digital literacies through off-line engagement.

Located a few blocks south of the University of Southern California, South Central High School is one of the oldest public high schools in the city of Los Angeles. With a student population of approximately 3,400, South Central High School is one of the largest in the city. Its demographics mirror those of its surrounding community: 83 percent Latino, 15 percent black, and 2 percent multiracial, with an English Language Learner group that makes up 39 percent of the students. Eighty-seven percent of the students receive free or reduced lunch (California Department of Education, 2010). Only 35 percent of students graduate from South Central High School; the majority of these students do not graduate eligible to enroll in most four-year universities (UCLA IDEA, 2010).

All participant and place names have been changed in this study. I have chosen to rename our school South Central High School not only as a signal of the general geographic location in which this school and this study are immersed, but also to validate the counter-narrative of cultural prosperity that persists in urban Los Angeles; a counter-narrative tells a historical account of events from a point of view that differs from a dominant one and provides a perspective that is often underrepresented. Due to historical depictions of poverty, violence, and squalor in films, music, and news headlines, for the past several years, the community of South Central Los Angeles has been in a state of flux. In a deliberate effort to erase a cultural past of uprising, resistance, and negative press through renaming the community, mainstream media and the governing agencies of Los Angeles now refer to the community as "South Los Angeles." However, despite the flooding of "South Los Angeles" messaging in media, I have never heard any of my students refer to this community as anything but "South Central."

DESIGNING SCALABLE, PARTICIPATORY, CRITICAL PLAY

Currently, we see that urban youth have increasing access to technology, and many scholars have shown that youth are engaging technology outside of school in increasingly sophisticated ways (Ito et al., 2010; Norris, 2001; Warschauer, 2003). Because of this, technology and gameplay are being called upon as antidotes to educational inequity. These tools can be used not only to engage students in meaningful learning experiences, but also to shape ways people participate and interact with the world (Lievrouw, 2011). However, while there is burgeoning research around the role that participatory media play in improving learning, educational researchers have identified challenges in their implementation. For example, "research on teaching in urban schools suggests that teachers' limited skills and limiting beliefs about their students lead to a steady diet of low-level material coupled with unstimulating, rote-oriented teaching" (Darling-Hammond, 2010).

Though numerous studies point to the learning potential that new media pose in the changing landscape of education (Bonk, 2009; Plester, Wood, & Bell, 2008; Schuler, 2009; Wood, & Bell, 2008), little research focuses specifically on their use in formal learning environments. Even more significant is the dearth of research focused on utilizing technology with and in underserved urban communities. With technology ushering in new learning challenges for the first "always-connected generation" (Lenhart, 2009), the role that this technology also plays in the growing global economy is taking a sharp turn, connecting individuals into productive networks despite geographical distance.

Recognizing the increasing need for students to critically examine their digital media use instead of merely consuming software, films, and games, as well as the limitations of many teachers' experiences with technology in the classroom, this project focused on using mobile media in ways that would be either intuitive or extremely adoptable for educators. Aside from a specific functional literacy tools, formal use of the iPod Touches in the class centered around the basic features of most mobile media devices: students took lengthy notes, texted writing to me, conducted online research, and heavily documented their research process through photo and video production. The specific tool, installed as an application on the iPod, was a Quick Response (QR) code creator and reader; QR codes are square black-and-white barcodes that contain customized information: text, hyperlinks, email addresses, etc.

In developing the opportunity for critical inquiry in and around the South Central community, this project is framed as an alternate reality game that guides students and educator through Youth Participatory Action Research (YPAR). As part of this inquiry, a custom-designed game, "Ask Anansi" (described below), guided students toward a process of identifying specific topics for critical inquiry and *playing* through the act of engagement and participation.

At the beginning of the class, the students independently wrote candid reflections about what they appreciated about their school and what they felt they could improve. Before the class wrote, I emphasized that their suggestions should look at specific areas of improvement that students felt they could affect. Through initial role-playing and storytelling, the students in the class identified six areas of exploration for our collective inquiry: trash, violence, graffiti, pollution, stereotypes, and love. Following this, larger class discussion and activities focused on honing student reflections into the specific areas of inquiry that students stated as interesting to them. In doing this, the students donned various roles to help them manage the task of identifying, researching, and communicating the topics students selected. These roles included:

- Diplomat: Helps facilitate work between group members
- Engineer: Oversees construction and presentation of work
- The Checkered Flag: Keeps group working in a timely manner
- Tourist: Examines the work from the lens of the "other"
- Portal: Communicates and sends updates to Anansi

The class then began writing narratives of individual and collective experience related to the six topics. A narrative account of how a fight on the first day of middle school affected Solomon, for instance, became a tool for critiquing and questioning the ephemeral influence of violence within the school community.

With these areas of focus, the class began enacting critical digital literacies practices in both online and physical environments. These instructional practices combined tenets of critical pedagogy with critical and sociocultural literacies. Here critical pedagogy is understood as a liberatory approach to education that guides students, as co-constructors of knowledge, to build their own meaning and critique of the inequities within their lives (Duncan-Andrade & Morrell, 2008; Freire, 1970). In formal school settings such as the one in which this study was conducted, critical pedagogy helps guide students toward academic achievement as a means of social empowerment; this effort still calls for a seismic shift in the current capitalist school structures and also encourages significant group achievement (Perry, 2003). This "conscientization" finds students and teachers alike questioning social and historical inequities (Freire, 1970).

Present literacy research points to the multimodal and productive nature of digital literacies (Gee, 2004; Kress, 2009; New London Group, 1996). Often, these conversations disregard the potential of *critical* within the nascent field of digital literacies. While this chapter expands definitions of critical digital literacies, I begin rooted in analog critical literacies. For me, these are critical literacies that are not tied to digital media; by focusing on analog digital literacies and seeing the ways these literacies inform decisions with digital media, a stronger understanding of how digital media products are shaped by critical literacies is clearly parsed. In making literacies relevant to the larger experiential context of society and culture, Freire and Macedo describes the need to read "the *world*" in order to engage in reading "the word" (1987). Freire's view fits into sociocultural understandings of literacy as developing socially constructed meaning. As Gumperz and Cook-Gumperz (Ogbu, 1983) explain, "The move into literacy requires children to make some basic adjustments to the way they socially attribute meaning to events and the process of the everyday world in order to be able to loosen their dependence upon contextually specific information and to adopt a decontextualized perspective" (p. 231). This constant process of reinterpreting and re-reading the world as part of literacies development signals opportunity for critique and counter-narrative. Critical literacies allow space for questions and multiple frames of understanding and interpretation. Positioning part of the role of literacies as understanding underlying power structures, Moje and Lewis (2007) point to the need for a "critical sociocultural literacy" as a means of merging these similar interests.

ASK ANANSI: A PEDAGOGY OF TRANSFORMATIVE SOCIAL PLAY

The work that is described follows nearly six weeks of alternate reality gameplay in my classroom. While the products that students created and analyzed speak to the transformative power of critical digital literacies, these activities function within a larger pedagogy of transformative social play.

> Transformative Social Play: forces us to reevaluate a formal understanding of rules as fixed, unambiguous, and omnipotently authoritative. In any kind of transformative play, game structures come into question and are re-shaped by player action. In transformative social play, the mechanisms and effects of these transformations occur on a social level. (Salen & Zimmerman, 2004, p. 475)

In *Homo Ludens: A Study of the Play Element in Culture*, Huizinga (1949) describes the space in which games are played as a "magic circle," emphasizing that the main characteristics of play are "that it is free"; furthermore, "[p]lay is not 'ordinary' or 'real' life. It is rather a stepping out of 'real' life into a temporary sphere of activity" (p. 8). The magic circle of gameplay is one in which role-playing, acting, and behavior exceeds social norms; so it is here that students can comfortably pose, flex, and experiment in ways they may not typically be expected to participate or behave. Casting this magic circle around the activities in my classroom and shielding our inquiry from pressure of student social conformity, I created an Alternate Reality Game (ARG) that steeps student action and problem-posing in a tradition of West African folklore called "Ask Anansi." The learning and activities in this ARG find students acting within communities of practice; a game's setting and multiple scenarios rely on situated student learning within specific contexts and provide key roles for students to undertake (Lave & Wenger, 1991).

In Ask Anansi, student participation is community centered; students engage in inquiry-based problem-solving by communicating with, and helping to unravel the stories they are told by Anansi. The trickster spider god of Caribbean folklore, Anansi has answers and solutions to any question students can imagine. Anansi's responses, however, are not always the most clear: he likes tricks, riddles, and befuddlement. As a result, students honed critical literacies skills to unravel the web of Anansi's hints and instructions. Some clues were found outside the walls of the classroom and may appear as posters, barcodes, or phone calls. Anansi's dialogue with students is one that challenges concerns of power, dominance, and agency in a capitalist environment. And while Ask Anansi operates within a fictitious narrative and the students (correctly) assumed I embodied the Anansi persona when communicating with them via text messages and emails, the gaming environment allowed students to act, question, and engage in simultaneously critical and playful inquiry.

Below, I describe the conclusion of Ask Anansi. Students were recruited to write an empowering counter-narrative about their community and dominant stereotypes. Though the main product of this game is one of problem-posing critical thinking and civic participation, the goal of the game is one based in the ARG's fiction: they must satisfy the insatiable need of Anansi for a *good* story. The topics that students chose—trash, violence, graffiti, pollution, stereotypes, and love—are discussed and repositioned through counter-narrative and critiquing dominant stories told by and about the community through popular media texts. Next, students proposed actionable solutions to move from repositioning stories of the community's past to threading the narrative toward the future. The scavenger hunt that follows focuses on the way students' past inquiry merges with their future. This data comes from my own daily field notes as the class teacher and co-researcher with my classroom as well as from the work students turned in, the text messages, photographs, and digital products sent to me, and from transcriptions I made of class conversations and focus groups. I coded my data using an inductive approach (Emerson, Fretz, & Shaw, 1995). In analyzing the qualitative data in this study, my main units of analysis were specific literacy events (Barton & Hamilton, 2005) and student-created critical textual products (Morrell, 2008).

While computational literacies, by their nature, focus on digital tools and dispositions like hacking and online media remixing, part of the work I've been doing with my students in this project is centered around extending these skills into a physical world and deliberately offline environment. These activities serve several purposes, including:

- Alleviating teachers from the strain of a digital participation gap
- Fostering physical world relationships among students in classrooms
- Illustrating the connections between 21st-century literacies and the academic literacies that are most heavily emphasized by standardized curricula, tests, and policies

INFORM, PERFORM, TRANSFORM

This scavenger-hunt sequence illustrates the ways youth may recontextualize their physical surroundings. This sequence followed a key thematic approach to critical transformative practice: Inform, Perform, Transform. This was adapted from my own experiences with the Black Cloud Game (Niemeyer, Garcia, & Naima, 2009), in which students' actions focused on improving local air quality and were informed by data collected at various nearby locations.

Each of the three thematic components to this approach had distinct activities tied to them:

Inform: Students gather, analyze, and collate information in order to produce their own, original work. Students furthered three types of knowledge during this phase:

1. Indigenous expertise of their communities
2. Conceptual understanding of the function of gameplay and problem-posing inquiry
3. Functional literacies skills including creating and reading QR codes, writing challenging and engaging clues, and properly logging and reflecting on found items.

Perform: Utilizing the knowledge and information acquired through their informational inquiries, students produce/perform new work that is tied to a larger critical, conceptual, and/or academic goal.

Students developed scavenger hunt clues for their classmates, hid them in and around their school space, and later searched for each other's clues.

Transform: Extending their performance toward publicly shared knowledge and action, students focus on directly impacting and critically transforming their world.

Students adapted the closed, class-only scavenger hunt into a publicly curated exhibit to impact the public's reading and interpretation of the South Central community.

"Inform, Perform, Transform" mirrors this research project's methodological approach. In allowing students to develop their own body of knowledge, with the teacher acting as facilitator in this process and encouraging transformative performative action, this process is a way to make explicit a YPAR design. I will go into further detail below about how each of these separate components unfolded within this project, the kinds of literacies and civic practices they developed, and the ways that this three-step process highlights a shift toward transformative social pedagogy in English Language Arts classrooms.

INFORMING: FOSTERING INDIGENOUS KNOWLEDGE AND DEVELOPING FUNCTIONAL CRITICAL LITERACIES

In the first phase of this scavenger-hunt process, I relied on traditional pedagogical practice. I modeled what I felt was an engaging learning process for students, asked them to share their own knowledge in regards to this topic, and then guided them through ways to explore and apply new critical literacies skills.

I scaffolded the searching process in the practice scavenger hunt, and then the class collectively analyzed clues that led them to QR code badges hidden at SCHS. The first clue was intentionally easier and in extremely close proximity to the students. The final clue I provided was significantly more difficult: the vocabulary utilized to describe the location, the spatial thinking required, and the fact that the clue was located in a place many students had not explored before led to a more challenging and collaborative problem-solving process.

In the anecdote below, I recount the process of watching the first scavenger-hunt clue move students from tepid, required participation, to out-of-the-seat ownership of the class curriculum:

As I handed out the printed paper that described the location of the first clue, students took the papers with their standard nonchalance for schoolwork. Here is what the students read:

> "This badge is tucked away in the corner of one of Mr. Garcia's favorite things: a book! There are many here ... so which one is it? To successfully find this badge, you need to find a book someone wrote about his own life, just like you have. He had many names: Homeboy, Satan, Minister, El Hajj Malik El Shabazz. This badge can be yours if you look on page 165."

As soon as Dante realized that he was looking for something within the class and that this was a sort of game, he stood up and started pacing and looking for things that might be askew among the disheveled bookcases. While many of the students looked uncertain and looked back and forth from their paper to me for further instruction, Dante had now roused Solomon and Jay and all three had now congregated around the bookcase.

As Dante and his friends focused on looking through myriad books, Tess focused on the final sentence of the clue description. She pulled out her iPod and, with the device placed in the middle of her table to collaborate with Holden, tapped "el hajj malik el shabazz" into her Wikipedia mobile application. The result redirects users to the page for Malcolm X. While more students continued to congregate around the bookshelves, Tess sat and took stock of our room: to her left, nearly half of the class was looking at or in books. Scattered in front of her, the rest of the class, including myself, was looking at the scavenger-hunt clue or at the mass by the bookshelves; the walls were cluttered with student work.

And then she saw it.

Perched high above the white board, strikingly out of place once noticed, a single paperback leaned casually by itself. She nodded to Holden and they slowly rose from their desks attracting nobody else's attention. She dragged her chair to the shelf and Holden stood on it, retrieved the black book, and handed it down to Tess. Flipping to page 165, seeing a QR code paper clipped above an underlined passage, Tess looked at Holden who yelled, "We found it!" Surprised comments (and disappointed grumbling from Dante) came from across the room.

I asked Tess to explain how she and Victor found the clue and then she read the underlined passage aloud for the class:

> The devil white man cut these black people off from all knowledge of their own kind, and cut them off from any knowledge of their own language, religion, and past culture, until the black man in America was the earth's only race of people who had absolutely no knowledge of his true identity.

Minerva, after the quote was read—before anyone could speak or reflect, and specifically before I could ask the class any guiding discussion questions, as is my wont—quickly said, "That's a nice quote. Okay what's the next clue?" The rest of the class looked to me expectantly.

Though Dante seemed somewhat disappointed that he didn't find the clue, the class was interested in the process of looking for and eventually finding a tangible object. As a game, the scavenger hunt increased participation for the day; entanglement with critical theory became a product of this pedagogical instrument.

To tie into an ongoing theme in the class of empowering individuals through webs of counter-narratives, the remaining badges (and the ones that students would subsequently create and hide) were wrapped scroll-like inside the ring portion of black plastic spider rings—the kinds typically given out to children around Halloween.

The next clue eventually led students to examine the portable desk that Mr. Raskol utilized to travel from room to room. I asked the students why they thought I ended up hiding a clue in the bright red desk that Mr. Raskol affectionately called "The Armadillo." Before handing out the third clue, the class spent a few minutes discussing my intentions as the game designer for the clue.

Elizabeth, the student to successfully locate the badge in a paper tray, said, "I think you wanted us to think about the fact that Mr. Raskol doesn't have his own classroom."

"Maybe you wanted us to look at the big-ass desk that Raskol has to move every period," Solomon added.

"This school can't even afford to give its teachers their own rooms and it will still probably fire Raskol at the end of the year," Jay said.

After discovering each clue, students were required to document their findings by logging a brief entry into a Scavenger Hunt Finding Log. The log prompted students to write down the factual information about the clue: what it was called, who authored it, when and where it was found. The log also briefly asked students, "What do I think this space's story is? How does it help tell a story about the community?"

After a second clue that led students to discover a clue hidden on the principal's desk, students were given a final clue I named the "Hidden Vestibule," which led students to an abandoned classroom space in an upstairs alcove of one of the school's buildings. Students were signaled that they were in the right location by a solitary spider dangling from a string in the doorway of the rundown room.

Marjane quickly grabbed the plastic spider and posed to highlight her win. Other students shuffled into the cramped space. Katherine let out a sigh of dismay, "It's so dirty up here. Oh my god." She said this while also holding her iPod up to her eye level and began snapping pictures of the disarray. Holden and Elizabeth also walked into the room and began snapping photos. Dante brooded in the back of the pack, dismayed that he'd only discovered one of the four badges for the day.

It is worth noting the fluid nature with which Katherine and our other co-researchers internalized the process of documentation. After nearly a month of being asked to photograph, document, or text qualitative data about their community for Ask Anansi, it was now a natural performative element of how the students understood their role when engaging in academic work.

In later class reflections, students would point to the scavenger hunt—both the model I've described and the version described later in this chapter—as a "fun" component of the class. It was also a significant pedagogical step forward for how the students interacted within the class and with their community. In many ways, this was the foundation for transformative youth voice becoming a primary goal as articulated by students. While the class continued to maintain competitiveness in searching for badges and in writing "difficult" clues, these became anchored in challenging the hegemonic norms of their surroundings. This was a transparent goal I'd designed into the gameplay curriculum and it was one that was understood by students and articulated in their textual products: SMS messages, scavenger-hunt clues, and video reflections.

Student iPods were utilized throughout the class to document the experience; the creation of QR codes was the only component of this scavenger hunt that required digital media tools. At the same time, the QR codes—as they are essentially a personalized text themselves—are no different a productive tool than the ability to create a text message, an essay, or a photograph.

Further, the QR code isn't even a crucial element of the scavenger hunt; all of the elements of hiding and of seeking would still be in place regardless of whether or not QR codes were used. In addition to being a functional literacy tool to add to students' bodies of knowledge, the QR codes were adopted for this unit to add feelings of exclusivity and, as a result, strengthen class community. Though QR codes are becoming more and more a mainstream media tool seen on advertisements, magazine covers, and even functioning as business cards, the students in my class and in the focus groups I conducted as part of this research project did not know QR codes by either sight or by name. With this in mind, they seemed like a foreign, "secret" language that my students were able to detect, create, and dialogue *through*. Like a digital Pig Latin or other playful language system, QR codes allowed students to communicate with each other, with me, and with those who found their clues in a way that was occluded from the public, dominant gaze.

These functional literacies did much more than simply mirror the way that literacy acquisition occurs in traditional ELA classrooms. Specifically, students understood how to use QR codes in ways that related back to their own identity development. In terms of learning to use a tool like a QR code reading application on a mobile media device, this is a significant negotiation that pedagogically plays out in the learning environment. Instead of purely *pulling* student-endorsed mobile media into the classroom through appropriation of youth tools and culture, the QR code application is instead engaged in a "third space" (Gutierrez, 2008); it is necessary for class participation, but it also becomes an additional ascribed layer of how students practice, flaunt, and share their mobile media repertoires of practice.

During this first process of playing, the class and I developed three key knowledge sets that would be used throughout the rest of the activity:

1. Indigenous expertise of their communities
2. Conceptual understanding of the function of gameplay and problem-posing inquiry
3. Functional skills including creating and reading QR codes, writing challenging and engaging clues, and properly logging and reflecting on found items

PERFORMING: PRODUCING CLUES TANGLING WITH WEBS

By the time the class finished the first scavenger hunt that I prepared for them, students had expressed interest in creating their own scavenger-hunt clues and hiding badges. Minerva and Dede had formed a team and began plotting locations to hide clues. Likewise, Dante was thrilled about the competitive prospect of potentially finding a clue before others did.

Students had opportunities to write clues and hide scavenger-hunt badges in pairs before being given asked to produce them independently. This aspect of the game transitioned the class from being merely a community of shared practice and shared production to a space where students highlighted and presented individual work to a shared space. In this way, it speaks to the balance between workplace environments that deemphasize individual work products, and academic spaces where original work is what often receives the most merit. Although I asked each student to hide a minimum of four badges and turn in four clues, eight students, nearly half of the class, turned in additional clues.

In a clue titled "Captain Green!" Dede attempted to draw her classmates' attention to the few plants and vegetation on the campus:

> We all know where we study but we don't seem to take a look at this Green friend of ours. After school some of us walk right next to it its real close. Notice how you see this everyday when you come in. Why is Captain Green all alone? [sic]

Dede's clue is similar to many of her peers' in that it is simultaneously playful and provoking. Though the clues point toward critical thought, they do so while also allowing students to enjoy the scavenger hunt as a game. Likewise, Minerva's clue, leading to a spider taped beneath the building's water fountain, helps her classmates look at how the poor conditions of her school environment are normalized. In the middle of her clue she writes: "We use it or have used it before but still we think it comes out nasty. It's where we walk by every day and sometimes we don't even look at it."

With three days to write and hide their clues, students in class spent much of the week busily creating and revising their clues. Meanwhile, the class service worker, Bruce, acted as the collator of clues: as students finished revised clues, Bruce would make a class set of the clue and collate them for impending distribution. By Friday, each student was given a sizeable workbook of more than 80 original clues. With a class period and a weekend to search on their own, students hunched over clues and copies of campus maps plotting how to not only retrieve clues based on where they speculated they were hidden, but how to do so efficiently: two students—Elizabeth and Marjane—grouped clues by proximity to each other, in an effort to find badges that were closest to one another and build a mapped journey of searching across the campus. Elizabeth started with searching for several badges that were in our building before venturing to the outside quad, the neighboring building, the main lunch area, and two badges that were located near the school's auditorium.

In preparing students to hide and search for each other's badges, I deliberately attempted to incorporate a subtle identity shift for the students. As the Ask Anansi narrative culminated in students sharing the storytelling duties of and about their community, Anansi revealed that the members of the class were recruited as "Agents of Anansi." Students were provided badges that allowed them to move around the campus on specified dates and times in order to look for appropriate hiding places and to place their badges in the correct locations. By wearing a physical badge that labeled the students as Agents of Anansi, student classroom identity shifted once again—no longer were they simply doing "English work" or playing a game, students could interpret their actions as embodied role-playing, performing a specific identity practice.

As students abruptly shifted their roles from hiding clues to now seeking them, it was enlightening to see the different ways students played and attempted to deal with the bulk of data that was presented to them—with such a large stack of clues to work through, students problem-solved their assignment in very different ways. Dante, donning his Agent of Anansi badge, took his clues and immediately left the room on his own accord. Unaccompanied, Dante would end up finding more clues than any other class member. In contrast, Elizabeth slowly riffled through the clues, sorting them as mentioned by location but also by what she felt was the difficulty that they were to "solve" and, in her own words, the clues "that [Dante's] probably already gone found by the time I went out there [sic]."

CRITICAL LITERACIES AT WORK AND AT PLAY

The role-playing component of this activity also meant students embodied qualitative research practices while also searching for scavenger-hunt badges. By filling out searching logs and reflection forms after the hunt, students captured data based on their observation and participation with the world at large. When understood that being an Agent of Anansi also meant being an indigenous anthropologist, the role of the game acts as an additional layer of educational value: students engaged in ELA curriculum that simultaneously fulfilled generic "school" functions while also prepping these participants for "society" positions that hold scholarly, political, and economic value.

The scavenger hunt ensured that critical literacies were embedded within students' school practices well beyond a single classroom activity. By definition, critical pedagogy challenges the dominant narrative and "hidden curriculum" (Anyon, 1997) of school. And while this curriculum, too, looked to push back on dominant and positivist constructions of literacies, it functioned to do this while also preparing students for meaningful post-secondary engagement and employment. By approaching critical literacies from a pedagogy of transformative social play, students incorporate literacies of resistance and, in turn, amplify their own emerging critical viewpoints through performance.

Similarly, this activity encouraged ninth graders facing three more years of secondary schooling to approach future classes with questions, criticality, and playfulness. While the duration of the activities that took place were limited due to the school's rigorous testing schedule, the literacy practices were purposefully developed to be applicable to myriad environments and circumstances. Exploring space, questioning author or producer intent, game-design thinking: these literacy-building skills helped students for classes that would likely not engage in alternate reality gameplay. Through these approaches, young people are guided through humanistic practices of critical literacies that extend beyond the ELA classroom, the walls of the socially sequestered school space, and into the liberatory and pragmatically relevant realm of the civic.

TRANSFORMING: ENSNARING PUBLIC DISCOURSE IN THE WEBS OF CRITICAL TRANSFORMATIVE ACTION

Once students had completed the scavenger hunt, we discussed what students encountered on their journey, who the class considered "the winner" of the hunt, and next steps. As a principal of most, but not all, games is the way that they are competitive (Salen & Zimmerman, 2004), the students were intent on quantifying their experiences to determine the winner.

As I did not anticipate the need to select a "winner," I attempted to shift the class discussion to focus on how the game could be taught to others. We engaged in a discussion of what fairness means. Most students felt that the game was played fairly when students independently searched for badges and relied on no other individuals while searching. I pointed out to the class parallels between gameplay and school structures and that fair gameplay and equitable gameplay essentially establish similar patterns of inequality.

Fair also meant making a "reliable" clue. As Jay explained, "Some clues were just like finding a piece of grass on the lawn. It was impossible." The specificity was of a degree that made finding some clues more tedious than provoking. It is worth noting, however, that even these clues that were too detailed in location, were still critical of the location to which they directed students. As Holden said when discussing the single blade of glass example, "I wasn't going to search every piece of grass on the field and I could see the point of the clue—the field is dirty and looks all dangerous."

As we continued to discuss the game, Elizabeth opened up a discussion of what made playing successful: for her, winning this game was about mutual participation in both aspects of the play performance, which meant writing challenging and enlightening clues and searching "with all your energy" for the clues that could be found.

Looking over their experiences transforming the experiences for their class-mates, the final step was to invert this game. The "magic circle" of gameplay made it acceptable to perform the role of the clue-placer/writer and searcher; the strict social rules that students learn as part of the informal curriculum of going to South Central High School were eschewed for the experience of "play."

Selecting two of their locations, I asked students to write very short descriptions of what they encountered, along with an informative or intriguing title. The assignment also asked the students to conclude their descriptions by posing a question to the individuals that read them. After these cards were written and revised by a classmate, students used tape to post them prominently in the spaces where they had originally hid the clues. The hidden badges morphed into prominent public displays of knowledge and dialogue. Minerva's clue, once hidden underneath the dusty water fountain outside our classroom, for instance, was later translated into a note-card that was taped directly above the water fountain, unavoidably within the line of sight of anyone using the fountain.

Pedagogically, this exercise places the critical practices of understanding hidden narratives of power within the community as a component of transformative, empowering voice. As educators and policymakers explore ways to weave participatory and mobile media practices into classroom practice, the potential demonstrated here suggests the value of mobile media to empower not only the individual learner but the community at large through easily replicable critical digital literacies instruction.

Further, the transition from making this a "closed" game only available to the students in my class into an open dialogue with the community is the most transgressive element of this curricular endeavor. Like graffiti or billboard advertisements, curating the space and reconfiguring how people see their environment is invasive. Though the notecards that students wrote can be removed and nothing permanent was added to the spaces, when they were up participants were confronted with a counter-narrative to the way space is interpreted and engaged.

In writing placards and physically curating the experiences of their community members, students express critical digital literacies as an opportunity to expand beyond reading the word and reading the world (Freire & Macedo, 1987) into a productive process of *writing* the world. Later, the digital world, too, was written upon by the class since the students took to the official Wikipedia page for South Central High School Wikipedia. They edited it using Standard English and the database's citation format. Students included details on the Wikipedia page that, while just as factually sound as the existing information about the school's history and alumni, allowed students to voice what they felt was necessary, important, and relevant to the public that may want to access the Wikipedia page. Students captured qualitative data about student opinion about the food, emphasized the school's dropout rate, and noted the small number of custodial staff for the large school.

TOWARD A PEDAGOGY OF PARTICIPATORY MEDIA

In 1932, Counts wrote that "teachers must bridge the gap between school and society and play some part in the fashioning of those great common purposes which should bind the two together." With participatory and mobile media tools, there is more potential to bridge this gap than ever before. The tools are already owned and understood by the students in our classroom and traditional pedagogy disregards this fact.

Through examining existing hegemonic narratives of their community and reappropriating space through textual performance, students developed critical literacies that sought to directly engage in community dialogue. While their use of mobile media facilitated and made easier the types of productive practices that are embedded in this curricular exercise, this unit emphasized that a pedagogy of participatory media can instill 21st-century critical literacies development without overly relying on complicated digital tools. Though students regularly engaged with mobile throughout this project—documenting evidence, looking up Wikipedia-related research, and writing discursive notes as both game designers and game players—it was never the central pedagogical spotlight of this work. Ultimately, the research that the students and I conducted yielded critical practice that decentered learning from a traditional classroom; it located engagement in spaces that students explored critically and instilled literacies instruction within experiential community knowledge.

Too often, I hear my teaching colleagues and administrators pass off mobile media as a novelty at best, and—more often—a significant distraction to learning. When educators and policies deliberately exclude the opportunities demonstrated through mobile media and participatory media pedagogy, they are perpetuating an achievement gap that further cleaves society by race and class (Jenkins, 2008).

Getting students to move more freely beyond the walls of traditional classroom pedagogy required recognizing the types of practices that students engage in through their informal practices and adapting them for formal, critical engagement with literacies. Similarly, even when the pedagogical design of this game-based activity meant students were not using their iPods during many parts of this work, the project was designed to replicate online participatory media shifts. The tools and forms of critical digital practices are insignificant. Students need to be exposed to ways that engagement with media and with society has shifted, regardless of the tools used. In this study, iPods were used. However, even if my students and I were unable to utilize these devices in our co-research, we would have been able to still participate in critical digital literacies instruction and learning. A pedagogy of participatory media, as demonstrated in this chapter, responds to the needs and interests of youth and engages them in practices they are familiar with to develop a transformative, community-driven voice.

REFERENCES

Anyon, J. (1997). *Ghetto schooling: A political economy of urban educational reform.* New York: Teachers College Press.

Barton, D., & Hamilton, M. (2005) Literacy, reification and the dynamics of social interaction. In D. Barton & K. Tusting, *Beyond communities of practice: Language, power, and social context* (pp. 14–35). New York: Cambridge University Press.

Bonk, C. (2009). *The world is open: How web technology is revolutionizing education.* San Francisco, CA: Jossey-Bass.

California Department of Education. (2010). *California basic educational data systems.* Retrieved from http://www.cde.ca.gov/ds/

Darling-Hammond, L. (2010). *The flat world and education: How America's commitment to equity will determine our future.* New York: Teachers College Press.

Duncan-Andrade, J. M. R., & Morrell, E. (2008). *The art of critical pedagogy: Possibilities for moving from theory to practice in urban schools.* New York: Peter Lang.

Emerson, R. M., Fretz, R. I., & Shaw, L. L. (1995). *Writing ethnographic fieldnotes.* Chicago, IL: University of Chicago Press.

Freire, P. (1970). *Pedagogy of the oppressed.* New York: Continuum.

Freire, P., & Macedo, D. (1987). *Literacy: Reading the word and the world.* Westport, CT: Bergin & Garvey.

Gee, J. P. (2004). *Situated language and learning: A critique of traditional schooling.* New York: Routledge.

Gee, J. P. (2008). Learning and games. In K. Salen (Ed.), *The ecology of games: Connecting youth, games, and learning* (pp. 21–40). Cambridge, MA: MIT Press.

Gutierrez, K. (2008). Developing a sociocritical literacy in the third space. *Reading Research Quarterly, 43*(2), 148–164.

Huizinga, J. (1949). *Homo Ludens: A study of the play-element in culture.* Boston, MA: Beacon.

Ito, M., et al. (2009). *Hanging out, messing around, and geeking out: Kids living and learning with new media.* Cambridge, MA: MIT Press.

Jenkins, H. (2008). *Convergence culture: Where old and new media collide.* New York: New York University Press.

Kelty, C. (2008). *Two bits: The cultural significance of free software.* Durham, NC: Duke University Press.

Kress, G. (2009). *Multimodality: A social semiotic approach to contemporary communication.* London, UK: Routledge.

Lave, J., & Wenger, E. (1991). *Situated learning: Legitimate peripheral participation.* Cambridge, UK: Cambridge University Press.

Lenhart, A. (2009). *Teens and mobile phones over the past five years: Pew Internet looks back.* Pew Internet & American Life Project. Retrieved from http://pewinternet.org/Reports/2009/14—Teens-and-Mobile-Phones-Data-Memo/1-Data-Memo.aspx

Lievrouw, L. (2011). *Alternative and activist new media.* Malden, MA: Polity Press.

McIntyre, A. (2000). Constructing meaning about violence, school, and community: Participatory action research with urban youth. *Urban Review, 32*(2), 123–154.

Moje, E. B., & Lewis, C. (2007). Examining opportunities to learn literacy: The role of critical sociocultural literacy research. In C. Lewis, P. Enciso, & E. B. Moje (Eds.), *Reframing sociocultural research on literacy: Identity, agency, and power* (pp. 15–48). New York: Routledge.

Morrell, E. (2008). *Critical literacy and urban youth: Pedagogies of access, dissent, and liberation.* New York: Routledge.

New London Group. (1996). A pedagogy of multiliteracies: Designing social futures. *Harvard Education Review, 66*(1), 60–92. Retrieved from http://wwwstatic.kern.org/filer/blogWrite44ManilaWebsite/paul/articles/A_Pedagogy_of_Multiliteracies_Designing_Social_Futures.htm

Niemeyer, G., Garcia, A., & Naima, R. (2009). Black cloud: Patterns towards da future. Paper presented at the Proceedings of the 17th ACM International Conference on Multimedia, Beijing, China.

Norris, P. (2001). *Digital divide: Civic engagement, information poverty, and the Internet worldwide.* New York: Cambridge University Press.

Ogbu, J. U. (1983). Literacy and schooling in subordinate cultures. In E. R. Kintgen, B. M. Kroll, & M. Rose (Eds.), *Perspectives on literacy* (pp. 227–242). Carbondale: Southern Illinois University Press.

Perry, T. (2003). Achieving in post–civil rights America: The outline of a theory. In T. Perry, C. Steele, & A. Hilliard III (Eds.), *Young, gifted, and black* (pp. 87–108). Boston, MA: Beacon Press.

Plester, B., Wood, C., & Bell, V. (2008). Txt msg n school literacy: Does texting and knowledge of text abbreviations adversely affect children's literacy attainment? *Literacy, 42*(3), 137–144.

Salen, K., & Zimmerman, E. (2004). *Rules of play: Game design fundamentals.* Cambridge, MA: MIT Press.

Schuler, C. (2009). *Pockets of potential: Using mobile technologies to promote children's learning.* New York: The Joan Ganz Cooney Center at Sesame Workshop.

Thomas, D., & Brown, J. S. (2011). *A new culture of learning: Cultivating the imagination for a world of constant change.* Seattle, WA: CreateSpace.

UCLA IDEA (2010). *California educational opportunity report,* UC Regents. Retrieved from http://idea.gseis.ucla.edu/educational-opportunity-report/2011/eor-search.php

Warschauer, M. (2003). *Technology and social inclusion: Rethinking the digital divide.* Cambridge, MA: MIT Press.

CHAPTER SEVEN

Beyond Technology Skills

Toward a Framework for
Critical Digital Literacies in
Pre-Service Technology Education

SARAH LOHNES WATULAK & CHARLES K. KINZER

INTRODUCTION

In this chapter, we propose a theoretical framework of critical digital literacies. We believe that a critical digital literacies perspective used in conjunction with Koehler and Mishra's (2009) Technological, Pedagogical, and Content Knowledge (TPACK) framework can provide important guidance for meeting the standards advocated by the International Society for Technology in Education (ISTE) and others concerned with the effective preparation of our nation's teachers in areas related to technology. ISTE's National Educational Technology Standards (NETS) for Teachers (2008) encourages teachers to "understand local and global societal issues and responsibilities in an evolving digital culture and exhibit legal and ethical behavior in their professional practices" (para. 4); likewise, students are expected to "understand human, cultural, and societal issues related to technology and practice legal and ethical behavior" (ISTE, 2007, para. 5). These standards ask students and teachers to engage with the broader social and cultural contexts of their technology use, concepts that move beyond the ability to manipulate a keyboard or create an interactive PowerPoint presentation.

Yet much pre-service education technology instruction focuses overly on the use of technology as a tool for digital creation. Perhaps this occurs, in part, because of the emergence in the United States of a participatory culture that features "relatively low barriers to artistic expression and civic engagement, strong support for creating and sharing one's creations, . . . members believe their contributions matter, and feel some degree of social connection with one another" (Jenkins, 2006, p. 3). These acts of sharing, collaboration, and expression—central to engagement in a participatory culture—are enabled and supported by free or low-cost web-based digital technologies such as blogs, wikis, YouTube, and other social media. There is both subtle and overt pressure to focus on teaching technologies as tools, without incorporating an understanding of their uses within participatory culture, and without integrating technology instruction fully into the pre-service curriculum in ways that result in critical analysis of content or alignment with pedagogy.

Technology integration strategies and models in pre-service education have traditionally focused on technology skills development (Polly, Mims, Shephard, & Inan, 2010), although Koehler and Mishra's (2009) Technological, Pedagogical, and Content Knowledge (TPACK) framework is increasingly used to address weaknesses in this approach because of its holistic focus on technology alongside pedagogy and content knowledge. However, while critical and reflective components are largely absent from current skills-based conceptions of technology instruction in teacher education, neither are they explicitly addressed by TPACK. This may raise concerns for pre-service educators and others who expect that future teachers be able to model successful participation in a digital society and teach their students to be technologically literate in the fullest sense. To address such concerns, we propose a theoretical framework of critical digital literacies.

We begin, below, with an overview of the current state of technology integration efforts in pre-service teacher education. Next, we develop a theoretical framework for critical digital literacies, which we define as encompassing four main elements: understanding cultural, social, and historical contexts of technology use; critical thinking and analysis; reflective practice; and facility with the functional skills and tools of digital technology production. Although discussions of technology integration most often fall under the purview of the field of instructional technology, we feel that a literacies approach in general, and a critical digital literacies approach in particular, has much to contribute to helping pre-service technology education move away from a skills-focused approach to digital literacy. We conclude with implications and suggestions for using critical digital literacies in conjunction with TPACK, within pre-service technology course curricula, to develop critical, reflective teacher practitioners who understand the uses, functions, and influences of technology.

TECHNOLOGY INTEGRATION IN TEACHER EDUCATION PROGRAMS

Not surprisingly, technology instruction has become a component of the vast majority of teacher preparation programs, in recognition of the need for pre-service teachers to be prepared to teach and to live in a digital society. Teacher education programs that seek to infuse technology into their curricula have used a variety of strategies to do so, including: a single course that focuses on technology; integrating technology throughout the pre-service curriculum, perhaps through the use of multimedia and e-portfolios; training education faculty, often through voluntary or required workshops (sometimes providing additional payment for workshop attendance); modeling strategies for teaching with technology (either in a single course, or integrated); collaboration with public schools to set up field-based programs, often involving a teacher mentor; increasing access to technology; and various combinations of strategies (Kay, 2006).

Recent studies have found that most teacher preparation programs in the United States employ a stand-alone course model, and to a lesser extent, technology-intensive field experiences (Gronseth et al., 2010) to encourage technology integration. In our own teaching, we attempt to integrate technology into every course, in order to introduce and model skills, practices, and ways of thinking for our students. The first author has also taught a version of the stand-alone technology course, the model employed at her institution. The population of learners served by this course includes primarily sophomore and junior undergraduate students, who have been accepted to an education major with teaching certification (including elementary education, secondary education, and special education). This course is taken prior to the students' field experience. The range of models and experiences described above aim to help pre-service teachers "see connections between current technology applications and the appropriate uses in a classroom" (Vannatta & Beyerbach, 2000, as cited in Gronseth et al., 2010, p. 30).

However, the literature does not present a clear picture as to the effectiveness of various technology integration strategies. Kay (2006) reviewed 68 studies on the effectiveness of integration strategies on pre-service teacher skills, beliefs, or attitudes toward technology (the three factors most often tested in the studies). Although a useful overview of integration strategies, Kay ultimately was unable to draw a conclusion regarding the effectiveness of these strategies, citing weaknesses in the methodological and theoretical orientation of the studies. Furthermore, there are many factors that can impact successful technology integration. For example, in studying the implementation of an online, case-based instructional system, Kinzer, Cammack, Labbo, Teale, and Sanny (2006) found several factors mitigating the instructors' desired integration of technology, including faculty frustrations with university IT departments, lack of readiness of equipment in time for classes, lack of appropriate software, and lack of awareness by university administrators of classroom issues when attempting to integrate technology.

Thus, while teacher educators must be prepared to assist their students in learning the skills and competencies that will provide a foundation for successful infusion of technology into their teaching, they may be constrained by a lack of access to technology, and/or insufficient support for use of technology in their own teaching (Wepner, Tao, & Ziomek, 2006); their skill level with the technologies; their understanding of best practices for using various technologies to promote learning and engagement; and by a lack of time to develop this expertise, especially given teaching, service, and research duties. Many of these factors are also present and must be considered with regard to field placements as well, in addition to considerations of mentor teachers' skill levels, and the match between the technologies that students were introduced to in their university classrooms, and what is available in the respective placement (Gronseth et al., 2010).

The pedagogies employed by teacher educators and curricular cohesiveness in university pre-service programs also factor in the eventual success of pre-service teachers' technology integration efforts. Groth, Dunlap, and Kidd (2007) found that the pre-service teachers in their study did not apply the hands-on technology training from their literacy methods courses during their student teaching because they did not see a clear connection between the literacy methods content and the technology instruction. Gronseth et al. (2010) advocate for "maintaining a level of authenticity in technology experiences" as a means of providing a real-world context for technology training (p. 30). Indeed, technology instruction that focuses primarily on developing students' technology skills has been criticized for leading to ineffective technology integration once in the in-service classroom (Harris, Mishra, & Koehler, 2009; Polly et al., 2010). Pre-service teachers may know how to create a blog, for example, but lack the ability to use this knowledge to create activities and environments that promote a deeper understanding of literacy content when they enter the profession as practicing teachers. Below, we describe a framework for technology integration that addresses some of the critiques of skills-focused technology instruction.

OVERVIEW OF THE TPACK FRAMEWORK FOR TECHNOLOGY INTEGRATION

Within the field of instructional technology, the TPACK framework for technology integration has gained a great deal of traction over the last five years. At the 2010 annual meeting of the Society for Instructional Technology in Teacher Education, for example, TPACK was included in the list of session topics used by the program committee to categorize posters and presentations; this category comprised 33 accepted paper presentations (4.5 percent of accepted papers). In 2011, the number rose to 72 (8.9 percent of accepted papers). Papers that address TPACK as a model for technology integration have been published in top-tier journals in the instructional technology field, including the *Journal of Research on Technology in Education* (i.e., Schmidt, Baran, Thompson, Mishra, Koehler, & Shin, 2009), the *Journal of Technology in Teacher Education* (i.e., Hur, Cullen, & Brush, 2010), and the *Journal of Digital Learning in Teacher Education* (i.e., Niess, van Zee, & Gillow-Wiles, 2010).

The recent popularity of this model stems from its attempt to address the weaknesses in skills-only technology instruction by providing an ecological approach to technology integration that focuses on the interplay between content knowledge, pedagogical knowledge, and technology knowledge (Koehler & Mishra, 2009). The model has gained traction, particularly among instructional technologists and teacher educators in university settings, who have used it as a framework to (a) design or redesign pre-service technology instruction (including the stand-alone technology course at Towson University), and (b) guide pre-service teachers in developing their own technology-supported instruction. For example, Spires, Hervey, and Watson (in press) and Spires, Zheng, and Pruden (in press) have found TPACK to be useful in helping educators understand the relationships between content, pedagogy, and technology, especially as related to new literacies.

Koehler and Mishra (2009) describe teaching as an ill-structured domain "requiring teachers to apply complex knowledge structures across different cases and contexts" (p. 61; see also Simon, 1973; Voss, 1988; Spiro & Jehng, 1990; and Ge & Land, 2003 for discussions of problem solving and learning in ill-structured domains). Shulman (1986; see also Berliner, 1986) argued that in order to be successful in this type of environment, teachers must be able to integrate knowledge across relevant domains, on demand, including knowledge of their content area (for our purposes here, literacy), and knowledge of pedagogy (general teaching methods, how people think and learn). He also identified a third domain of knowledge that combines the two, pedagogical content knowledge: "an understanding of how particular topics, problems, or issues are organized, represented, and adapted to the diverse interests and abilities of learners, and presented for instruction" (Shulman, 1987, p. 8). To these, Koehler and Mishra (2009) add the domains of technology knowledge (TK), knowledge of technology tools and affordances; technological content knowledge (TCK), knowledge of how tools can be used to support specific content and objectives; and technological pedagogical knowledge (TPK), knowledge of how particular technologies can be used to support specific pedagogical approaches.

In practice, the model suggests that successful technology integration—that is, technology integration that is seen as having a meaningful impact on pre-service teachers' learning—would occur at the intersection of content knowledge (CK), pedagogical knowledge (PK), and technological knowledge (TK): TPACK. Teachers must have a deep understanding of how to select pedagogical strategies and technologies, to further the understanding of specific content, within particular contexts and environments.

In order to scaffold this understanding, Harris and Hofer (2009) developed a framework of learning activity types that provide a content-focused structure for planning instruction that integrates these knowledge domains. See Tables 1 and 2 for examples of learning activity types for elementary and secondary literacy learning (Schmidt, Harris, & Hofer, 2011; Young, Hofer, & Harris, 2011). While these learning activity types provide a "preliminary organizational structure to help scaffold teachers' thinking about how one might design engaging literacy learning activities" (Schmidt et al., 2011, p. 1), the authors emphasize that these activity types provide a starting point only; as teachers develop their TPACK knowledge, they will find new ways to integrate content, pedagogy, and technology in ways that best fit their own context.

Although a relatively new model of technology integration, examples of research that examine TPACK outcomes exist in the literature. Much of this research uses survey and self-report to measure students' increased understanding in each of the TPACK domains separately (CK, PK, and TK), as well as the overlap between them (TPACK). For example, courses designed around the TPACK model have been shown to promote positive changes in students' self-efficacy as related to TPACK domains (Abbitt, 2011a; Schmidt et al., 2009). Koehler, Mishra, and Yahya's (2007) qualitative analysis of pre-service teacher discourse around a semester-long design-based activity revealed the development of connections between technology, pedagogy, and content domains over the course of the semester. Despite these positive outcomes, Abbitt's (2011b) review of research methods and instruments used by researchers to assess gains in TPACK knowledge by pre-service teachers points to future research questions that must be answered in order to fully understand the usefulness of the TPACK model for technology integration:

> How much knowledge of technology, pedagogy, content, or within the blended domains such as TPK, TCK, TPACK, etc., is sufficient for a beginning teacher? (p. 140)

Although a more robust and complex approach to technology integration than previous models, technological knowledge (TK) primarily refers to the development of technology skills, and understanding the affordances of particular tools. As we discuss below, this conceptualization falls short of perspectives that advocate moving beyond skills-based notions of digital literacy.

Table 1. Example of Fluency Learning Activity Type for Elementary Literacy Learners[1]

Activity Type	Brief Description	Example Technologies
Drama	Students perform, usually by memorization, a play or story for an audience	Video recording, digital storytelling, video sharing sites (e.g., TeacherTube), podcasting

1. Schmidt, Harris, & Hofer, 2011, p. 2.

Table 2. Example of During-Writing Activity Type for Secondary Literacy Learners[2]

Activity Type	Brief Description	Example Technologies
Writing Other Forms of Text	Students engage in a variety of writing activities including other forms of text (e.g., academic notes, poetry, screenplay, storyboard, multimodal, multi-genre, multimedia, web-based text, participatory media, comic creation, texting, etc.)	Word processing software / other writing software, comic creation software, video creation software, VoiceThread, blog, wiki

2. Young, Hofer, & Harris, 2011, p. 8.

CRITICAL DIGITAL LITERACIES

"Digital literacy" has been used to signify a variety of concepts in recent years, and remains a contested term. The phrase has roots in and relationships with a variety of disciplines, including computer literacy, ICT literacy, media literacy, information literacy, and e-literacy. This is reflected in the range of definitions of digital literacy, from mastery of digital-technology-related basic skills and competencies

(Bawden, 2008), to digital literacy as "ideas, not keystrokes" (Gilster, 1997, as cited in Martin, 2008, p. 18). This latter concept is embedded in the growing body of work in the theory and practice of digital literacy currently under development at Futurelab, a United Kingdom–based nonprofit dedicated to 21st-century teaching and learning. Futurelab's digital literacy framework emphasizes "social awareness, critical thinking, knowledge of digital tools" (Hague & Williamson, 2009, p. 8). Martin (2008) integrates ideas from information and media literacy with an emancipatory agenda, defining digital literacy as

> The awareness, attitude and ability of individuals to appropriately use digital tools and facilities to identify, access, manage, integrate, evaluate, analyze and synthesize digital resources, construct new knowledge, create media expressions, and communicate with others, in the context of specific life situations, in order to enable constructive social action; and to reflect upon this process. (pp. 166–167)

In these definitions of digital literacy, functional technology skills are only one piece of a complex digital literacy picture. Indeed, the latter definition represents an expanded view of digital literacy, echoing sociocultural perspectives that acknowledge the generative interplay between literacy and the contexts in which literacy occurs (Lankshear & Knobel, 2007).

Similarly, Gillen and Barton (2010) advocate a social practices approach to digital literacy, drawing on literacy frameworks such as the New London Group's conception of multiliteracies (1996), Kress' multimodality (2010), and Hutchins and colleagues' notion of distributed cognition (Hutchins, 1991; Hollan, Hutchins, & Kirsh, 2000). In their view, digital literacies are "the constantly changing practices through which people make traceable meanings using digital technologies" (Gillen & Barton, 2010, p. 9). From this perspective, what it means to be "literate," "successful," "appropriate," "constructive" are defined contextually, as in Street's (1984) ideological model of literacy, in which literacies "are always rooted in a particular world-view and in a desire for that view to dominate and to marginalize others" (Street, 2003, p. 2). The notion that definitions of literacy are contextually based and must continually change has also prompted arguments that literacy has become a deictic term due to the link between literacy practices, rapidly developing and changing technologies, and societal demands and expectations of literate individuals who must use such technologies (e.g., see Leu, 2000; Leu, Kinzer, Coiro, & Cammack, 2004).

This understanding of digital literacy and its practices provides the foundation for *critical* digital literacies, an emerging concept within discussions of digital literacy. From the perspective of sociocultural frameworks of literacy, one might argue that digital literacies are by definition critical. However, we employ the specific term "critical digital literacies" to de-emphasize the relative importance of technology skills, and emphasize the critical understanding of and engagement with functional technology skills within the broader contexts of technology use. One of the first authors to employ the phrase in the literature on digital literacy, Merchant (2007), drew on critical pedagogy and critical literacy to argue for infusing digital literacy with criticality: "it is important to examine and critique discourses that relate to wider social issues, power relationships, prejudices or inequities, and indeed that it is part of the function of educational institutions to engage in this sort of work" (p. 125). In a similar vein, Dowdall (2009) defined critical digital literacy as "a mastery of the wider sociocultural and economic context in which text production in digital spaces occurs" (p. 51). Note that both of these positions acknowledge the functional aspect of digital literacy (i.e., digital text production, broadly defined), but focus their attention on understanding the broader contexts in which production occurs, and their potential impacts and outcomes.

Thus, in our view critical digital literacies are not as much a departure from previous concepts of digital literacy as an intentional emphasis on the "critical" component, which is often de-emphasized. In other words, critical digital literacies are part of a broader digital literacy framework, embedded within personal and professional contexts, environments, and practices. Drawing on earlier definitions of digital literacy, as well as emerging understandings of critical digital literacies, we see them as encompassing four central elements located within professional and personal contexts, environments, and processes, and within the broader category of digital literacy. Figure 1 illustrates the relationship between the factors that comprise a critical digital literacies approach.

In its fullest sense, each of the factors represented in Figure 1 encompass those situated within. Thus, professional contexts, environments, and processes include aspects of personal contexts; digital literacy; critical digital literacies; critical thinking; reflective practice; understanding of social, historical, and cultural contexts; and functional knowledge. The figure illustrates visually that digital literacy must encompass critical digital literacies, and its four central elements:

- Understanding cultural, social, and historical contexts of technology use, including ethical and appropriate practices
- Critical thinking and analysis
- Reflective practice
- Functional skills with digital technologies

Each of these elements of critical digital literacies are described in detail below, after a brief discussion of professional and personal contexts and their application.

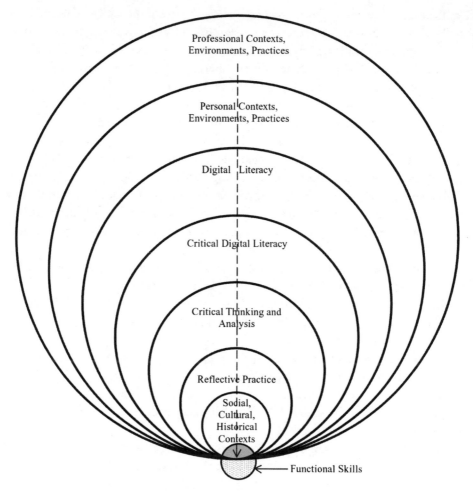

Figure 1. Elements and Positioning of Critical Digital
Literacies from a Pre-service Technology Integration Perspective.

Professional and personal contexts, environments and processes

Keeping in mind the focus of technology integration within pre-service experiences, we begin with professional contexts, environments, and processes. Using technology for professional purposes, such as teaching within a subject area, requires content-specialized knowledge. A science teacher, for example, may need to know about using probes linked to a computer, while this may not be relevant for a language arts teacher. Similarly, the contexts within which professional activities are performed influence the technology selection, as well as its use. Professional activities conducted with home-based technologies might include the use of specific software or Internet tools (perhaps Google Scholar or Gradebook software, or software developed by designers or publishers for specific professional uses in a given content area) and hardware that differs from professional uses in classroom contexts (where hardware might include interactive white boards or projection capabilities). Communicative activities, both in form and content, may also differ in the context of professional uses when compared to personal or informal uses; the structure and content of communication on a professional forum would differ from informal communication targeted at friends or family. Pre-service technology integration must, therefore, consider the affordances and constraints of professional contexts and technologies when planning for instruction. As noted by the TPACK framework, a one-size-fits-all approach to technology integration may not develop the specific expertise that content-area teachers require in their professional activities.

Lohnes and Kinzer (2007) and Lohnes Watulak (2012) have shown that different personal contexts, environments, and processes also lead to differences in technology selection and use. Personal contexts may be physical, experiential, or based on levels of expertise. For example, personal contexts may encompass a family situation with computers shared across family members versus a laptop that never leaves one's side; knowledge of, and sophistication with, certain types of software tools over others may all lead to different affordances and constraints. Such factors should be acknowledged when considering technology integration.

In Figure 1, we place professional contexts within its outer ring given that the framework targets pre-service instructional considerations. We recognize that personal contexts and factors in technology use spill into and influence professional uses as well. Teachers with always-available computers function in different ways than those who share computers, as do teachers who feel that social software is integral as opposed to peripheral to their personal lives. Clearly, on a personal level, technologies can be leveraged in powerful ways to communicate both personal and professional identities. Dowdall (2009) uses the example of social network site profile creation to illustrate the knowledge of the wider social and communicative contexts that young people draw upon while participating in social network sites, using a carefully chosen mix of words, images, and actions to perform their digital identity via their profile.

Arguably, one might say that personal factors may override professional ones; and, if the framework focused on general factors of use, the two outer rings may be reversed. However, with pre-service courses that attempt to integrate technology into their curricula as our present focus, we feel that planning for instruction and technology integration should begin with professional aspects that acknowledge the influence of personal factors.

Critical thinking and analysis

At its core, critical thinking represents thinking that is "purposeful, reasoned, and goal-directed" (Halpern, 1997, p. 4). Dictionary.com provides a second definition of critical thinking as well, drawn from their "21st Century Lexicon": "the mental process of actively and skillfully conceptualizing, applying, analyzing, synthesizing, and evaluating information to reach an answer or conclusion" (dictionary.com, n.d.). This definition shares much in common with information literacy, and also overlaps with elements of Martin's (2008) definition of digital literacy. It also reflects a shift in how critical thinking is understood by the general public, in part due to the discourse surrounding what have come to be known as 21st-century skills and competencies—though critical thinking, evaluation, analysis, and distinguishing fact from propaganda have been a part of literacy curriculum guides for decades. Nila Banton Smith, for example, cites Stauffer, a coauthor of the popular *Winston Basic Readers* published between 1960 and 1962, who notes that the first- through sixth-grade reading series includes "Deliberately selected stories [that] focus on problem-solving situations . . . [inviting] children to value and improve their skill in critical thinking" (Smith, 2002, p. 308).

The Partnership for 21st Century's (2009) Framework for 21st Century Learning lists "critical thinking, problem solving, communication and collaboration" as core skills that students need in order to be successful in today's workplace in a digital society (p. 1). Within the 21st Century Framework, critical thinking is applied specifically within the context of our "technology and media-driven environment, marked by access to an abundance of information, rapid changes in technology tools and the ability to collaborate and make individual contributions on an unprecedented scale" (p. 2). It has always been necessary to think critically about the evidence available for decision making, in order to make informed, rational decisions; however, the vast amount of information available requires us to apply the process-oriented second definition in order to achieve the first.

Our understanding of critical thinking within the context of critical digital literacies draws on both of these perspectives. In his discussion of the collaborative inquiry group research method, Reason notes that participants are asked to develop "critical attention . . . the ability to look at their experience with affectionate curiosity" (1999, p. 212)—in other words, to question the taken-for-granted elements of their lives. This is an apt description of what we see as the "critical" component of critical digital literacies. We ask students to question the taken-for-granted elements of their lives—in this case, their experiences around technology—and to develop more disciplined thinking about their technology use, informed by an understanding of both the technologies and their contexts of use. This disciplined thinking and understanding can be developed through the process described by the second definition of critical thinking: conceptualizing, synthesizing, evaluating, applying, and so on.

Finally, we note that we differentiate our understanding of the "critical" aspect of critical digital literacies from critical literacy, a framework that is "intended to help the marginalized unveil unequal power relations and transform their lives through the empowerment of literacy education" (Lee, 2011, p. 96). While we advocate for a self-reflective understanding of our position and practices within a digital society (see next section), these understandings are focused on changing personal and professional practice, rather than on uncovering power inequality and social injustice.

Reflective practice

A critical digital literacies perspective incorporates the idea that digital citizens should be reflective practitioners who must possess awareness of social, cultural, and historical contexts and functional skills, but also should reflect on their position and practices within these contexts and the outcomes of the uses of their functional skills. Reflection is an important aspect of a critical digital literacies approach, and one that needs to be explicitly articulated in any definition of critical digital literacies. Martin's (2008) description of the three stages and "key elements" of digital literacy emphasizes reflective practice through a conscious, reflective engagement with the technologies in our lives. According to Martin, reaching "digital transformation" (the third stage of digital literacy) requires "the ability to be aware of oneself as a digitally literate person, and to reflect on one's own digital literacy development" (2008, pp. 166–167) in order to bring about change within one's life.

Within a professional context, Martin's digital transformation brings to mind what Schön (1987) calls "reflection-in-action (the 'thinking what they are doing while they're doing it') that practitioners sometimes bring to situations of uncertainty, uniqueness, and conflict" (p. xi). Reflection-in-action arises from an in-the-moment recognition that a change is needed in a particular situation, and leads to immediate experimentation with ways to bring about a change. Our future teachers need to have the resources to resolve challenges that occur within complex classroom spaces, including those arising from attempts to integrate technology into instruction. In the context of a technological challenge, we require knowledge arising from reflection on our own digital literacy practices, including the limits and needed extensions to our functional technology skills.

Thus, digital transformation begins with self-reflection, when we bring the types of critical attention, awareness, and thinking described above to bear on our digital literacy practices. Transformation occurs when we extend the understanding gained through reflection to the outside world in order to bring about conscious changes in ones' technology practices. Within the context of a participatory culture, reflection may be social and collaborative, as well as personal and individual.

Care must be taken, however, to ensure that reflection activities are designed around important issues and require deep thinking. Reflective practice has a long history and many advocates. Yet, Risko, Vukelich, and Roskos (2002) remind us there are many things to consider when talking about reflective critique. Following a critical review of research that focused on reflection activities with pre-service teachers, they found that

> the professional literature is thick on describing researchers' goals and intentions but thin on providing guidance for teaching students how to reflect. . . . [and the] goal to initiate reflective critique as an intellectual practice was not met. (p. 135)

Risko, Vukelich, and Roskos suggest that in order to encourage effective reflective practices, instructors must consider the social contexts within which reflection is expected to occur. While they do not directly address technology as a tool for collaborative reflection by pre-service teachers, pre-service technology instruction can encourage reflection in a number of ways, including individual and/or shared collaborative activities in face-to-face classroom settings, or asynchronous reflection via technology tools. This must be done with care and planning, and instructors will need to incorporate the various factors shown in Figure 1.

Understanding cultural, social, and historical contexts of technology use

Technologies are not value-neutral objects. As users of digital technologies, we must understand that technology and its uses are both shaped by social and societal forces, and synergistically shape how we interact with and make meaning in the world (Pinch & Bijker, 1984). Leu, Kinzer, Coiro, and Cammack (2004; see also Leu, Kinzer, Coiro, Castek, & Henry, in press) note that there is a synergistic relationship between technologies and cultural and social factors, and that these often overlap economic interests. For example, they point to relationships between changing technologies of literacy and societal needs initially in the use of cuneiform tablets, which arose due to the need to record business transactions in Sumerian society in the fourth millennium BC; the emergence of the printing press and resulting societal changes that threatened religious dogma and autocratic governments; the distribution of books influencing the development of public education in the United States; and so on. More recently, we have seen the role of social software and technology as instrumental in supporting efforts of resistance against governments in the Middle East (Howard, Duffy, Freelon, Hussain, Mari, & Mazaid, 2011; Taylor,

2011) and to organize protests throughout the world within what has come to be known as the "Occupy" movement (Preston, 2011). Clearly, technology and literacy are intertwined and are linked through historical, cultural and societal contexts.

Leu, Kinzer, Coiro, and Cammack (2004) also note the importance of technology to increased personal fulfillment and economic benefits. They argue, "global economic competition within economies based increasingly on the effective use of information and communication" is a social force that shapes our literacy and technology practices (p. 1573). Within all of these contexts—cultural, historical, and social—particular technologies, skills, and the practices in which they are embedded are valued above others. Jenkins (2006) suggests that a participatory culture privileges "social skills developed through collaborating and networking" (p. 4). Other valued skills and competencies include the ability to effectively use information and communication technologies to find and organize information, to communicate, collaborate, solve problems, and think critically, all of which form a part of a critical digital literacies perspective.

Understanding the broader, often less-visible frameworks that shape our interactions with technology has implications for the design of instruction at all levels. For example, pre-service teachers can use this understanding to maintain a level of authenticity within the formal instructional environment, asking their students to blog in order to connect with others, rather than using the blog space to reproduce a traditional three-part essay. At the same time, we must also understand that there is more at stake than whether or not students are capable of creating a Facebook profile or crafting a blog post that becomes a platform for engaging discussion. What are the implications for students who do not have access to the technologies themselves (the traditional digital divide), and/or who do not have access to the privileged practices (the second digital divide)? These are the types of questions and issues with which pre-service teachers must be prepared to engage when planning a curriculum that integrates technology.

Functional skills with digital technologies

Functional skills—the ability to manipulate technological tools for a specific purpose—are the foundation of traditional definitions of digital literacy, and are an important aspect of a digital literacy approach. Teachers and students must be able to identify and use appropriate technological tools to further their pedagogical and communicative goals, thus skills training is often a central goal of pre-service technology education. We see a parallel with contested definitions of traditional, text-based literacy that view literacy as a series of skills to be mastered rather than defining literacy as skills embedded within practices. To be literate in the first sense is to master sub-skills; to be literate in the second is to both master sub-skills and be able to deploy those skills in contextually appropriate ways. To be digitally "literate" in the fullest sense means incorporating functional skills and the other components of critical digital literacies to understand the practices and cultures of use within which these skills are deployed.

However, focusing only on teaching technology skills is less than optimal for another reason as well: the fast pace of technological change means that many of the functional skills deemed important today will be different than the functional skills necessary for success in the future. For example, we heard colleagues and students exhibit varying degrees of frustration when our campuses updated to a newer version of Microsoft Office, which has a different interface from previous versions. Some people, who exhibited mild frustration when trying to find command locations that were moved (print, save, etc.), took the change in stride, knowing that the commands must be there—it was simply a matter of finding them. These users were secure in the knowledge that they could master the change. Some other users seemed stymied by the changes. Those who exhibited high degrees of frustration seemed to resent the change and had difficulty with the transition, viewing the changes as inappropriate and burdensome, and worrying that they might not be able to function well with the updated software.

Indeed, Standard 3 of ISTE's (2008) NETS for Teachers, Model Digital-Age Work and Learning, asks teachers to "demonstrate fluency in technology systems and the transfer of current knowledge to new technologies and situations" (para 3). This requires not only functional skills knowledge, but also a framework that provides a critical understanding of how technology can be used, why changes occur, why they may be necessary, and how they can be implemented across personal and professional contexts. We believe that teaching with a purely functional skills focus discourages the flexibility needed to maximize the potential to adapt to technological change.

Figure 1 shows functional skills as being both within and outside the factors that should form a part of pre-service technology education. The lower part of the functional skills circle, outside the rest of the diagram, shows the location of many technology programs at present. We feel that functional skills are best taught at the point where all of the circles in the diagrams insect within the functional skills circle. At that intersection point, functional skills would be taught and incorporated with all of the other factors represented in Figure 1. When creating pre-service technology courses or integrating technology instruction into content-area methods classes, keeping this intersection in mind will help ensure that students learn functional skills, understand their application within their professional and personal contexts, and understand the implications of technology on society, as well as their own and their students' lives.

TOWARD CRITICAL DIGITAL LITERACIES IN TEACHER EDUCATION PROGRAMS

At the beginning of this chapter, we set forth the challenge to envision technology integration within teacher education programs that prepares future teachers (and their students) to be successful, full participants in today's digital society. Although the research literature does not provide conclusive evidence as to the best way forward in terms of technology integration strategies, it appears that strategies that focus primarily on technology skills instruction—whether in a stand-alone course or a field experience—tend to fail (Harris et al., 2009; Polly et al., 2010). With the introduction of the TPACK model for technology integration, the field has been reminded that successful technology integration begins with a deep understanding of the intersection of content, pedagogy, and technology tools and affordances. This has been viewed as a positive step toward improving how we envision technology integration in university as well as K–12 classrooms.

However, even within the TPACK framework, technology knowledge (TK) is discussed primarily in terms of functional skills—how to manipulate technology tools—and is reminiscent of a skills-based definition of digital literacy. Critical perspectives are largely absent from the discussion. The notion of context is incorporated into the TPACK model, but its role is not explicitly addressed. Pre-service teachers are sometimes asked to reflect on their TPACK knowledge after completing technology-related projects (e.g., Wetzel, Foulger, & Williams, 2008), which taps into the notion of reflective practice within professional contexts. However, the model does not explicitly address social and institutional contexts, nor does it address self-reflection on our digital participation in a digital society.

We suggest that a critical digital literacies framework, used in conjunction with TPACK, may serve to bring a critical, reflective lens to technology use within personal and professional contexts. From a practical standpoint, a critical digital literacies perspective suggests that formal and informal learning concerned with digital literacies must involve more than functional (digital) skill instruction. Below, we present two example activities that incorporate critical digital literacies and TPACK into their design. Teacher educators can use these activities in stand-alone technology courses, or in any content-area or methods courses that incorporate technology. Through these activities, teacher educators work with their pre-service teachers to become technologically literate in the fullest sense. Functional skills should be taught as needed. Knowing how to create and post to a blog, use Comic Life (http://plasq.com), create a graphic novel, and so on would be taught as needed in order to fulfill the larger goals of the assignment. We also include the Common Core English Language Arts College and Career Readiness (CCR) Anchor Standards

(Common Core State Standards Initiative, 2010) to connect these general activities to a literacy content framework.

Activity 1. Instructors employ this instructional activity to engage pre-service teachers in a critical exploration of the concept of participatory culture, a concept central to understanding the current social and cultural contexts of our technology use. In addition to pre-service education, this activity may be used in any course that deals with digital culture, youth culture, or technology topics.

Pre-service teachers would blog their technobiographies—autobiographical accounts of the role technology plays in their lives—in order to reflect on themselves as participants in a digital culture. To critically explore their context, they would choose, explore, and analyze a topic related to participatory culture, and produce a video mashup (created by recombining original source material) that represents their understanding of the topic. The video is shared on YouTube; students are expected to use comments left on their video by other YouTube users to revise their work. After the activity, pre-service teachers blog again, reflecting on the experience of digital authoring within a participatory context. They may also reflect collaboratively, using a wiki or Google Docs to look back together on the development of their skills and knowledge as related to their teaching practice. See Table 3 for the alignment of the activity with critical digital literacies components, TPACK components, and the Common Core CCR Anchor Standards.

Activity 2. This activity asks teacher educators to use the TPACK learning activity types (see Table 2; also Harris & Hofer, 2009) to provide authentic, content-based experiences for their pre-service teachers. Incorporating activities based on the learning activity types provides pre-service teachers with an opportunity to practice using technologies to support specific content objectives and pedagogical approaches. The learning type activities can then be modified to include elements of critical digital literacies.

For this example, we refer back to Table 2 and the Writing Other Forms of Text learning activity. To modify this activity to incorporate a critical digital literacies perspective for pre-service teachers, the instructor would ask her students to create a short graphic novel that represents their understanding of a class topic, as an alternate to writing a traditional research paper. Before beginning the assignment, the pre-service teachers write a blog post about what they know about graphic novels, and share their experiences with reading or creating graphic novels. During the research and pre-writing process, they also investigate the graphic novel genre, and how they are embedded in popular culture, in order to use the technology to represent their understandings via images and text in a way that appropriately reflects the discourse. Pre-service teachers then use Comic Life or other comic-creation software to create their assignment. After completing the assignment, they write a final blog post reflecting on the experience of making their graphic novel, with a focus

Table 3. Alignment of Participatory Culture Inquiry Activity With Common Core English Language Arts College and Career Readiness Anchor Standards, Critical Digital Literacies, and TPACK

Instructional goal: Understanding the historical, social, and cultural contexts of our technology use.

Activity Components

1. Understanding participatory culture and cultures of relevant technology tool use (mashups, YouTube, wikis, Google Docs)
    o   English Language Arts College and Career Readiness Anchor Standards
            Several, across content areas, dealing with understanding cultural and historical contexts
    o   Critical digital literacies components
            Understanding context
    o   TPACK components
            None

2. Evaluating issues surrounding participatory culture
    o   English Language Arts College and Career Readiness Anchor Standards
            Research to Build and Present Knowledge
            Standard 7. Conduct short as well as more sustained research projects based on focused questions, demonstrating understanding of the subject under investigation.
            Standard 9. Draw evidence from literary or informational texts to support analysis, reflection, and research (Common Core State Standards Initiative, 2010).
    o   Critical digital literacies components
            Critical thinking and analysis

    o   TPACK components
            Content knowledge (CK)

3. Reflecting on participation in digital society
    o   Critical digital literacies components
            Reflective practice—personal
    o   TPACK components
            Pedagogical knowledge (PK)

Table 3. (*continued*)

---

4. Reflecting on the development of technology skills and knowledge
   o Critical digital literacies components
      Reflective practice—professional
   o TPACK components
      Pedagogical knowledge (PK)

5. Video editing and sharing via the web
   o English Language Arts College and Career Readiness Anchor Standards
      Text Types and Purposes
      Standard 1. Write arguments to support claims in an analysis of substantive topics or texts using valid reasoning and relevant and sufficient evidence.
      Standard 2. Write informative/explanatory texts to examine and convey complex ideas and information clearly and accurately through the effective selection, organization, and analysis of content.
      Production and Distribution of Writing
      Standard 6. Use technology, including the Internet, to produce and publish writing and to interact and collaborate with others (Common Core State Standards Initiative, 2010).
   o Critical digital literacies components
      Functional skills
   o TPACK components
      Technological knowledge (TK)

---

on translating their experience to future classroom teaching. Alternatively, they may use a visual format such as the graphic novel, or digital storytelling (a video combining images and audio narration), to create a multimedia reflection. See Table 4 for an overview of the alignment of the activity with critical digital literacies components, TPACK components, and the Common Core CCR Anchor Standards.

Table 4. Alignment of Writing Other Forms of Text Activity With Common Core English Language Arts College and Career Readiness Anchor Standards, Critical Digital Literacies, and TPACK

Instructional Goal: Understanding and writing other forms of text

Activity Components
1. Exploring cultures of use around graphic novels, including collective intelligence
   - English Language Arts College and Career Readiness Anchor Standards
     - o Research to Build and Present Knowledge
       7. Conduct short as well as more sustained research projects based on focused questions, demonstrating understanding of the subject under investigation (Common Core State Standards Initiative, 2010).
   - Critical digital literacies components
     - o Understanding context
   - TPACK components
     - o None

2. Applying understanding of graphic novel genre and discourse to final product
   - English Language Arts College and Career Readiness Anchor Standards
     - o Research to Build and Present Knowledge
       Standard 9. Draw evidence from literary or informational texts to support analysis, reflection, and research (Common Core State Standards Initiative, 2010).
   - Critical digital literacies components
     - o Critical thinking and analysis
   - TPACK Components
     - o Content knowledge (CK)

3. Multimodal writing (using words and images to create narrative)
   - English Language Arts College and Career Readiness Anchor Standards
     - o Text Types and Purposes
       Standard 2. Write informative/explanatory texts to examine and convey complex ideas and information clearly and accurately through the effective selection, organization, and analysis of content (Common Core State Standards Initiative, 2010).

Table 4. (*continued*)

- Critical digital literacies components
  - o Critical thinking and analysis
  - o Functional skills
- TPACK components
  - o Content knowledge (CK)
  - o Pedagogical knowledge (PK)

4. Reflecting on own experiences with graphic novels
   - Critical digital literacies components
     - o Reflective practice—personal
   - TPACK components
     - o Pedagogical knowledge (PK)

5. Reflecting on the experience of creating a graphic novel
   - Critical digital literacies components
     - o Reflective practice—professional
   - TPACK components
     - o Pedagogical knowledge (PK)

6. Creating a graphic novel with Comic Life or other comic-creation software
   - English Language Arts College and Career Readiness Anchor Standards
     - o Production and Distribution of Writing
       Standard 6. Use technology, including the Internet, to produce and publish writing and to interact and collaborate with others (Common Core State Standards Initiative, 2010).
   - Critical digital literacies components
     - o Functional skills
   - TPACK components
     - o Technological knowledge (TK)

These activities draw on elements of TPACK and critical digital literacies to engage pre-service teachers in experiences that move beyond technology skills, toward an understanding of what it means to be a digital practitioner (Hague & Williamson, 2009) in a participatory culture that emphasizes technology as a preferred means of producing and communicating information and other texts (Jenkins, 2006).

CONCLUSION

In one of the earliest articles to explicitly articulate a need for critical digital literacies, Merchant (2007) concluded that students have a "common entitlement with respect to critical digital literacy" based on these rights:

- The right to access and use up-to-date new technologies building on everyday (or out-of-school) practices
- The right to an education that supports and develops the skills, knowledge and dispositions needed for the effective use of digital media, and also provides opportunities for critical digital literacies practice
- The right to explore and experiment with one's own digital space
- The right to critique and resist dominant or dominating discourses in digital domains (p. 126).

These are rights of pre-service teachers, and of their future students. Though traditionally focused on technology tools, pre-service technology instruction has an opportunity to play a role in securing these rights for our current pre-service teachers. This requires an acknowledgment that successful participation in our digital society includes the ability to understand, think critically about, reflect on, and respond to the societal, cultural, and economic forces that shape our interactions with and through technology, both in our professional lives as educators, and in our everyday lives. We hope that the critical digital literacies framework and activities presented in this chapter offer both theoretical and practical guidance for teacher educators to conceptualize pre-service technology instruction that incorporates, but moves beyond, teaching technology skills.

REFERENCES

Abbitt, J. (2011a). An investigation of the relationship between self-efficacy beliefs about technology integration and technological pedagogical content knowledge (TPACK) among preservice teachers. *Journal of Digital Learning in Teacher Education, 27*(4), 134–143.

Abbitt, J. (2011b). Measuring technological pedagogical content knowledge in preservice teacher education: A review of current methods and instruments. *Journal of Research on Technology in Education, 43*(4), 281–300.

Bawden, D. (2008). Origins and concepts of digital literacy. In C. Lankshear & M. Knobel (Eds.), *Digital literacies: Concepts, policies, and practices* (pp. 17–32). New York: Peter Lang.

Berliner, D. C. (1986). In pursuit of the expert pedagogue. *Educational Researcher, 15*(7), 5–13.

Common Core State Standards Initiative. (2010). *College and career readiness anchor standards for reading.* Retrieved from http://www.corestandards.org/the-standards/english-languagearts-standards/anchor-standards-hssts/college-and-career-readiness-anchor-standards-for-reading/

Critical thinking. (n.d.). *Dictionary.com's 21st century lexicon.* Retrieved from http://dictionary.reference.com/browse/critical thinking

Dowdall, C. (2009). Masters and critics: Children as producers of online digital texts. In V. Carrington & M. Robinson (Eds.), *Digital literacies: Social learning and classroom practices* (pp. 43–62). London: Sage.

Ge, X., & Land, S. M. (2003). Scaffolding students' problem-solving processes in an ill-structured task using question prompts and peer interactions. *Educational Technology, Research and Development, 51*(1), 21–38.

Gillen, J., & Barton, D. (2010). *Digital literacies: A research briefing by the Technology Enhanced Learning phase of the Teaching and Learning Research Programme.* Retrieved from http://www.tlrp.org/docs/DigitalLiteracies.pdf

Gilster, P. (1997). *Digital literacy.* New York: Wiley.

Gronseth, S., Brush, T., Ottenbreit-Leftwich, A., Strycker, J., Abaci, S., Easterling, W., et al. (2010). Equipping the next generation of teachers: Technology preparation and practice. *Journal of Digital Learning in Teacher Education, 27*(1), 30–36.

Groth, L., Dunlap, K., & Kidd, J. (2007). Becoming technologically literate through technology integration in PK-12 preservice literacy courses: Three case studies. *Reading Research and Instruction, 46*(4), 363–386.

Hague, C., & Williamson, B. (2009). *Digital participation, digital literacy, and school subjects: A review of the policies, literature, and evidence.* Bristol, UK: Futurelab. Retrieved from http://www.futurelab.org.uk/sites/default/files/Digital_Participation_review.pdf

Halpern, D. (1997). *Critical thinking across the curriculum: A brief edition of thought and knowledge.* Mahwah, NJ: Lawrence Erlbaum.

Harris, J., & Hofer, M. (2009). Instructional planning activity types as vehicles for curriculum-based TPACK development. In C. D. Maddux (Ed.), *Research highlights in technology and teacher education 2009* (pp. 99–108). Chesapeake, VA: Society for Information Technology in Teacher Education (SITE).

Harris, J., Mishra, P., & Koehler, M. (2009). Teachers' technological pedagogical content knowledge and learning activity types: Curriculum-based technology integration reframed. *Journal of Research on Technology in Education, 41*(4), 393–416. Retrieved from http://mkoehler.educ.msu.edu/OtherPages/Koehler_Pubs/TECH_BY_DESIGN/AERA_2007/AERA2007_HarrisMishraKoehler.pdf

Hollan, J., Hutchins, E., & Kirsh, D. (2000). Distributed cognition: Toward a new foundation for Human-Computer Interaction research. *ACM Transactions on Computer-Human Interaction, 7*(2), 174–196.

Howard, P. N., Duffy, A., Freelon, D., Hussain, M., Mari, W., & Mazaid, M. (2011). *Opening closed regimes: What was the role of social media during the Arab Spring?* University of Washington: PITPI (Project on Information Technology and Political Islam; Working Paper 2011.1). Retrieved from http://dl.dropbox.com/u/12947477/publications/2011_Howard-Duffy-Freelon-Hussain-Mari-Mazaid_pITPI.pdf

Hur, J. W., Cullen, T., & Brush, T. (2010). Teaching for application: A model for assisting preservice teachers with technology integration. *Journal of Technology and Teacher Education, 18*(1), 161–182.

Hutchins, E. (1991). The social organization of distributed cognition. Perspectives on socially shared cognition. In L. B. Resnick, J. M. Levine, & S. D. Teasley (Eds.), *Perspectives on socially shared cognition* (pp. 283–307). Washington, DC: American Psychological Association.

International Society for Technology in Education. (2007). *NETS for students*. Retrieved from http://www.iste.org/Libraries/PDFs/NETS-S_Standards.sflb.ashx

International Society for Technology in Education. (2008). *NETS for teachers*. Retrieved from http://www.iste.org/standards/nets-for-teachers/nets-for-teachers-2008.aspx

Jenkins, H. (2006). *Confronting the challenges of participatory culture: Media education for the 21st century*. Retrieved from http://digitallearning.macfound.org/atf/cf/%7B7E45C7E0-A3E0–4B89-AC9C-E807E1B0AE4E%7D/JENKINS_WHITE_PAPER.PDF

Kay, R. (2006). Evaluating strategies used to incorporate technology into pre-service education: A review of the literature. *Journal of Research on Technology in Education, 38*(4), 383–408. Retrieved from http://www.eric.ed.gov/PDFS/EJ768720.pdf

Kinzer, C. K., Cammack, D. W., Labbo, L. D., Teale, W. H., & Sanny, R. (2006). The need to (re)conceptualize pre-service literacy teacher development: Technology's role and considerations of design, pedagogy and research. In M. C. McKenna, L. D. Labbo, R. E. Keiffer, & D. Reinking (Eds.), *International handbook of literacy and technology* (Vol. 2, pp. 211–233). Mahwah, NJ: Lawrence Erlbaum.

Koehler, M., & Mishra, P. (2009). What is technological pedagogical content knowledge? *Contemporary Issues in Technology and Teacher Education, 9*(1), 60–70. Retrieved from http://www.citejournal.org/articles/v9i1general1.pdf

Koehler, M. J., Mishra, P., & Yahya, K. (2007). Tracing the development of teacher knowledge in a design seminar: Integrating content, pedagogy and technology. *Computers & Education, 49*(3), 740–762.

Kress, G. (2010). *Multimodality: A social semiotic approach to contemporary communication*. New York: Routledge.

Lankshear, C., & Knobel M. (2007). Sampling the "new" in new literacies. In M. Knobel & C. Lankshear (Eds.), A new literacies sampler (pp. 1–24). New York: Peter Lang.

Lee, C. J. (2011). Myths about critical literacy: What teachers need to unlearn. *Journal of Language and Literacy Education* [Online], 7(1), 95–102. Retrieved from http://www.coe.uga.edu/jolle/2011_1/lee.pdf

Leu, D. J., Jr. (2000). Literacy and technology: Deictic consequences for literacy education in an information age. In M. L. Kamil, P. Mosenthal, P. D. Pearson, & R. Barr (Eds.), *Handbook of reading research* (Vol. III, pp. 743–770). Mahwah, NJ: Erlbaum.

Leu, D.J., Kinzer, C.K., Coiro, J., & Cammack, D. (2004). Toward a theory of new literacies emerging from the Internet and other information and communication technologies. In R. B. Ruddell & N. Unrau (Eds.), *Theoretical models and processes of reading* (5th ed., pp. 1568–1611). Newark, DE: International Reading Association.

Leu, D. J., Kinzer, C. K., Coiro, J., Castek, J., & Henry, L. (In press). New literacies: A dual level theory of the changing nature of literacy, instruction, and assessment. In R. B. Ruddell & N. Unrau (Eds.), *Theoretical models and processes of reading* (6th ed.). Newark, DE: International Reading Association.

Lohnes, S., & Kinzer, C. K. (2007). Questioning assumptions about students' expectations for technology in college classrooms. *Innovate, 3*(5). Retrieved from http://www.innovateonline.info/index.php?view=article&id=431

Lohnes Watulak, S. (2012). "I'm not a computer person": Negotiating participation in academic Discourses. *British Journal of Educational Technology*, *43*(1). doi: 10.1111/j.1467–8535. 2010.01162.x

Martin, A. (2008). Digital literacy and the "digital society." In C. Lankshear & M. Knobel (Eds.), *Digital literacies: Concepts, policies, and practices* (pp. 151–176). New York: Peter Lang.

Merchant, G. (2007). Writing the future in the digital age. *Literacy*, *41*(3), 118–128. Retrieved from http://blog.rogerfrancis.info/files/9/2/2/3/1/121276–113229/Merchant.pdf

New London Group. (1996). A pedagogy of multiliteracies: Designing social futures. *Harvard Educational Review*, *66*(1), 60–92.

Niess, M., van Zee, E. H., & Gillow-Wiles, H. (2010).Knowledge growth in teaching mathematics/science with spreadsheets: Moving PCK to TPACK through online professional development. *Journal of Digital Learning in Teacher Education*, *27*(2), 42–52.

Partnership for 21st Century Skills. (2009). *Framework for 21st century learning*. Retrieved from http://www.p21.0rg/overview/skills-framework

Pinch, T., & Bijker, W. (1984). The social construction of facts and artifacts: Or how the sociology of science and the sociology of technology might benefit each other. In W. Bijker, T. Hughes, & T. Pinch (Eds.), *The social construction of technological systems: New directions in the sociology and history of technology* (pp. 17–50). Cambridge, MA: MIT Press.

Polly, D., Mims, C., Shephard, C., & Inan, F. (2010). Evidence of impact: Transforming teacher education with preparing tomorrow's teachers to teach with technology (PT3) grants. *Teaching and Teacher Education*, *26*, 863–870.

Preston, J. (2011, November 24). Protesters look for ways to feed the web. *New York Times*, p. A28. Retrieved from http://www.nytimes.com/2011/11/25/business/media/occupy-movement-focuses-on-staying-current-on-social-networks.html

Reason, P. (1999). Integrating action and reflection through co-operative inquiry. *Management Learning*, *30*(2), 207–227.

Risko, V. J., Vukelich, C., & Roskos, K. (2002). Preparing teachers for reflective practice: Intentions, contradictions, and possibilities. *Language Arts*, *80*(2), 134–144.

Schmidt, D. A., Baran, E., Thompson, A. D., Mishra, P., Koehler, M. J., & Shin, T. S. (2009). Technological pedagogical content knowledge (TPACK): The development and validation of an assessment instrument for preservice teachers. *Journal of Research on Technology in Education*, *42*(2), 123–149.

Schmidt, D., Harris, J., & Hofer, M. (2011, February). *K–6 literacy learning activity types*. Retrieved from http://activitytypes.wmwikis.net/file/view/K-6LiteracyLearningATs-Feb2011.pdf

Schön, D. A. (1987). *Educating the reflective practitioner: Toward a new design for teaching and learning in the professions*. San Francisco, CA: Jossey-Bass.

Shulman, L. S. (1986). Those who understand: Knowledge growth in teaching. *Educational Researcher*, *15*(2), 4–14.

Shulman, L. S. (1987). Knowledge and teaching: Foundations of the new reform. *Harvard Educational Review*, *57*(1), 1–22.

Simon, H. A. (1973). The structure of ill-structured problems. *Artificial Intelligence*, *4*(3–4), 181–201.

Smith, N. B. (2002).*American reading instruction*. Newark, DE: International Reading Association.

Spires, H. A., Hervey, L., & Watson, T. (in press). Scaffolding the TPACK framework in reading and language arts: New literacies and new minds. In C.A. Young & S. Kadjer (Eds.). *Research in English language arts and technology.* Charlotte, NC: Information Age Press.

Spiro, R. J., & Jehng, J.-Ch. (1990). Cognitive flexibility and hypertext: Theory and technology for the nonlinear and multidimensional traversal of complex subject matter. In D. Nix & R. Spiro (Eds.), *Cognition, education, and multimedia: Exploring ideas in high technology* (pp. 163–204). Hillsdale, NJ: Lawrence Erlbaum.

Street, B. (1984). *Literacy in theory and practice.* New York: Cambridge University Press.

Street, B. (2003). What's "new" in New Literacy Studies? Critical approaches to literacy in theory and practice. *Current Issues in Comparative Education, 5*(2), 1–14.

Taylor, K. (2011, September 13). Arab Spring really was social media revolution. *TG Daily.* Retrieved from http://www.tgdaily.com/software-features/58426-arab-spring-really-was-social-media-revolution

Voss, J. F. (1988). Problem solving and reasoning in ill-structured domains. In C. Antaki (Ed.), *Analyzing everyday explanation: A casebook of methods* (pp. 74–93). London: Sage.

Wepner, S., Tao, L., & Ziomek, N. (2006). Broadening our view about technology integration: Three literacy teacher educators' perspectives. *Reading Horizons, 46*(3), 215–237.

Wetzel, K., Foulger, T., & Williams, M. K. (2008). The evolution of the required educational technology course. *Journal of Computing in Teacher Education, 25*(2), 67–71. Retrieved from http://www.eric.ed.gov/PDFS/EJ834102.pdf

Young, C. A., Hofer, M., & Harris, J. (2011, February). *Secondary English language arts learning activity types.* Retrieved from http://activitytypes.wmwikis.net/file/view/SecEngLangArts LearningATs-Feb2011.pdf

PART 3

Resisting Dominant Narratives

CHAPTER EIGHT

"They Get What They Deserve"

Interrogating Critical Digital Literacy Experiences as Framed in a Québec Alternative High School Context

DANA E. SALTER

In this chapter I would like to make two interconnected arguments. First, I argue for the interrogation of the way alternative schools are framed in order to explore what range of literacy practices are enabled and/or constrained by how critical digital literacies practices and experiences get produced and taken up in this education context. There are three frames that help me make this argument: (1) the nuanced frame of defining the alternative-school context, (2) English Language Arts curriculum in the alternative-school context, and (3) digital literacy definitions produced in the alternative-school context. These frames were distilled from my interviews and conversations with teachers and students in a Québec alternative school, as well as curriculum and policy document analysis. Taken together, these three frames highlight how the underlying structure and values associated with the alternative school in my study produces a definition of in-school literacy and student engagement with literacies—critical digital literacies in particular—that narrows, rather than expands, literacy engagements for students in this schooling context.

Second, I argue the vital importance of interrogating the pre-formed images of the schools, students, and learning that critical digital literacies teachers and researchers bring to alternative education contexts and how these taken-for-granted ideas about these schools and research sites shape the way we frame our critical digital literacies research through how we interact with the sites themselves, our inter-actions with research participants, and our expectations of what we'll find. This is particularly true for contexts and people who have been framed around discourses of deficit, pathology, exclusion, and marginalization. The two arguments go hand in hand and have not been widely explored in alternative education, literacy, and crit-ical digital literacies in alternative education context literature. I conclude by not-ing that we should "think big" (Greene, 1995; Kim, 2010) about critical digital literacies in alternative- school contexts so that all students, and especially students in alternative schools, get the education—literacy education in particular—framed and taught in ways they "deserve."

WHAT IS THE STORY?

So how did I arrive at the above arguments in this chapter? While analyzing my data, several emergent themes kept taking me back to an observational vignette that I captured early on in my field notes as I conducted my research at Opportunities High School (OHS) (all names are pseudonyms), an English-language alternative school in Québec, Canada. The alternative school in my study is part of a group of publicly funded schools in Québec that educate students who have been "invited to leave" or have been "pushed out" of traditional/regular high schools for a variety of reasons and who struggle to complete high school (Hemmer, 2009; Kim, 2008, 2011; Kleiner, Porch, & Farris, 2002; Smith, Peled, & Albert, 2008; Wishart, 2009; Wright et al., 2008). This vignette turned out to be a pivotal moment in my research in terms of how I began to "see" the OHS contextually.

Vignette: "They get what they deserve"

Opportunities High School (OHS) is an alternative high school located in a work-ing-class neighborhood in Québec that provides education for about 60 young peo-ple ages 14–20. The computer lab there has about 25 old PCs in it and on any given day, fewer than half of them are fully working. There is a row of about 12 broken computers lined up on the floor in the back of the lab. Their black screens are cov-ered in a fine layer of dust.

Outside of the computer lab at OHS is an old piano with well-worn keys. Some of the ivory has chipped off the keys and the piano is obscenely out of tune. But that doesn't stop students from playing it. And that is the point of its existence there. In fact, on the day I'm writing about, one student, Shawn, was teaching himself to play piano by watching YouTube videos and playing this very piano.

During the morning of my fourth day of fieldwork, I walked into the computer lab and met Linda, the technology support person who worked for the IT department at the school board. Linda was at the school to check for software updates on the computers in the lab. What fascinated me about Linda's presence was an interaction she had with Mary and Joanne, the teachers I was working with on the critical digital literacies graphic-novel digital story and comic book projects.

Both teachers asked Linda when someone was going to come and pick up the defective/non-working computers so that they could fix up the computer lab. Linda's response was to talk about the organization of picking up computers and that they have to be picked up in batches of 20 or more. There were only about 12 sitting on the floor. Linda said that it would be a useless trip for them to pick up a few computers. Joanne was irritated about this and said so. She couldn't believe that no one could come and get the computers so that she and Mary could make their school look nice. I noted in my field notes that it didn't seem like an unusual protocol for computer pick up and so Joanne's response seemed off to me or disproportionate to what I thought the situation called for.

Mary added that one of the main reasons they wanted the computers out of there is that they have "new" donated computers, and having me volunteer showed the kids that they (the teachers and the school) take pride in kids and in the school's appearance—and that this goes a long way towards improving student perceptions of the school. Joanne apologized for her line of questioning and asked if they could just rent a truck and move the computers. Linda said no, as each computer had to be scanned and accounted for.

Linda continued that it was a shame that OHS didn't have more money because there are other schools that have so many new computers. There was a pause in the conversation as the echo of Linda's statement hung in the air. Linda continued that in some schools she goes into, there are all these new computers and so no computer maintenance is needed—she basically has nothing to do when she goes to these schools. Mary and Joanne continued to look at Linda. There was no conversation about why this school wasn't getting new computers.

I left the room because Shawn popped his head in and asked me to watch a YouTube video and play the piano with him. When I returned, Linda was in the middle of explaining that the kids in this school have to take care of their things and why fix them up or get new ones if the OHS students weren't going to take care of them anyway. Linda said the OHS students had to learn to accept the consequences of their actions. She concluded: "These kids get what they deserve." Mary and Joanne, visibly angry, looked at the clock on the wall and left to start the school day.

How this vignette begins to illustrate "the story"

I took a step back from the data and asked my own follow-up question to Linda's observation: "What do 'these' students 'deserve'?" The dictionary defines "deserve" as meaning "to be qualified for reward, punishment, recompense, etc." (Dictionary.com, 2011). The idea of the students in the alternative school being qualified for having old computers with outdated software and a broken-down piano got me thinking about what else we think these young people are qualified for. The moment that Linda, the technology support person at OHS, uttered these words and I observed Mary and Joanne's reaction to them ultimately proved to be a pivotal turning point in my research, because this vignette helped me begin to articulate the frames that produce the context of the school, the way English Language Arts curriculum is taken up and how critical digital literacies get defined in this context. Re-reading my field notes as I explored the emerging themes in the data brought the vignette to the forefront of my research analysis because of the questions it raised in light of my emergent findings. Particularly, what pre-formed images do we have about alternative schools? How are these images constructed? How are these images operationalized in the literacy curriculum at this school? What happens when we introduce critical digital literacies into this context? How are critical digital literacies then framed in this education context?

To begin to address these questions, I again returned to my analysis, which helped me see that while Linda's words were upsetting to hear, I had to try to place myself in Linda's shoes and think about what pre-formed images of the alternative school could have possibly shaped her response. Again, how was that image constructed and operationalized in Linda's discussions of the OHS students and technology with Mary and Joanne? What story of the school could this image create and how did Linda "see" the students? How did Mary and Joanne "see" the students? How did I "see" and frame the students, teachers, the school, and the critical digital literacies praxis in the school?

OVERVIEW OF THE STUDY

As I begin to talk in more detail about the story of the OHS context as revealed through the vignette, I will first briefly outline my study. In this study, I worked with the Secondary 4 and 5 (equivalent to high school grades 9–11) students, English Language Arts teachers, and resource teachers at the school to create two separate critical digital literacies projects that had never been done before at OHS: a graphic novel-based, digital story unit and a self-reflection comic book unit. Briefly, my working definition of critical digital literacies builds upon Dockter and Lewis' (2009) definition by viewing them as digitally mediated social practices that envision and frame literacy as a form of critical civic engagement "so that [students] can 'read' [and I would add produce and act upon] the linguistic, visual, and aural signs and symbols that inundate their lives, both public and private" (p.17; see also Merchant, 2009). The critical digital literacies projects I helped design with the students and teachers at OHS used this working definition as the foundational theoretical frame as we aligned the project with the Québec English Language Arts curriculum (MELS, 2001).

In this chapter, I focus on the graphic novel-based digital story unit where students chose a pre-approved graphic novel and produced a digital story of their own critical literacy response to the book. After the students completed these projects, I interviewed them and their teachers. At that point in the research, I saw that I needed to step back and explore more deeply what the students, teachers, and my analysis of the curriculum was revealing, because my findings were bumping up against my taken-for-granted pre-formed images about the school context and my research.

As I analyzed the data, I was compelled to look at three emerging themes that I hadn't anticipated as having such a profound impact on my critical digital literacies research in this context: contextual characteristics of alternative schools; stories/narratives associated with students/teachers in alternative schools; and literacy and critical digital literacy as defined at OHS. I didn't think I entered into the research context naively; I had researched the alternative education and critical digital literacies literatures to think through issues of literacy, power, critical digital literacies, and context. I did note that I found minimal research relating to critical digital literacies praxis in alternative-school contexts. However, I didn't anticipate how meaningful that research silence would be in my work. These themes did not make sense with my initial research focus, but they brought forward important conversations about how alternative schools are framed that I subsequently learned were rarely mentioned in relation to critical digital literacies and alternative schools in the literature.

To illustrate my point, I return to Shawn, the student in the vignette who used YouTube to teach himself how to play piano. Shawn really embraced the project, going beyond the assigned work to create not one but two digital stories about his process in creating the assignment. This project was a particularly generative moment for Shawn and his teachers because it showcased a side of him that the teachers and his peers had not seen. Because of the highly enthusiastic and surprised response to his project, I obtained Shawn's permission to show his digital story to other teachers and students and interview the teachers and students immediately after viewing the digital story. One teacher responded that this project "completely changes his story! I had no idea he could do this…what other talents do these kids have that we just don't know about because of the way we're teaching them?" This project seemed to provide a more complex and rich way to frame critical digital literacies research in alternative education contexts. But again, that was not the full story.

In the next sections, I discuss in greater detail the three frames for interrogating critical digital literacies praxis in an alternative school context that emerged from my data. These three frames are context, curriculum, and critical digital literacies definitions produced in this context. Taken together, they begin to construct what I call "messy" contextual understandings of how, when not interrogated, the alternative school context can produce a narrowed, rather than expanded, literacy engagement spectrum for students in this school.

FRAME NUMBER 1: NUANCED DISCUSSION OF THE OHS CONTEXT

The first frame for interrogating critical digital literacies in the alternative school context is the frame of a nuanced discussion of context itself. Through a focus group conversation and interviews with the teachers in the school, in which I asked them to respond to Shawn's project, I began to see how "messy" yet crucially important framing a nuanced discussion of the context of OHS was for understanding the role and impact of critical digital literacies praxis in the school. Quickly and tellingly, my goals for the conversations to be about Shawn's project morphed as they were taken up by the teachers and repurposed to discuss both the need for schools like OHS and the teachers' own experiences of the challenges of the very existence of the school. The longer we talked, the messier my understanding of the alternative school context became, and the clearer I began to see the need for this messy frame in thinking through the consequences and affordances of critical digital literacies engagements in alternative schools like OHS. Based upon the teachers' conversations, there are three key parts to this frame: the alternative school identity crisis, the Québec education landscape, and the sloganization of inclusive education.

The alternative school identity crisis

The excerpt below is from a teacher focus group conversation about Shawn's project. This conversation quickly turned into a discussion of the challenges of defining the school context itself through my question regarding the teachers' perceptions of the impact of this project at this school. The teachers sought to define the school and subsequently revealed three different images of alternative schools that shape how they are defined, and ultimately help us begin to understand the pre-formed image people may have about the school (Kim, 2008, 2010).

PATRICIA:	[OHS] is a dumping ground—
HOPE:	Yea, we don't know who we are. We don't know if we're a special ed school or—
BRIAN:	Or...or socio-environmental—
TRICIA (TEACHER):	Yea, we kind of have an identity crisis going on . . .

The theme of "not knowing who we are," the image of the school as a "dumping ground" and having an "identity crisis" are observable in the emerging alternative school literature (Becker, 2010; Kim, 2008, 2010; Munoz, 2004; Rhymes, 2001). As the excerpt from the teacher interview shows, depending on how the alternative school is framed from its conception and in relation to its context, the alternative school can have a staggering amount of definitions. As Patricia noted, it can be defined as being a "dumping ground" or "warehouse" for young people who don't fit into or are falling behind in "regular" school contexts (Kim, 2008, p. 207). It can be defined as an education space for students with behavioral challenges, psychosocial and emotional needs (Quinn & Poirier, 2006; Smith, Peled, & Albert, 2008). It can also be understood as a space for education that is less regimented and more aligned with the specific needs of students and community (Wishart, 2009). Additionally, these schools can be defined as charter schools and other alternative education programs (Raywid, 1999). Finally, alternative schools can be understood as combinations of all of the above school conceptualizations (Kim, 2010; Rymes, 2001). Importantly, even with the myriad of definitions, alternative education in North America has been minimally researched in relation to the ongoing role they have had in public education (Kim, 2008).

Returning to the teacher excerpt, Kim (2008) discusses the concept of identity crisis by arguing that the alternative school in her study existed "in a multidimensional state of disequilibrium" (p. 217) that impacted and shaped a range of schooling practices. This identity crisis or disequilibrium caused Kim to wonder "who truly benefited from this kind of alternative education" (p. 217). These teachers seem to be asking the same question, which is important since this conversation happened just after viewing Shawn's project. What is obscured by this confusion around defining alternative education in general and OHS in particular and "not knowing who [they] are" is the larger discursive framework that produces these schools and out of which the schools produce students, teachers, and learning experiences.

The challenge of the Québec context

Continuing my discussion of the first frame for interrogating critical digital literacies in the alternative school context, I turn my attention to locating alternative education in the Québec geopolitical context. In this focus group excerpt, Patricia, the head teacher, explains why she believes the alternative school is needed in Québec, while also speaking to the challenge of being heard in a context that seems indifferent to your existence:

> ...but there are kids out there that are different, absolutely, and...I think the school system has to cater to that...[the Québec Ministry of Education has] begun to understand that there definitely is a need for [Opportunities High School and schools like it] but I think...we need to be heard. There has to be...a louder voice because we are definitely not getting enough funding in order for us to succeed. And to feel that we've succeeded in catching all these kids...we need to have more funding and very slowly people are beginning to understand that we're the ones that are keeping the dropout rate low.

Patricia's argument that the school system needs to not just acknowledge but include and cater to the students who "are different" invites us to question what it means for a student to be "different" in Québec, where the education system has recently (within the last ten years) undergone sweeping curriculum reform (MELS, 2001; Smith, Foster, & Donahue, 1999). It also begs us to ask how that difference translates to schooling practices. For example, to date, recent studies and public discussions have addressed how issues related to difference, such as dropout and retention rates (McKinsey & Co., 2010), immigration, French- and English-language laws and policies (Breton-Carbonneau & Cleghorn, 2010; Lamarre, 2008), local, national, and global socioeconomic policy discourses (Edgerton, Peter, & Roberts, 2008; Henchey, 2007), and the aforementioned curriculum reform (Bhardwaj, 2011; Lafortune, Prud'homme, Sorin, et al., 2011) create a complex education context that seems to simultaneously provide space for and limit a spectrum of education options. Alternative school education seems to be produced as one of these options (Wright et al., 2008).

However, while these schools may be produced as an option, Patricia observed that her school and other schools like them fill an ever-growing need to reduce the high Québec dropout rate (McKinsey & Co., 2010); yet they still "need to be heard," amplifying the silence about these schools in the Québec research literature—even in light of the above-mentioned geopolitical context. As the Canadian education system is organized around provincial education policies and funding practices (Edgerton et al., 2008; Wotherspoon & Schissel, 2000, p. 2), it is difficult to get a clear picture of the scope and frame of alternative education across the country because, to the best of my knowledge, there is not a multiple provincial or national discussion or repository of alternative education research and studies (e.g., Carver, Lewis, & Tice, 2010; Stanford University's California Alternative Education Research Project, 2008). The dearth of research and analysis on alternative schools in the Québec context, especially in light of what it means to be "different" in this context as briefly outlined above, has an impact on the questions asked and research done regarding the learning experiences of increasing number of Québec students who are struggling in school. Extending this conversation, in the absence of sustained research and wide-ranging nuanced discussions of alternative education in Québec, how do we understand the image of schools like OHS that are produced in an opaque system and the impact of that image on framing learning experiences (Munoz, 2004, p. 14)?

The consequences of the sloganization of inclusive education

Since alternative schools are minimally discussed in Québec research, an insightful way to try to view the alternative school context in my study is through Québec's adoption of an inclusive education policy stance towards education (Lupart, 2000, 2008; MELS, 2000; Porter, 2008; Slee, 2011), since this policy is aimed at framing educational avenues for students who struggle in school. Briefly, inclusive education in Québec, like alternative education, has a long history and a host of definitions that are fraught with deep tensions around defining and diagnosing students who struggle in school, how the barriers for learning should be removed and high-quality equitable schooling provided for all students, but especially students who have been diagnosed with learning disabilities/difficulties and/or who struggle to fit in to so-called "regular schooling" (Advisory Board on English Education Special Education, 2006; Allan, 2009; Benjamin, 2002; Lupart, 2008; Slee, 2011). By law, each Québec school board constructs and implements their own inclusive education provisions and these can range from "integration" of students to providing special-education schools (MELS, 2006). Keeping this in mind, the question then becomes, how do alternative schools like OHS fit into inclusive education conversations?

During our teacher focus group conversation about Shawn's digital story, a teacher named Hope opens up this question by making the following statement:

> It used to be that...a lot of the students that are here now probably...wouldn't have been kept in schools. It's just recently that Québec has adopted this whole inclusion [inclusive education policy] thing...so now they're deciding to not separate these students who are learning disabled who used to be in special ed classes or resource rooms or stuff like that. Now they are trying to incorporate these students into a regular classroom and when you have 30 kids in a classroom...or you have maybe one person following the child and it just creates the behaviour difficulties. So a lot of these schools are trying to...it seems like they are just trying to get rid of these kids. So now the alternative school has also become kind of like a special ed center.

Taking up Hope's observation that certain understandings of inclusive educa-tion policy and practice allow regular schools to use the alternative school as a way to remove the students who struggle, I argue that she is alluding to the impact of the sloganization of inclusive education. The way that the many inclusive educa-tion definitions and policies get produced and taken up in education contexts has led to the sloganization of inclusive education—where, as Benjamin (2002) notes, "a framework for understanding and engaging with student failure has not been developed and failure itself becomes elided through complicated narratives of reme-diation and 'banal and vacuous' versions of 'inclusion' (Wilson, 2000)" (Benjamin, 2002, p. 50). In Hope's statement, a version of inclusion is the "dumping ground" of the alternative education. Inclusion becomes just another slogan.

Pushing back against the sloganization of inclusive education, Slee (2011) reminds us that "[i]nclusive education...requires that we seek understandings of exclusion from the perspectives of those who are devalued and rendered marginal or surplus by the dominant culture of the regular schools" (p. 107). While many alter-native schools, including the one in my study, are framed as inclusive education spaces that can provide positive and rich learning spaces for students who have strug-gled in traditional schools and help them be successful in their post-school lives (Kim, 2010; Slee, 2011; Wishart, 2009; Wotherspoon & Schissel, 2000), as the head teacher Patricia noted above, these schools also serve as places to "catch" the surplus students. While this can seem laudable on the surface, it also produces a certain kind of student in a certain kind of education context—an "at-risk" surplus student in an education context that is rendered invisible (Gee, 2001). This alternative education context frame has enormous ethical and emotional costs for students, teachers, their communities, and society as a whole. In particular, the frame of context impacts how curriculum is shaped and implemented in general, and critical digital literacies cur-ricular practices in particular.

FRAME NUMBER 2: ENGLISH LANGUAGE ARTS CURRICULUM IN THE OHS CONTEXT

The second frame for interrogating critical digital literacies praxis in the alterna-tive school context is curricular. In this section, I argue that the OHS context pro-duces a version of the English Language Arts curriculum that bumps up against the stated goals of the official English Language Arts curriculum. Examining the stated goals and desired competencies of the Québec Education Program curricu-lum raises important questions about the role of context in literacy/critical digital literacies education in the alternative school.

The Québec Education Reform English Language Arts Curriculum and Critical Digital Literacies

I would argue that according to the Québec Education Program, the curricular expectations for literacy in all Québec high schools is, in theory, very much aligned with definitions of critical digital literacies that call for a renewed examination of what critical digital literacies engagement looks like in classrooms with historically marginalized students (Dockter & Lewis, 2010; MELS QEP, pp. 4–5). The Québec Education Program states that high school Cycle 2 (Secondary 4 and 5) English Language Arts is a critical literacy curriculum that "focuses on fluency in the reading and production of spoken, written and media texts." (MELS QEP, pp. 1 & 5). Teachers and students are encouraged to work from an integrated "interactive and collaborative" inquiry approach to literacy education that is deliberate about addressing the sociocultural nature of the codes and conventions of different genred literacy experiences (MELS QEP, pp. 7 & 11).

Indeed, as I mentioned previously, in my study, my working definition of critical digital literacies builds upon Dockter and Lewis' (2009) arguments by seeing them as digitally mediated social practices that envision and frame literacy as a form of critical civic engagement "so that [students] can 'read' [and I would add produce and act upon] the linguistic, visual, and aural signs and symbols that inundate their lives, both public and private" (p.17; see also Merchant, 2009). Working with students in alternative schools to have a range of literacy experiences is at the heart of my definition, and I see it echoed in the stated English Language Arts curriculum. In the Québec Education Program, there is an explicit directive for literacy education that provides a robust range of literacy experiences that are reflective, and that provide degrees of civic engagement and prepare students for post-school life (MELS QEP, pp. 5–7).

Re-thinking the Québec Education Program and the alternative school context

On the surface, the Québec Education Program seems to align nicely with critical digital literacies discussions. However, as with any curriculum, not all education contexts where the curriculum will be implemented are equal, and taking up the Québec Education Program English Language Arts curriculum in the OHS context magnifies the constraining force of context. When I use my emerging frame of the little-studied messy context of OHS, I get another view of the Québec Education Program English Language Arts curriculum and how literacy is framed in this context that compels me to question how we conceptualize critical digital literacies in alternative schools like OHS (Munoz, 2004). For example, the Québec

Education Program has been critiqued as being produced within and advocating a neoliberal discourse that privileges a direct linking of school knowledge with the knowledge-based economy (Bhardwaj, 2011). This coupling of school knowledge with economic structures is not new (Apple, 2001; Cuban, 1989; deCastell & Luke, 1983; Franklin, 1994; Stevens, 2011), but what is important to consider is how emergent discussions of critical digital literacies are being produced and taken up within this equation that subsequently frames how literacy discussions and curriculum are produced and implemented for historically marginalized students who are rendered surplus and are in alternative education contexts (Alvermann, 2006, 2009; Franzack, 2006; Hull, Zacher, & Hibbert, 2009; Janks, 2010; Vasudevan & Campano, 2009, p. 328). That is, we must consider how critical digital literacies are defined and the range of literacy experiences that are subsequently expected within the alternative school context based upon how the school itself is framed (Luke & Woods, 2009, pp. 198–200). In the next section, I begin to discuss specifically how the frames of OHS context and English Language Arts curriculum in this context help us see how critical digital literacies discussions are produced and taken up at OHS.

The pull of context: The Québec Education Program English Language Arts curriculum, OHS, and narrowed definitions of literacy

In discussing their experiences of the tension between the stated goals of the Québec Education Program English Language Arts curriculum and what happens when it is taken up at OHS, Nora, one of the two support teachers I interviewed who work closely with the OHS English Language Arts staff, explained:

> Really, it's depressing. When you read about [the high dropout rate]…when you read about these kids and the outcomes and all of that, it's…it's not positive at all. Why are we giving up? I mean it's scary to think…when you think about…what…what is going to happen to them? That's what I think about. What is going to end up happening? Because there is such a high demand in the workforce for literacy, for social skills, and all of these skills that you know…and here we are working in piecemeal…you know, past-tense verbs and are they able to understand this or that or spell a word right. You know, very discrete little skills that, in the end, who cares. Once we get into the world, it's not about whether or not they can spell "because" exactly, right?

Nora's comments pull together our previous discussions to this point in this chapter. She begins by talking about the public engagement with the messy context of how OHS is framed by talking about the negative images of the school and students in it in public discourse (Branswell, 2009) such as newspapers, social media, and TV. She moves the conversation from the theoretical to the emotional by noting that there is a strong element of fear associated with thinking about the lived experiences of students in alternative schools. The emotional connection that Nora voices when she asks, "What's going to end up happening" to the students relates to my earlier discussion of how the school is framed as an inclusive school, but we must closely examine how inclusion and exclusion are framed from the perspective of those who are rendered surplus. What is inclusion in this context and what happens after one is excluded?

Finally, similar to the framing of the Québec Education Program, Nora links literacy engagements and neoliberal knowledge-based economic conversations by noting that a range of literacy skills are in demand in the workforce. But interestingly, she immediately draws attention to how all of these issues converge in the alternative school context by stating, "here we are working in piecemeal." For Nora, in this alternative school context, she cannot even get to addressing the literacy experiences outlined in the Québec Education Program, because "here" literacy is framed as remediation within a larger deficit construction of students' literacy practices and engagements (Valencia, 2010).

And while this view of literacy as a set of remedial piecemeal practices may be foregrounded at OHS, I would like to return our attention to the nuanced discussion of context. The school itself is produced at the intersection of a range of issues, and rarely researched and discussed, thus producing a "thick" silence that Patricia, the lead teacher, articulated, where these important literacy/critical digital literacies conversations remain in isolation. The students, teachers, and staff work piecemeal to teach and acquire literacy practices. I am not interpreting Nora's comments as arguing that there are not specific skills that young people need to have in order to take care of themselves and be successful (e.g., being able to read and write to do well in a job). What I am saying is that Nora's comments highlight the point that these skills cannot be divorced from the context in which their value was produced (Gutierrez, Morales, & Martinez, 2009). We value certain kinds of literacy skills in certain kinds of contexts. And in the alternative school context, a narrowed literacy spectrum that focused on job-readiness literacy skills seems to be most valued (Franzak, 2006). Again, I understand why, especially in light of the high dropout and unemployment rate for young people who struggle in school. However, that is not the only reason for literacy practices. We must expand the literacy spectrum and value a range of literacy experiences for all students, and students in alternative schools like OHS in particular.

FRAME NUMBER 3: CRITICAL DIGITAL LITERACIES IN THE OHS CONTEXT

How do we begin to expand the literacy spectrum for students in alternative schools like OHS? I argue that critical digital literacies are one way to begin. In this next section, I return to my conversations with teachers and students after they viewed Shawn's digital story. What I found most interesting from these conversations was that even in a project designed to engage with critical digital literacies, the pull of the context (e.g., the need for the project to lead to post-school, work-related, literacy-skills development) almost overshadowed the critical components of the digital literacy engagements. Revealingly, as the researcher, I was a key part of encouraging this line of reflection. I feel this is important to acknowledge for methodological reasons as we conduct critical digital literacies research in alternative education sites and other historically marginalized and underserved contexts. If the messiness of the alternative school context is not considered, critical digital literacies can be shaped and taken up as "more of the status quo" of literacy instruction and learning. At the same time, when the messy context is engaged with, it can provide a way to loosen the constraining, narrowly defined literacy discourse that may be produced in this context.

Reinscribing narrow critical literacy visions

The excerpt below took place immediately after two support teachers and I had watched Shawn's digital story together:

TARA:	But to use [this project] as an alternative…why not? I mean it's…they're doing…they're using the same basic skills…they're researching, they're having to plan it out, they're having to present, to express themselves…so what is the difference, really? But I think this is even better because they're using…they're using technology that they will likely have to use at some point when they're working, you know?
DANA:	And that's one of the things I said to him that, you know, we can…we can start to think about your CV and get more digital storytelling…experience.
NORA:	It really just focuses in, centers in […] so that he's able to find a career or some kind of job at least that…that he can use his strengths in.

Astoundingly, the very first thing the teachers and I mentioned about the project is the isolated skill sets that Shawn employed. I argue that while my good intentions were aimed at working with the teachers and Shawn to make a project that we hoped would begin to expand his range of in-school literacy experiences, part of the way we framed and discussed the project bore the traces of a discourse of risk and deficit constructions mentality (Slee, 2011; Swadener & Lubeck, 1995; Valencia, 2010) that reduces literacy discussions in alternative schools to, in this case, making sure to emphasize how this project, and projects like this, might help Shawn and students like him get jobs and be "successful" in their post-school lives (Benjamin, 2002, p. 50).

A key assumption or pre-formed image we had was the role that increased new literacies opportunities can have in helping historically marginalized young people participate in the global knowledge economy. As Tara asked, "what was the difference, really" between this project and a non-critical digital literacies project? Shawn did take ownership of the project and engage in some critical elements of meaning-making, but during the course of the project, we (researcher and teachers) got so excited about the fact that it was happening at this school in this context that we didn't look carefully at the literacy engagements that were being produced. We focused on the discrete narrow skill sets Shawn was practicing. Again, yes, this is important, but it tends to be the default conversation in alternative school contexts (Hemmer, 2009; Kim, 2008). While the teachers and I did talk about the decontextualized nature of testing and how the culture of the school impacts learning, that exchange took place later in the conversation, not directly after viewing Shawn's digital story.

And here we can see the pull of the messy context. I am not arguing that our response is only localized to the alternative school context (Alvermann, 2009); I am instead arguing that this kind of response is even more the case for a schooling contexts made explicitly for students who have been "rendered surplus" and marginalized from regular or traditional education system—no matter the good intentions (Kim, 2011; Slee, 2011). It is this idea of default thinking about literacy experiences in the alternative school context that can make the introduction of critical digital literacies seem to be one more initiative along the continuum of approaches introduced into this context. But there are ways to reframe this default conception.

The potential role of critical digital literacies in expanding the literacy spectrum at OHS

In light of all three frames for looking at critical digital literacies praxis in an alternative school like OHS, a lightning-rod moment in the study was the conversation I had with Eric, a recent graduate of OHS, just after he viewed Shawn's digital story. Our conversation immediately shifted from one that focused on an instrumental view of critical digital literacies, to one that looked at it as socially mediated civic engagement view, and this shift was led by Eric.

> You know, I think projects like this are good, right? They get you active and doin' stuff in school. [School] is more interesting, right. But you know, well, you know, when I think about school and stuff, I remember how I, like, lived in three different countries while in high school, right? South America, U.S., and Canada. And I had a lot of trouble in regular schools, but there's reasons, you know? There's many reasons...like sometimes I would

come to school hungry—and [OHS] school is good, they feed you if they see you're hungry. But this school gets to be a place where like, you can put kids, you know? Anyway, other kids have to take three buses and to get to school and there's all [these things going on] at home. Like, our parents work hard and but it's tough, you know? So, I get to school and then I'm supposed to just learn in class—like, write some essay or something? So, I guess video games and digital [stories] could be a part of that but there,…I don't know…it's a lot to think about, [students at OHS] have a lot of things going on already so the [work] in school has to, I don't know….[the teachers] have to think if they're gonna do [these projects] here …

Eric's words put my conversation with Tricia and Nora in sharp relief as we discussed Shawn's project. This moment underscored the importance of considering how students in the alternative school understand their literacy experiences before critical digital literacies are introduced—something I had not focused on in my research. Eric brought up several of the points that I've previously discussed in this chapter as being vital for thinking about critical digital literacies in the alternative school context. For example, in talking about the "regular schools," he notes that while he did get into trouble, he was "rendered surplus" by the regular school and one of the reasons he got in trouble was that he would come to school hungry. As a side note, upon reading this chapter, Eric asked me to add that he is not excusing his getting into trouble, just calling out the factors that greatly influenced his in-school experiences.

Eric continued that, on top of what was happening outside of school, when he got there he was supposed to "just learn in class—like, write some essay or something." This speaks to the clash of the Québec Education Program, which calls for a range of literacy experiences, and Patricia's comment that the school needs more funding, among other resources, to serve the students they get. Eric, and students experiencing out-of-school lives that are similar to his, don't "just" learn. Like any student, they need meaningful, rich, and critically engaging curricular experiences designed with a nuanced understanding of students' existence across multiple (sometimes competing) contexts. If his school is rarely discussed and not visible in research literature or public discourse, how can the curriculum become rich in this silence? Eric's in-school experience with literacy was one that was greatly shaped by his out-of-school context. Again, we know that research and conversations with students, teachers, parents/guardians, and community members supports this, but little research has explicitly documented it in the alternative school critical digital literacies context. This thinking through or interrogating how students' literacy experiences are understood helps students themselves, and their teachers, better understand how the messy context of the alternative school shapes the literacy expectations for students—and how to push back against those frames.

CONCLUSION: SO WHAT DO THEY DESERVE?

Circling back to the vignette at the beginning of this chapter, I hope I've created the beginning of a matrix-like layout of the complex messy construction of the alternative school context in my study and the implications of that context on critical digital literacies praxis. My intention is that this discussion of the context in which the school is produced can help us think through and frame how we see comments like the one made by the technology-support person, Linda. I also hope we are able to hold our (well-intentioned?) pre-formed images of the school up for analysis to see how our assumptive ideas and unexplored frames about a site like Opportunities High School can potentially produce a narrow vision of critical digital literacies engagement in context—from conception to implementation.

How we conceptualize the alternative school context frames our image of the school, which impacts how we design and implement literacy curriculum in this context. Creating so-called critical digital literacies experiences, like the project I did, to help push back against marginalization and myopic literacy engagements can on the surface appear to be helpful. However, if we are not mindful of the alternative school contexts, these projects can essentially champion a narrow spectrum of literacy possibilities and practices for young people who have already historically been marginalized. Again, going back to Franzak (2006), "[b]ecause marginalized adolescent readers [and learners] are initially identified as such within the school context, the underlying structure and values of school literacy are built into definitions of struggling readers [and learners]" (p. 219). Extending this understanding to the alternative school context in my study, I argue that the underlying structure and values of the alternative school, as it is produced in the messy "identity crisis" context, produces a definition of literacy and student engagement with literacy that narrows, rather than expands literacy engagements.

My goal in this chapter has been twofold. First, to show how the three frames that emerged in conversation with OHS teachers, staff, and students and myself—the frames of context, curriculum, and critical digital literacy defined in context—produce a narrow version of literacy and critical digital literacies when they are not interrogated and brought into the forefront of literacy policy, research, and pedagogical discussions. Second, as Eric showed and reminded me, we must expand and "think big" (Greene, 1995, p. 10; Kim, 2010) about how we (researchers and teachers) conceptualize critical digital literacy in the OHS context. While on the one hand, the teachers and I were excited about the project, Eric reminded us of larger critical issues related to expanded notions of literacy. I draw upon Greene's (1995) discussion of "thinking big":

To see things or people small, one chooses to see from a detached point of view, to watch behaviors from the perspective of a system, to be concerned with trends and tendencies, rather than the intentionality and concreteness of everyday life. To see things or people big, one must resist viewing other human beings as mere objects or chess pieces and view them in their integrity and particularity instead. One must see from the point of view of the participant in the midst of what is happening if one is to be privy to the plans people make, the initiatives they take, the uncertainties they face. When applied to schooling, the vision that sees things big brings us in close contact with the details and with the particularities that cannot be reduced to statistics or even to the measurable. (p. 10)

As Vasudevan and Campano (2009) argue regarding historically marginalized young people, "the language of innovation and discovery does not permeate the levels most frequently used to describe the youth on whom we have been focused in this review" (p. 329). The same can be said for students like Shawn at Opportunities High School. Because the language of innovation and discovery, though present in the English Language Arts curriculum, has not permeated the context of the school, it is easy to view any introduction of innovative critical digital literacies approaches as being a positive move. However, as my study showed, it must be conceptualized as "big" and brought "into close contact with the details and the particularities" of alternative education context so that it is a part of expanding, not the continued narrowing, of literacy experiences for students in these schools. This is all in a continued effort to help these and all students get the education they deserve.

REFERENCES

Advisory Board on English Education Special Education (Commission de l'éducation en langue anglaise). (2006). Issues of inclusion and integration in the classroom. Brief to the Gouvernement du Québec, Minister of Education (Ed.). Retrieved from http://www.mels.gouv.qc.ca/cela/pdf/AvisInclusionIntClasseResume_a.pdf

Allan, J. (2009). *Rethinking inclusive education: The philosophers of difference in practice*. Dordrecht, the Netherlands: Springer.

Alvermann, D. (2006). Struggling adolescent readers: A cultural construction. In A. McKeough, L. M. Phillips, V. Timmons, & J. L. Lupart (Eds.), *Understanding literacy development: A global view* (pp. 95–111). Mahwah, NJ: Erlbaum.

Alvermann, D. (2009). Sociocultural constructions of adolescence and young people's literacies. In L. Christenbury, R. Bomer, & P. Smagorinsky (Eds.), *Handbook of adolescent literacy research* (pp. 12–28). New York: Guilford.

Apple, M. (2001). Comparing neo-liberal projects and inequality in education. *Comparative Education, 37*(4), 409–423.

Becker, S. (2010). Badder than "just a bunch of SPEDs": Alternative schooling and student resistance to special education rhetoric. *Journal of Contemporary Ethnography, 39*(1), 60—86.

Benjamin, S. (2002). *The micropolitics of inclusive education: An ethnography.* Buckingham, UK: Open University Press.

Bhardwaj, P. (2011). *Neoliberalism and education: A case study of Québec.* Montreal, QC: McGill University Press.

Branswell, B. (2009, February 15). In your face at Options II. *Montreal Gazette,* pp. 4–6.

Breton-Carbonneau, G. L., & Cleghorn, A. (2010). What's language got to do with it?: An exploration into the learning environment of Québec's classes d'accueil. *Canadian and International Education/Education Canadienne et Internationale, 39*(3). Retrieved from http://ir.lib.uwo.ca/cgi/viewcontent.cgi?article=1062&context=cie-eci

Carver, P. R., Lewis, L., & Tice, P. (2010). *Alternative schools and programs for public school students at risk of educational failure: 2007–2008* (NCES 2010–026). Washington, DC: U.S. Department of Education, National Center for Statistics.

Cuban, L. (1989). The "at-risk" label and the problem of urban school reform. *Phi Delta Kappan, 70*(10), 780–784, 799–801.

de Castell, S., & Luke, A. (1983). Defining "literacy" in North American schools: Social and historical conditions and consequences. *Journal of Curriculum Studies, 15*(4), 373–389.

Dictionary.com. (2011). Retrieved from http://dictionary.reference.com/browse/deserve

Dockter, J., Haug, D., & Lewis, C. (2010). Redefining rigor: Critical engagement, digital media, and the new English/language arts. *Journal of Adolescent and Adult Literacy, 48,* 418–420.

Dockter, J., & Lewis, C. (2009). Redefining academic rigor: Documentary film making in the new English/language arts classroom. *CURA Reporter.* Retrieved from http://www.digitalmedia-astudies.org/uploads/4/2/5/5/4255278/cura_reporter_article.pdf

Edgerton, J., Peter, T., & Roberts, L. (2008). Back to the basics: Socio-economic, gender, and regional disparities in Canada's educational system. *Canadian Journal of Education, 31*(4), 861–888.

Franklin, B. (1994). *From "backwardness" to "at-risk": Childhood learning difficulties and the contradictions of school reforms.* New York: SUNY Press.

Franzak, J. (2006). Zoom: A review of the literature on marginalized adolescent readers, literacy theory, and policy implications. *Review of Educational Research, 76*(2), 209–248.

Gee, J. (2001). Identity as an analytic lens for research in education. *Review of Research in Education, 25,* 99–125.

Greene, M. (1995). *Releasing the imagination.* San Francisco, CA: Jossey-Bass.

Gutierrez, K. D., Morales, P., & Martinez, D. (2009). Re-mediating literacy: Culture, difference, and learning for students from nondominant communities. *Review of Research in Education, 33,* 212–245.

Hemmer, L. (2009). Critical analysis of "at-risk" policy discourse: Implications for administrators and teachers. Unpublished thesis: Doctor of Philosophy, Texas A&M University.

Henchey, N. (2007). The state and the curriculum: Questions and options for Québec. *McGill Journal of Education, 42*(3), 443–456.

Hull, G., Zacher, J., & Hibbert, L. (2009). Youth, risk, and equity in a global world. *Review of Research in Education, 33,* 117–159.

Janks, H. (2010). *Literacy and power.* New York: Taylor & Francis.

Kim, J. H. (2008). An alternative for whom?: Rethinking alternative education to break the cycle of educational inequality. *Journal of Educational Research, 101*(4), 207–219. Retrieved from http://krex.k-state.edu/dspace/bitstream/2097/9169/1/KimJER2008.pdf

Kim, J. H. (2010). Narrative inquiry into (re)imagining alternative schools: A case study of Kevin Gonzales. *International Journal of Qualitative Studies in Education, 24* (1), 1–20.

Kleiner, B., Porch, R., & Farris, E. (2002). *Public alternative schools and programs for students at risk of education failure: 2000–2001* (NCES 2002–2004). U.S. Dept. of Education. Washington, DC: National Center for Education Statistics. Retrieved from http://nces.ed.gov/pubs2002/2002004.pdf

Lamarre, P. (2008). English education in Québec: Issues and challenges. In R. Y. Bourhis (Ed.), *The vitality of the English-speaking communities of Québec: From community decline to revival.* Montreal, QC: CEETUM, Université de Montréal.

Luke, A., & Woods, A. (2009). Policy and adolescent literacy. In L. Christenbury, R. Bomer, & P. Smagorinsky (Eds.), *Handbook of adolescent literacy research* (pp. 197–219). New York: Guilford.

Lupart, J. (2000). Students with exceptional learning needs: At-risk, utmost. Paper presented at the Pan-Canadian Educational Research Agenda Symposium: Children and Youth at Risk, Ottawa.

Lupart, J. (2008). Achieving excellence and equity in Canadian schools: Can inclusion bridge the gap? Paper presented at the International Inclusive Education Research (IIER) Professorial Series (2011).

Lafortune, L., Prud'homme, L., Sorin, N., et al. (2011). *Manifeste pour une école compétente.* Presses de l'Université du Québec, Québec, Canada.

McKinsey & Co. (2010). Knowledge is power: Toward a Québec-wide effort to increase student retention. In McKinsey & Co., *Report of the action group on student retention and success in Québec, Québec, Canada.* Retrieved from www.bmo.com/bmo/files/images/7/1/knowedge_is_power.pdf

MELS (Gouvernement du Québec, Ministère de l'Éducation, du Loisir et du Sport). (2001–present). *Québec Education Reform (QEP): Secondary English Language Arts Curriculum.* Retrieved from http://www.mels.gouv.qc.ca/sections/programmeFormation/index_en.asp

Merchant, G. (2009). Literacy in virtual worlds. *Journal of Research in Reading, 32*(1), 38–57.

Munoz, J. S. (2004). The social construction of alternative education: Re-examining the margins of public education for at-risk Chicano/a students. *High School Journal, 88*(2), 3–22.

Porter, G. (2008). Making Canadian schools inclusive: A call to action. *Canadian Education Association, 48*(2), 62–66.

Quinn, M., & Poirier, J. (2006). *Study of effective alternative education programs: Final grant report.* Washington, DC: American Institute for Research.

Raywid, M. (1999). History and issues of alternative schools. *Education Digest, 64*(9), 47–51.

Rymes, B. (2001). *Conversational borderlands: Language and identity in an alternative urban high school.* New York: Teachers College Press.

Slee, R. (2011). *The irregular school: Exclusion, schooling, and inclusive education.* New York: Routledge.

Smith, W., Foster, W., & Donahue, H. (Eds.). (1999). *The contemporary education scene in Québec: A handbook for policy makers, administrators, and educators.* Montréal, QC: McGill University: Office of Research and Educational Policy.

Smith, A., Peled, M., & Albert, M. (2008). *Making the grade: A review of alternative education programs in British Columbia.* Vancouver, BC: McCreary Center Society.

Stanford University (2008). *California Alternative Education Research Project*. Retrieved from http://jgc.stanford.edu/our_work/alt-ed.html

Stevens, L. P. (2011). Literacy, capital, and education: A view from immigrant youth. *Theory Into Practice, 50*(2), 133–140.

Swadener, B., & Lubeck, S. (Eds.). (1995). *Children and families "at promise": Deconstructing the discourse of risk*. Albany: SUNY Press.

Valencia, R. (2010). At-risk students or at-risk schools? In *Dismantling contemporary deficit thinking: Educational thought and practice* (pp. 101–125). New York: Routledge.

Vasudevan, L., & Campano, G. (2009). The social production of adolescent risk and the promise of adolescent literacies. *Review of Educational Research, 33*, 310–353.

Wilson, J. (2000). Doing justice to inclusion. *European Journal of Special Needs Education, 15*(3), 297–304.

Wishart, D. (2009). *The rose that grew from concrete: Teaching and learning with disenfranchised youth*. University of Alberta Press.

Wotherspoon, T., & Schissel, B. (2000). Risky business?: "At-risk" designations and culturally diverse schooling. Discussion paper presented to the Council of Ministers of Education Canada, Pan-Canadian Education Research Agenda. Retrieved from http://www.cesc.ca/pceradocs/2000/00Wotherspoon_Schissel_e.pdf

Wright, A., Frenay, M., Monette, M., Tomen, B., Sauve, L., Smith, C., et al. (2008). *Institutional strategy and practice: Increasing the odds of access and success at the post-secondary level for under-represented students*. Montreal, QC: Canada Millenium Scholarship Foundation.

CHAPTER NINE

Relocalization IN THE Market Economy

Critical Literacies and Media Production in an Urban English Classroom

CYNTHIA LEWIS, CANDANCE DOERR-STEVENS,
JESSICA DOCKTER TIERNEY, & CASSANDRA SCHARBER

"But Ms. Haas, you spent all year teaching us that this stuff is corrupt!"

Ms. Haas, an urban teacher who taught an 11/12 English class focused on critical media analysis and production, shared with one of us that a student in her class had said these words. The student wanted Ms. Haas to consider that the public relations unit they were undertaking at the end of the school year seemed to contradict the critical media focus of the course itself. Ms. Haas smiled when she relayed the student's comment, pleased, as were we, to find that the critical focus of the course had taken hold to the extent that a student would challenge one of the course units. Ironically, Ms. Haas created this unit on public relations not as a tool for marketing corporate products or services, but rather as a tool for critical intervention. Specifically, Ms. Haas's purpose in this unit was to focus on using public relations techniques to promote the school, with the hope of producing a counter-narrative to the debilitating discourses that malign urban high schools such as this one. This scenario represents the conundrum that we wish to write about in this chapter: a tension inherent in critical literacies classrooms given the pervasiveness of a market economy that shapes student and institutional identities as well as classroom pedagogy.

English educators have long focused on critical media literacies in an effort to challenge the pervasive media content that persistently reproduces dominant ideologies. Although typically media literacy courses focus on close analyses of media, scholars in the field have claimed that media production should be at the center of any critical media curriculum in order to foster critical perspectives that cannot be developed through analysis alone (Fabos, 2008; Kellner, 2004; Sholle & Denski, 1994). The increasing use of digital media tools in schools has provided new avenues for critical media production within a critical literacies framework. However, some scholars contend that involving students in media production is not enough unless the social and political dynamics of this work are examined. Hill and Vasudevan (2008) and Morrell (2007), for example, argue that it is important for researchers and teachers to consider the particular conditions and contexts that shape how media producers resolve tensions between social reproduction and critique.

In an effort to understand how students as media producers resolve these tensions, our research examined media practices as students partnered with a multinational firm (hereafter called "The Firm") to use media content to market their own school (names of participants and school are pseudonyms). Having learned that the school had hired a public relations firm to promote the school, Ms. Haas convinced her principal that students in her media studies class be allowed to participate in the project. Trained by the marketing firm, the students produced promotional videos, news broadcasts, logos, and newsletters, all of which were published via an online social network software, in this case using Ning, which was publicly available at the time and through part of the following school year. After a discussion of the theoretical grounding for this chapter and a brief description of the context and methodology, we focus on the competing discourses that shaped the unit and the way that these discourses were taken up by the teacher and her students. We follow this section with an example of one student's navigation of the complex terrain of the classroom and conclude the chapter with implications for critical literacies research and practice.

GLOBAL AND LOCAL DISCOURSES AND PRACTICES

This study draws from interdisciplinary work in critical linguistics and social semiotics, especially contemporary work related to globalization and mediated discourse. Globalization is marked by increased "flows" (Appadurai, 2000) that expand the connectivity between ideas, bodies, and identities across local spheres, which are continually shaped by the global interdependence of economies and technologies. Social practices in local spheres are always navigated across different scales (e.g., local, institutional, and global scales) that represent differential access to discursive (and material) resources. Social theorists who study globalization view homogeneity as one effect of the global market (Bauman, 1998; Pennycook, 2010; Santos, 2006). Related to public education, globalization redefines local practices in schools amid intensely competitive notions of what counts as legitimate knowledge. Communities vie for market niches that appear to provide viable choices (e.g., specialized charter schools) but ultimately remain viable only if they meet homogeneous national and international measures of "accountability," such as the standardized ranking of academic achievement (e.g., the widely publicized rankings of the Programme for International Assessment). As Santos (2006) stated:

> Globalization seems to combine universality and the elimination of national borders, on the one hand, with rising particularity, local diversity, ethnic identity, and a return to communitarian values, on the other. In other words, globalization appears to be the other side of localization, and vice versa. (p. 393)

Pennycook (2010) argued that global discourses are "relocalized" (p. x) through local practices. These local institutional contexts and histories of participation create locally manifested ways of being, producing, and interpreting that are constituted in global spheres such as neoliberal notions of school choice and international assessments of student achievement. Practices at the classroom and school levels are integrally shaped by these distal factors and "reaccented" (Brooks, 2011, p. 75) locally. Like Santos, Pennycook (2010) discussed two seemingly conflicting effects of global forces on local practices. On the one hand, globalization demands homogenization—for example, a "standard" for what a school should look like in multiple localities: standardized achievement scores, graduation rates, and so forth. On the other hand, the homogeneity produced through globalization also has the potential to produce difference because global homogeneity can only be understood through its inflection in local practice, which is, in Pennycook's view, dynamic and capable of resistance and rearticulation. It is this side of the global market—this side of school "choice"—that the critical media is leveraging. East High School, the site for our study, was a case in point.

Our knowledge of East High developed over four years (2007–2011) during which several of us conducted research and participated in program development. We first conducted a study of critical engagement in a documentary film class (Lewis & Dockter Tierney, 2011) and later developed and studied a ninth- through twelfth-grade interdisciplinary digital media studies program (Scharber, Lewis, & Beach, 2010). The public relations unit that is the focus of this chapter occurred in the spring quarter of 2009, during the first school year of the digital media studies program. As already mentioned, the teacher initiated the unit as an impromptu part of her curriculum based on the opportunity she saw to incorporate The Firm's expertise and provide her students with a project that involved an authentic purpose and audience (creating public relations products for their school in order to "sell" it to potential students and boost its reputation in the district and neighborhood).

Keying into the popular discourse of 21st-century skills, the critical media course we studied was a site of resistance to the perception of East as a "default school," as one teacher put it. It was a site that attempted to rearticulate the meaning of rigor—the rigor of critical engagement in digital media production—which students described in interviews from an earlier study to be the "most intellectually challenging" and "hardest" work they've ever been asked to do in school (Dockter, Haug, & Lewis, 2010).

East High School was low status in this Midwestern metropolitan school district, with many problems typical of urban schools. Standardized test scores were low and school enrollment decreasing. The shift from neighborhood schools to "magnet" programs, each with a special academic focus drawing students from across the district, fueled the use of various discourses. Informed by neoliberal notions of school choice, district schools were placed in competition for student enrollment, forcing schools to market themselves as products to be consumed. When looking at the local discourses involved in the school's identity, East High School was located in a mostly white lower-middle to middle-class neighborhood, and had a history that included a good deal of pride as a neighborhood school. In recent years, few neighborhood families sent their children to East, yet its more illustrious history figured prominently in the language and lore surrounding the school (as gleaned from field notes and interview data). Teachers and students alike hoped that East could return to some version of its glory days, albeit one that celebrated the more recent demographics of its student body, which included at the time of this study, 83 percent who qualified for free and reduced lunch, 39 percent English-language learners, and 90 percent students of color (46 percent African or African American, 33 percent Latino/a, 8 percent Asian American, 3 percent American Indian). The class we studied was representative of this demographic distribution.

Informed by this view of classrooms as relocalized spaces, we were interested in the contradictions inherent in creating promotional media as part of a classroom that had been steeped all year in critical media literacies. We were especially interested in how students responded to these contradictions and negotiated competing purposes, audiences, and desires as they created promotional media.

MEDIATED DISCOURSE ANALYSIS AS THEORY AND METHOD

Our research is a close qualitative examination of a one-month unit focused on digital media analysis and production. We had 27 participants in the study representing all students in the class and the classroom teacher. Four students served as focal participants, one for each of the public relations media formats described below. The classroom teacher, Ms. Haas, a white female with 17 years of urban teaching experience, developed a similar process for each unit, which involved students accessing multiple media texts and genres; critically analyzing those texts for how technical elements positioned viewers to believe, feel, or think in certain ways; and creating, sharing, and reflecting on their own media projects. Units during this yearlong course focused on the following: how the media defines and creates our modern culture; media representations; power of the media to create awareness and change in the world; propaganda focused on news and advertising; and the 21st-Century Marketing Campaign for East High School (the unit focused on in this chapter). Major projects included media ethnographies, wikis that researched and exposed corporate ethics, spoof ads, and the promotional media discussed in this chapter.

For the public relations marketing unit, we served as participant-observers in the class three times weekly for four weeks. Each of us facilitated one of four student groups working on public relations for the school in one of the following formats: YouTube videos, logos for a billboard, a newsletter, and a Ning for social networking. Students' unfamiliarity with YouTube content creation and with Nings as a format for social networking caused them to gravitate to the more familiar formats of billboards and newsletters when initially asked to choose a group. However, once a representative from The Firm came to discuss the new media options of video creation and social networking, students became interested, and the groups were formed. As the project progressed, and in keeping with the way that media formats converge, the Ning group became blended with the YouTube and broadcast news groups. The broadcast news features were uploaded to YouTube, which was linked to the Ning. Students in the Ning group did not have end products to produce, such as a logo, newsletter, or video, and so had more time to participate in video production and use the videos to create a more engaging site with which to reach out to current and potential students.

Data sources included corporate documents, field notes, recordings of classroom interactions, interviews with focal students, and informal conversations with students as they produced media content. In analyzing this data, we applied the theory and method of mediated discourse analysis (MDA) and geosemiotic theory, which we drew from the work of Scollon (2001), Scollon and Scollon (2003) and Norris and Jones (2005). Briefly, this work regarded meaning-making to be both semiotically discursive and material. It foregrounded *action* in social spaces and provided a lens through which to understand the meaning of texts and tools in practice. Since social action is carried out by social actors/agents who interact with mediational means in sites of engagement, mediational means such as texts and language "are carriers of social, cultural and historical formations that amplify certain social actions and limit others" (Jones & Norris, 2005, p. 49). In the mediated action we highlight in the next section, the mediational means are the digital media tools of video editing and Ning, along with specific voice-enhanced "vocaloid" videos that one student, Ellen, viewed and appropriated in order to create her promotional video. Vocaloids are videos made using the Vocaloid software, which use synthesizer effects to blend voice and music along with images and video frequently appropriated from Japanese anime.

Scollon and Scollon in *Discourses in Place* (2003) used the term "emplacement" (142) to explain the relationship between objects and their environment. These texts *emplaced* in an English classroom seem commonplace to those for whom media analysis is an ordinary component of English studies and integral to this particular class with its regular use of media texts. However, the text as a site of meaning-making in the classroom can be interpreted and produced differently depending on repeated social performances that index the text as having a particular function or meaning in local practice (Lewis & Dockter Tierney, 2011). In other words, the way that teachers and students repeatedly responded to or interact with a text produces and reinforces the text's function in the local context. Naturally, given that there are many social actors in a classroom, texts can have multiple functions and meanings at once or over time. In the next section, Ellen's vocaloid serves as an example.

"Practice," in the language of mediated discourse analysis, is a linked chain of mediated actions and histories of participation. As Thibault (2004) explained:

> Meaning-making is a semiotic-discursive phenomenon in the sense that its dynamical processes enact meaningful patterns and relations that integrate the particular occasion or situation to the systems of semantic and other semiotic categories that the members of a given community or social network recognize and interpret as meaningful. Furthermore these categories serve to link the particular event and the particular individuals who participate in that event to other activities, other practices, other individuals and social institutions on diverse space-time scales that go beyond the particular here-now event. (pp. 6–7)

Particularly important in this passage is the concept of linkage across space-time scales that include the histories of participation—or practice, to use the mediated discourse term—within and outside the "site of engagement" (Scollon, 2001, p. 3) where the mediated action occurs. Such histories include the school's illustrious past and current low status, the teacher's passion for critical media analysis and fervent desire to revise the narrative about her school, and Ellen's identity as a white adolescent girl in a very diverse school as well as her de facto role as sole creator of the video. Our analysis depended on these linkages of actions and practice. "The place to look for struggles of power and ideology, according to MDA, is not, however, in any one of these practices, but in the way multiple practices converge to influence concrete social actions" (Jones & Norris, 2005, p. 10.) The next section explains the competing discourses and practices that played a role in the creation of Ellen's video and shaped the meaning of critical literacy in the classroom.

COMPETING DISCOURSES AND PRACTICES

In this section, we highlight the competing discourses and practices at work in the classroom that influenced the social actions of students as they created media products around the stated common goal of "marketing" the school. We demonstrate, at the same time, that students' own purposes and perceived audiences were often different than those outlined by the public relations firm and even, at times, by Ms. Haas. Like their teacher, most students were interested in offering positive representations of their school since they were very aware of the school's low status and declining enrollment. However, instead of using corporate- or school-sanctioned genres, students pursued their own agendas and styles of expression. This section offers an overview of conflicting discourses, purposes, and audiences interspersed with examples from multiple students and situations that reveal the complexity of digital media marketing within a critical literacies framework.

Competing discourses: Marketing versus advocacy

During their first session with students in the digital media studies classroom, the representatives from The Firm made the goal of the marketing unit clear. A slide from their first PowerPoint read: "Your Job: You are a junior marketing executive, helping to create and execute marketing for East High School." And another slide read: "Your Goal: to increase awareness of programs and opportunities available at the school among key audiences." The representatives went on to define the idea of branding for the students, explaining the concept by emphasizing the discrete skills of "defining a product," "distinguishing it from other competitive offerings," and "controlling an image."

Framing the discourses of the unit this way from the outset, representatives from The Firm established a discourse of business marketing within the classroom. For the students, this discourse was compelling because they believed they were being given a special assignment, or in terms of the marketing executives who presented the challenge, a special "job." Ms. Haas, too, promoted the discourse of marketing when talking with students about the unit. To one group of students, for example, she gave this praise: "[One of the public relations representatives] thinks your video is awesome. She thinks the Ning is awesome. I'm sure she went to the YouTube channel and saw the colors and banner and everything matched. She said to tell you all that I should give you a raise. You're junior account execs, right?" Despite being frustrated with The Firm in ways we describe below, Ms. Haas promoted the market discourse they established in order to frame the project and students' involvement as special and important.

At the same time that the unit carried with it a discourse of business shaped by notions of executives, earning raises, and being given a job, representatives from The Firm wanted to control the image of the public relations firm as not so much a multinational corporation, but a bold company of "advocates" who are "shaping the game." In fact, the firm's logo stated, "Advocacy starts here," and when one of the representatives described the firm as "part of a conglomerate," her colleague was quick to jump in and explain that conglomerate means they are a "family" with "a family of expertise." The public relations representatives used language that suggested diversity and variation, favoring terms such as "define" and "distinguish" in relation to the school as a product, and the language of personal connection—for example, "family" over "conglomerate." These terms served to obscure the power relations at work, including what it meant to "distinguish" a product so that consumers would believe they have the power to select the superior product among a field of choices. Ironically, despite the desire for uniqueness through the niche markets of public magnet and charter schools (including large public schools that create "brands" through small learning communities or a whole-school focus), consumers of schools seek typical indicators of success such as performance on achievement tests and strong statistics for college admission. Thus, schools that serve niche markets survive only if they meet homogenous indicators of success.

Tensions between the discourses of market and advocacy led to questions from some students about whether The Firm was providing their time and expertise free of charge, questions that both the teacher and the representatives skirted at various times. This, and the fact that one of the public relations representatives frequently talked about how special she thought it was for the school to offer a class like this one, also led to a mentality among some of the students that The Firm was there to help them save their low-status school, which was in serious danger of being closed. In reality, however, The Firm, which was paid by the school for three hours of prep time and two hours of travel time for every one hour of teaching (at $250 per hour), did not offer any assistance beyond their contract even when Ms. Haas sent inquiries via email and even when the newsletter, one of the media produced in the unit, was in danger of not getting printed because there was no money available to do so. At moments like this, some of the students saw The Firm in a new light. Sarah, from the newsletter group, said in class one day, "They got paid already and they can't shovel out like $200."

For Ms. Haas and the students in the media studies classroom, advocacy meant something different. Ms. Haas, for instance, wanted the project to promote a sense of continuity and history. She used the word "legacy" throughout the unit to remind students that this project would connect them to the history of their school—back to East's better days and a "better" reputation—and would also be something they would pass on. It was for this reason that she persuaded Sarah, a leader in the newsletter group whose family had a long history of attending East, to change the chosen name for the publication from *The East Side Gazette* to *The New Standard*, which echoed the publication's former name, *The Standard*.

In addition, Ms. Haas saw this unit as an avenue to regain a sense of community in the school. She was particularly excited about possibilities for the Ning, despite the fact that students were reluctant to sign up for this group because none had heard of a Ning before. When she shared the media tool with her classes, several students asked that they be switched into this group. Pictures from homecoming, pep rallies, and other events throughout the year as well as special groups created by students and staff caught their attention. In addition, the Ning posted information about upcoming school events such as the blood drive. Ms. Haas shared her excitement about the Ning with her students, telling them, "This is what we need."

Although The Firm set up a clear role for the students in the media studies classroom—to act as executives and market their school—and established a business discourse that motivated the students and their teacher, competing discourses around the school's need for a historical and future legacy as well as an avenue for community created a tension at the outset of the unit. Ms. Haas was a confident and creative teacher who advocated bringing The Firm into the classroom. She needed The Firm's expertise in order for her and her students to learn the basics of public relations, but was fully in charge of the groups and their progress after the initial workshop for each of the four public relations genres that students would produce. While Ms. Haas attempted to maintain the discourse of marketing in order to push her students to produce powerful media, she also felt very strongly about the need for students to be in charge of their own identity representations and speak back to a reputation of urban youth as apathetic and incompetent. In this way, marketing worked as both a tool for taking control of an image of urban youth while also demonstrating to students that, in the real world, money (and offering services only when being paid) could trump more ephemeral goals of maintaining a legacy and creating community. Ms. Haas's practice, in this case, was mediated by institutional histories as well as dominant ideologies about urban schools and urban youth that operate both locally and in broader contexts.

Competing purposes: Critical analysis versus production

Another tension that emerged during the unit was between critical analysis and production of media. Critical analysis of media was a cornerstone of the media studies course throughout the year, and Ms. Haas taught students that the best way to understand and challenge manipulation was through production. For example, in one unit, Ms. Haas had students analyze and identify various forms of propaganda and then had students create counter-propaganda in response. In another unit, Ms. Haas had students research the ethical practices and advertising of multinational corporations and create wikis to educate the public about the hidden practices of well-known companies such as Coca-Cola and Nike. And during the marketing unit, Ms. Haas reminded students again, "There is no better way to understand and be proactive than to produce something."

Yet students received a very different message from the public relations firm. Critical analysis according to the public relations representatives was a "landscape analysis" completed in order to further define a product. This analysis served the goal of controlling the image of a product, in this case, East High, and manipulating an audience, in this case, those who might attend East. For Ms. Haas, critical pedagogy involved a partnering of analysis with production in an effort to avoid manipulation and to create counter-narratives. For the public relations representatives, the benefit of the relationship between analysis and production *was* manipulation—and ultimately profit.

This tension was best demonstrated by an example from the first visit by the public relations firm during the unit. As they explained to the class that day, one of the main clients for The Firm was the U.S. Army; they gave the example of a public relations event where the Dallas Cowboy Cheerleaders visited high schools and challenged students to push-up contests to find out if they were "Army ready." Cynthia, who was observing the class on that day, was interested in students' responses to this example because earlier in the year Ms. Haas had used Army recruiting videos for the purposes of critique and students had identified clearly the videos' techniques of manipulation and propaganda. Surprisingly to us, neither the students nor Ms. Haas said anything nor responded in any way visibly to The Firm's Army connection.

Instead, as already mentioned, many of the students thought it was generous of The Firm to come and teach them. One student who was part of the Ning group, for instance, mentioned several times that she was so pleased that the public relations firm "funded us"—although the opposite was true. However, Ms. Haas later shared that one of her students (as reported at the start of this chapter) remarked that the public relations project seemed weird because "you spent all year teaching us that this stuff [corporate manipulation] is corrupt." To this, Ms. Haas responded by saying that they would be promoting their school, which was not the same as promoting a product. And yet, later, as students argued over the branding of the billboard during a class presentation of each group's work, Ms. Haas stated, "marketing is marketing"—no matter the product involved. In this way, the purpose of the marketing unit, while exciting to students for its real-world appeal, conflicted with the purpose of critical analysis that Ms. Haas had taught to the students all year. Was it possible to be critical consumers and producers of media while also being savvy product marketers? The next section further complicates this question and underscores Pennycook's (2010) concept of relocalization.

RELOCALIZED PRACTICE: AN ILLUSTRATION

Perhaps most helpful in understanding classroom practice as relocalized in relation to competing global discourses, audiences, and purposes is to look at one of the media products made by the students in the class. One such project was a promotional video (PV) created by Ellen and her group, developed for the purpose of attracting youth to enroll in this urban high school. In this district, families had some degree of choice in selecting a high school (although complicated by local politics, socioeconomics, and zoning and transportation factors beyond the scope of this chapter), and Ellen's video would need to appeal to several audiences, including parents, youth, classroom peers, and her teacher.

Ellen was the primary creator of the PV. Ellen and the other two students in her group were part of the YouTube Channel group, which was in charge of making and managing videos for a student-sponsored YouTube channel. The videos and channel were linked to the school Ning site. We discuss her video not because we think it represents an effective PV, but rather because her video and its process of production illustrate the competing forces discussed in the previous section and serve as an example of relocalized practice.

Relocalized production process

Ellen's media production process reflected conflicting definitions of "marketing." First, according to the multinational public relations firm working with the class, "marketing" involved defining and controlling the image of product via branding. Ms. Haas's definition of marketing differed from that of The Firm in that she focused on promotion and marketing as selling a product via product placement. In other words, Ms. Haas urged that the promotional video (PV) should educate the audience about East High School in a way that presented the school as a "desirable" product. In this situation, "marketing," with its various definitions, was a construct of the global market, which in Ms. Haas's class, was reframed for local purposes.

Ellen's preferred style of marketing involved selling an identity or lifestyle via product association, a further relocalization of the marketing construct. For Ellen, the purpose of her PV was to market an identity as a product and, in turn, market the institution (her school) through selling that particular identity. Ellen's understanding of "marketing" was informed by various sources including the media analysis class, the public relations firm, and her own media consumption, particularly that of Japanese anime. Ellen described the best PVs as those that play on big screens at "fun, exciting events," such as the "vocaloids" played at concerts or in dance clubs. While these PVs are not the main focus of the audience's attention, Ellen claimed that they were absorbed as part of the "cool event." While the other students in Ellen's group were more inclined to go with the teacher's vision of a PV, Ellen was persistent in putting forward her vision for the PV. These differing views of what it meant to market and promote a product led to much delay and conflict among the group members in terms of deciding on an idea and getting started with the filming and editing.

Production delays were further fueled by conflicting perceptions of intended audiences and purposes. While Ms. Haas made it clear to students that it was their perspective that would make the social media appealing to other students, telling them, "As adults, we come from a different point of view than you...as the teenagers who are using this site, we want to know what you think," she also named the intended audiences for the media pieces as parents of current and prospective students, district administrators or "gatekeepers," and her professional peers. Ms. Haas explained to her students the importance of attending to these different audiences:

> You have to keep a couple things in mind, you guys, is that we're trying to convince the school district, you know "gatekeepers" to open the gates and let you guys have some power, and in order to do that we have to play by some of their rules. So we can't be having people put up, you know, cursing, and things like that....This channel is going to say East High School, it is going to be public, so we want to make sure we are representing ourselves in a way that is responsible, and what not.

For Ms. Haas, the idea of audience and purpose in this unit was very tied to a sense of public performance of the digital media course. Her focus on rules and responsible representation highlighted a sense of public evaluation by other authorities. Thus, students were expected to use language and images that would appeal to teens, but at the same time keep in mind the reputation of the school and its students by framing it in a positive light for parents, teachers, and community members.

Ms. Haas was open with students about this dilemma over public content. "As adults," she told them, "we are worried about safety," and went on to explain that media content had to be carefully guarded for the well-being of students and with attention to copyright issues. While she, like her students, was excited about the Ning becoming a school-wide social media tool, she told students, "The Ning should grow beyond this class, as long as it's about East." Ms. Haas then suggested that they limit content to only events and images related to the school. With little resistance, students in the class agreed with Ms. Haas and decided that the student administrators of the Ning group would be in charge of controlling all content to ensure its appropriateness.

In this way, students' ability to share their identity affiliations beyond the walls of the classroom and the school became limited, a fact that frustrated Ms. Haas behind the scenes, but to her students, she resolved, "We need to start thinking about these issues as we become more global." The local practices of the classroom—where students' identity affiliations were valued and mobilized in media production—were "relocalized" (Pennycook, 2010) by global constructs of urban youth and by judgments about what counts as legitimate knowledge, and by whom, in competitive schools.

A concern for rules and responsible representation were not, however, among the criteria for the various audiences that Ellen perceived for the video. In viewing the piece as a PV to attract students to East, Ellen saw the main intended audience as prospective eighth graders choosing a high school. In particular she wanted to attract students like herself, whom she described as artistic students or "artsy kids." In addition, her audience involved her own peers. She talked about sharing the video with her friends who go to other schools, including art schools. When asked about her intended audience, Ellen described the group:

> I tried to do a specific group of people like eighth graders and more artistic people, like vocaloid people, cause they're artistic....I wanted, basically like any artist, to use pictures to tell a story. And they [artistic eighth graders] would probably understand that. They would think, "Oh, this is cool, maybe I can do this. I can express myself through the media and get credit for it." Maybe then hopefully they will come to East. And that's what I really wanted.

In Ellen's description of her intended audience, she positioned the PV not as a text that explicitly promoted East, but instead as an example of something students could do if they were to go to East. In other words, the PV was associated with freedom of expression in terms of students' academic work, a quality that Ellen believed would attract artistic eighth graders to East. Of course, expression is never purely transparent. It is mediated by many competing discourses, which often inspire and/or require relocalization. In the case of the students' media products, the global discourses of product branding and neoliberal concepts of school choice pushed and pulled at students' production decisions, leading to various product positionings or emplacements.

Product emplacement

In looking specifically at the media product and how it is emplaced, it is important to remember that texts as sites of meaning-making can be interpreted and produced differently depending on repeated social performances that index the text as having a particular function in local practice. In this case, the primary genre Ellen had in mind was vocaloid videos. Ellen described vocaloid videos as cool videos played at events to promote a hip, artsy youth culture. Ellen identified the *Hatsune Miku—Hiro Sai* as one of her favorite vocaloid videos. (The video can be viewed at http://www.youtube.com/watch?v=mUAAnDJ6060.) In this video, the female persona Hatsune Miku (created using the voice-synthesizing software Vocaloid 2) sings the song Hiro Sai. Similar to an animated music video, the song is illustrated by a series still anime drawings and video of Hatsune Miku running through the streets in search of a mysterious person or love interest.

Influenced by the vocaloid genre, Ellen's video also featured a love story, but instead of anime drawings and video, her video included a series of still photographs of the school and of two students as the characters who fall in love. All images were set to piano music with a hip-hop beat composed by one of the group members.

Ellen's initial plan was to make a vocaloid video similar the *Hatsune Miko—Hiro Sai* video described above. She had made anime sketches for the video and had hoped her group members would make the music. Yet through repeated conversations and discussions about what constituted a "promotional video" with her group members and Ms. Haas, the final media product showed a compromise of various elements that underscored that texts are produced and interpreted as having particular functions in local practice.

First, in terms of genre, Ellen's video followed the typical vocaloid narrative, which is that of a suspenseful love story; yet due to the urging of her teacher and peers that the product to be promoted, East High School, should be evident in the video, Ellen decided to situate the story in the school. She did this by including still photos of the school mural, a school basketball game and the school mascot. A group member digitally synthesized the music for the final piece.

It is perhaps with image selection and editing that Ellen, who did all of the video editing for the project, was most able to realize her original plans of making a vocaloid video. Similar to a vocaloid video, Ellen used a series of motion and zoom features to add motion to still shots. In particular, she mimicked and appropriated a series of profile shots used in the vocaloid video into her own video. (See Figure 1.)

This appropriation of image editing reveals Ellen's resistance to the more traditional forms of PV that were presented in class through incorporating elements of vocaloid videos, which she viewed as effective promotion. The repeated image of a girl's face from slightly different angles is resonant of the vocaloid video that served as Ellen's inspiration, but in the form of an actual student at East High emplaced in the school's hallway. Ellen's appropriation of semiotic signs can be understood in terms of the process of "entextualization," discussed by Blommaert (2005). This process involves a text that is removed from its context (decontextualized) and placed in a new context (recontextualized) in order to produce a "preferred reading" (Bauman & Briggs, 1990, p. 73). This process, we argue, is central to digital media

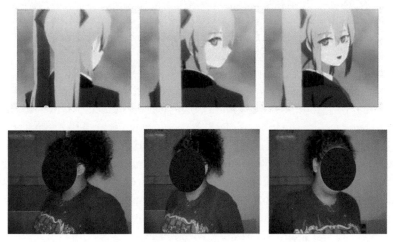

Figure 1: Image Editing in Ellen's Video and Vocaloid Video
Top: Hatsune Miku—Hiro Sai (Vocaloid Video)
Bottom: Project (Ellen's Video)

production and to critical literacy. In this case, Ellen's promotional video served the process of entextualizing Higo Sai's vocaloid video so that the initiating text was removed from its interactional setting and placed in a new context. This new context (a Ning) included other media meant to build community within the school and attract new families to the school. Thus, the recontextualized video is entextualized as a new text with a "metadiscourse" that stipulates how it should be interpreted (Blommaert, 2005, p. 47). This process resonates with a concept discussed by Scollon and Scollon (2003) that signs are emplaced in relation to other signs, producing a "double indexicality." Each sign "indexes a discourse that authorizes its placement" (p. 205), in this case vocaloid video, but "is never isolated from other signs in its environment, embodied or disembodied" (p. 205). The other signs were those within the Ning, within the images presented as examples appropriate for the marketing of East High, and within the competing discourses of marketing and advocacy, which regulated the processes of production and interpretation.

But these processes can never be entirely regulated. Ellen's post-production reflection essay revealed Ellen's use of the media production process as an active process of identity exploration both for herself and her school as a possible community that supports her. As Ellen explains,

> It was hard to put the marketing into something artistic, as I think the two are separate. But after talking with [fellow student], I remembered something we watched about ads and advertising. They said something along the lines of "we are just making ads for ourselves" and that struck home and made me able to continue.

In other words, her motivation for completing the PV was less about promoting her school on The Firm's terms and more about figuring out how she viewed her school and where she saw herself in that image. Through making the video, she was able to entextualize herself into the East school body.

Both Ellen and her teacher acted in ways that were constituted in global discourses. Ellen's work existed on multiple spatial and temporal scales. She was not only creating a video in the here and now, she was enmeshed in who she imagined herself to be as well as the kind of place she wanted her school to be. In a sense, she was creating what Holland, Lachicotte, Skinner, and Cain (1998) would call a "figured world" where particular ways of being and acting are valued over others (p. 52) but where meanings and structures are also transformed through ongoing cultural production (Bartlett, 2005). Ellen improvised within the figured world of her classroom to create a video that imagined another figured world with students whose artistic interests and identities meshed with her own.

CONCLUSIONS AND SIGNIFICANCE

Our focus in this chapter has been on how critical media literacies are influenced by global market forces interrelated with local practices. Although Ellen's PV was at odds with The Firm's examples, she used her video to rearticulate the concept of promotion rather than dismiss it. Ellen found a way to insert her interests and identities into the PV, but she did so with the intention of "selling" the school to other artistic youth like herself. She was not concerned about boosting enrollment for funding as were the administrators who originally hired The Firm, nor did she express her teacher's concern for rewriting the negative narrative that maligns urban schools. Nonetheless, the marketing focus permeated her discourse and practice as she sought to attract more students to the school and determined that the best way to accomplish this promotional goal was to represent the school through her own interests in (the globally marketed) vocaloids and anime—a kind of promotional affinity space, to use Gee's (2004) term for a space where social actors share interests, activities, and identities.

Pennycook (2010) argued that representational and embodied practices are always relocalized. We have tried to demonstrate how this relocalization occurred in an instructional unit that revealed how the global market economy discursively and materially shaped student and institutional identities as well as classroom pedagogy.

As described earlier in this chapter, students had engaged in highly critical analyses and production of media content throughout the year (e.g., corporate ethics wikis). However, their media content for this school promotion project did not reflect the same level of critique. Other media products for this unit included a school newsletter describing end-of-the-school-year events; billboards and school logos attempting to brand the East High mascot and school colors; video updates broadcasting topics of student interest; and the very popular Ning space, which hosted most of the final media products and much student discussion. While most of these media products were effective in distributing the news, events, and newly "branded" image of East High, they were not critical of school or corporate authorities, nor were they as genre adventurous in their expression as Ellen's video. We attribute this first to the competing discourses of doing school and performing media competency according to marketing goals. With these competing frameworks came conflicting knowledge economies and media practices (e.g., critique vs. branding). Second, given the expanded audience and visibility of the media content, students were concerned about how their work would be received. Because they were often ascribed identities of underachievers, this media production event offered opportunities to perform competency for their local and metropolitan communities.

As our example shows, students focused on performing media-literate identities rather than on producing critical media content. However, in reaccenting global discourses such as the language of neoliberalism associated with school choice, students actually produced what could be viewed as critical media literacies. Much like their teacher, many saw value in producing counter-narratives that would market their urban school. Global discourses are themselves various. Ellen's vocaloid vision was supported by an entertainment industry that markets to youth like her as a target audience. Although she viewed her artistic aesthetic as individual and expressive, rather than determined by market economies, she used what could be viewed as critical media literacies to fuse the artistic vision she thought would best sell her school with the vision of her teacher and classmates who wanted realistic profiles of students in the school setting.

The multinational marketing firm's participation in this unit placed in high relief the tension between critical literacies and market economy. However, we argue that this tension, which permeates all aspects of critical literacy pedagogy and practice, is under-examined. The students and teacher in this class were social actors whose relocalization of the global market produced a complicated and dynamic form of critical media literacies praxis. This has led us to reconsider what counts as "critical" in critical literacies pedagogy. Our examination of the mediated action involved in this example showed how objects, images, and language were used to both appropriate and remake global market discourses. It also showed that the social actors involved had competing desires and interests that they viewed as central to promoting their school in a competitive market based on niche offerings as well as standard indicators of success. We argue that the meaning of critical literacies should be re-examined through an analysis of how social actors in the classroom relocalize global discourses as they appropriate and remake texts and signs.

REFERENCES

Appadurai, A. (2000). Grassroots globalization and the research imagination. *PublicCulture, 12*, 1–19.

Bartlett, L. (2005). Identity work and cultural artifacts in literacy learning and use: A sociocultural analysis. *Language and Education, 19*, 1–9.

Bauman, R., & Briggs, C. L. (1990). Poetics and performance as critical perspectives on language and social life. *Annual Review of Anthropology 19*, 59–88.

Bauman, Z. (1998). *Globalization: The human consequences.* New York: Columbia University Press.

Blommaert, J. (2006). Sociolinguistic scales. *Working Papers in Urban Language & Literacies, 37*, 1–15.

Brooks, K. (2011). Resistance is futile: "Reaccenting" the present to create classroom dialogues. *Pedagogies: An International Journal, 6*, 66–80.

Dockter, J., Haug, D., & Lewis, C. (2010). Redefining rigor: Critical engagement, digital media, and the new English/language arts. *Journal of Adolescent and Adult Literacy 48*, 418–420.

Fabos, B. (2008). The price of information: Critical literacy, education and today's Internet. In D. J. Leu, J. Coiro, M. Knobel, & C. Lankshear (Eds.), *Handbook of research on new literacies* (pp. 843–874). Mahwah, NJ: Lawrence Erlbaum Associates.

Gee, J. P. (2004). *Situated language and learning: A critique of traditional schooling.* New York: Routledge.

Hill, M. L., & Vasudevan, L. (2008). *Media, learning, and sites of possibility.* New York: Peter Lang.

Holland, D., Lachicotte Jr., W., Skinner, D., & Cain, C. (1998). *Identity and agency in cultural worlds.* Cambridge, MA: Harvard University Press.

Jones, R. H., & Norris, S. (2005). Introducing meditational means/cultural tools. In S. Norris & R. H. Jones (Eds.), *Discourse in action: Introducing mediated discourse analysis* (pp. 49–51). New York: Routledge.

Kellner, D. (2004). Technological transformation, multiple literacies, and the re-visioning of education. *E-Learning, 1*, 9–37.

Lewis, C., & Dockter Tierney, J. (2011). Mobilizing emotion in an urban English classroom, *Changing English, 18*, 319–329.

Morrell, E. (2007). *Critical literacy and urban youth: Pedagogies of access, dissent, and liberation.* New York: Routledge.

Norris, S., & Jones, R. H. (2005). *Discourse in action: Introducing mediated discourse analysis.* New York: Routledge.

Pennycook, A. (2010). *Language as local practice.* New York: Routledge.

Santos, B. (2006). Globalizations. *Theory, Culture, and Society, 23*, 393–399.

Scharber, C., Lewis, C., & Beach, R. (2010). Analyzing critical engagement in an urban high school digital media program. Paper presented at the Digital Media and Learning Conference, San Diego, CA.

Scollon, R. (2001). *Mediated discourse: The nexus of practice.* London: Routledge.

Scollon, R., & Scollon, S. W. (2003). *Discourses in place: Language in the material world.* London: Routledge.

Sholle, D., & Denski, S. (1994). *Media education and the (re)production of culture.* Westport, CT: Bergin & Garvey.

Thibault, P. (2004). *Brain, mind and the signifying body: An ecosocial semiotic theory.* London: Continuum.

CHAPTER TEN

Hacker Literacies

User-Generated Resistance and Reconfiguration of Networked Publics

RAFI SANTO

INTRODUCTION

In this chapter, I want to address what I see as emerging forms of literacy in digital culture and in doing so answer what I believe to be important questions: What role might criticality play in the age of participatory media? How are values-based questions like those relating to corporate control most relevant in a world where the one-to-many broadcast media is but one component of a many-to-many participatory media culture? Where can we currently look to see critical and empowered digital practices at play? And how can these in situ cases that merge critical and participatory mind-sets guide us as we conceptualize emergent literacy frameworks?

In the first half of this chapter, I explore the theoretical contours of hacker literacies and share why I see them as necessary, and in the second half I aim to show how hacker literacies are currently being practiced in situ in order to ground the construct in lived experiences. I share examples of how users are currently resisting and reconfiguring networked public spaces, such as the mass uprisings in response to Facebook privacy changes, the invention of the hashtag on Twitter, and a teen-led protest movement in a virtual world.

Hacker literacies, characterized simultaneously by criticality and participation, are a response to a shifting media landscape. In the past, communications media evolved at a rate that pales in comparison to what we're experiencing in the 21st century. Even then, it was not a simple task to conceptualize what it meant to be literate with media. At the same time, despite what pundits and some watchers of the digital space might brashly proclaim, we are not entirely in a "brave new world" where "everything is different"; we have much to gain from looking at the rapid change before us through some existing, well-developed lenses, tinkering and adjusting them to our new circumstances as needed rather than starting from scratch.

What I call "hacker literacies" are just that—a cobbling together of two existing paradigms for understanding what it means and looks like to be literate with media: critical media literacy and participatory media literacies. (Use of the singular, 'literacy,' and plural, 'literacies,' is intentional here and based on how these existing bodies of literature characterize themselves.) Hopefully in this process of theoretical concoction, a Frankenstein isn't created, though the examples of hacker literacies I'll share here point, I believe, to the fact that not only does this synthesis already exist in real-world practices regardless of theory, but that those practices are not monstrous in their nature by any means. To the contrary, I believe the examples I will share later in this chapter are important signposts on the road to figuring out how we should be educating young people to be literate with media in the 21st century.

SYNTHESIZING MEDIA LITERACY FRAMEWORKS

What it means to be literate with communications media has always been a moving target (Hannon, 2000)—media inevitably change, and when they do, so do the social practices that surround and shape them. And so as a society we've always done our best to document and understand what it means to be literate in these practices.

What I refer to as the "first wave" of these literacy frameworks, critical media literacy, responded to the explosion of broadcast media in the 20th century. TV, radio, film, and the press enriched society—they provided new forms of artistic and popular culture, broadly accessible information about politics, and the possibility of understanding and connecting with a wider world. And they simultaneously presented risks. With media controlled by just a few interests, political bias, propagation of problematic stereotypes, and lack of attention to issues deemed unsavory by those in power became regular features, and, to many, flaws of the mass-media landscape. Critical media literacy offered itself up in response to these sorts of issues. It advocated practices that empowered young people in relation to the messages of mass media, asking them to question the intent, assumptions, and biases of media producers (Buckingham, 2003; Hobbs, 2006; NAMLE, 2007). Who made this TV show? What kind of culture is it promoting? Who is this ad targeting? What techniques is it using to make me want to buy the product? These are hardly questions that should go out of vogue.

Yet at the start of the 21st century, we saw a new paradigm for media literacy emerge. The advent of the Internet and the broader participatory culture surrounding it heralded a number of "second wave" media literacy frameworks, most prominently the new literacies studies (Gee, 2007; Lankshear & Knobel, 2006, 2007) and new media literacy (Jenkins, Clinton, Purushotma, Robison, & Weigel, 2009), that I refer to collectively as "participatory media literacies." This framework recognized that participatory forms of interaction through new media (blogs, wikis, social networks, virtual worlds, etc.) were becoming broadly accessible, and proposed that a new set of literacies were organically emerging that focused on how people can leverage and participate culturally through new media, empowering them not simply to be consumers of culture, but producers of it as well.

In practice, while critical media literacy would have a person ask how a cable news program might contain political bias, participatory media literacies would then have them engage in authentic blogging practices within a broader online civic community so that they could spread their own political views within a broader ecology. In short, one advocates criticality in response to media while the other encourages participation through it.

Both of these paradigms are crucial, and there remains significant work to promote the kinds of practices they value. At the same time, something is missing—the current conversation happening around participatory media literacies concerning empowerment *through* new media has seldom incorporated ideas about empowerment *in relation* to new media. For example, questions about what agendas are implicit in the very design of these new participatory tools don't get asked very often. These are the sorts of questions critical media literacy would ask about a media message. Additionally, more work could be done to understand the ways that the practices associated with participatory media literacies can be used to advocate for substantive changes to the design of these sociotechnical spaces when they fail to align with a person's values.

Drawing from many of the strengths of the critical media literacy and participatory media literacies traditions, there lies the potential to address this problem through the proposal of a "third wave" media literacy framework that I refer to as hacker literacies. Hacker literacies are a set of practices that support an individual to become empowered *in relation* to participatory digital media, such that the design and norms of sociotechnical spaces and the intentions of their creators and associated communities are not taken for granted. Rather, they are seen as malleable avenues for expression of the values and agendas of the individual user, as opposed to solely those of the designer or dominant community. Important to note is the fact that hacker literacies as a construct does not seek to impose any normative ideological "right response" to technologies or people aside from one that assumes active engagement with sociotechnical spaces based on the values one brings to them.

In defining hacker literacies, I take inspiration from many within the critical media literacy and participatory media literacies traditions, as well as from Constructionist learning theorists such as Papert (1980) who were interested in ensuring that it is the child who programs the computer, rather than the other way around.

I define hacker literacies in this way: empowered participatory practices, grounded in critical mind-sets, that aim to resist, reconfigure and/or reformulate the sociotechnical digital spaces and tools that mediate social, cultural, and political participation. These "critical mind-sets" include perceiving how values are at play in the design of these spaces and tools; understanding how those designs impact the users of those spaces and tools; and developing empowered outlooks, ones that assume that change is possible, in relation to those designs rooted in an understanding of their malleability. "Empowered participatory practices" include making transparent for others the values at play in and effects of sociotechnical designs, voicing alternative values for these designs, advocating and taking part in alternative designs when spaces and tools are misaligned with one's values, and employing new media as a means to change those digital spaces and tools whether on the social or technological level via social or technological means.

I will highlight how I'm conceiving of literacy and sociotechnical spaces below, but will for the most part let the examples in the second half of this chapter illustrate the construct of hacker literacies in terms of the critical mind-sets and empowered participatory practices that comprise it.

When I say literacy and literate practices, I am referring to existing sociocultural conceptualizations of literacy and looking specifically to a definition put forth by Lankshear and Knobel: "socially recognized ways of generating, communicating, and negotiating meaningful content through the medium of encoded texts within contexts of participation in Discourses (or as members of Discourses)" (2006, p. 64). A key idea in their notion of what counts as a literate practice is the intersection of a technology (though not confined to digital ones), knowledge (including values, attitudes, and beliefs) and skills and associated actions.

In this case, the technology is indeed digital—it is those sociotechnical digital spaces that increasingly mediate participation in civic, social, and political life. I refer to these spaces as sociotechnical since they are simultaneously made up of technical features and social actors existing in dialectic relationship with one another. Technical features afford and constrain certain social behaviors, and at the same time are always themselves shaped by social actors, whether they are users, designers, or other stakeholders. This dialectic relationship, of course, is what makes these spaces malleable, and so is foundational to their reformulation and reconfiguration through various practices.

While many digital spaces are explicitly social in their design, such as social network sites like Facebook or interest-driven community sites such as

AnimeMusicVideos.org, for the purposes of hacker literacies I also include digital technologies that are not explicitly social, such as media production tools like Photoshop or FinalCutPro as well as other computer applications. These tools have important roles in mediating what kinds of participation are possible in the 21st century, and are themselves, of course, designed and iterated upon by social actors and as such deserve our attention.

On Hackers

When I use the term "hacker" here, I'm not talking about any malicious or unethical people, a misapplication of the term often used in popular culture and mainstream news contexts,[1] but am pointing to the critical and participatory ethos of the hacker community that revels in collaborating around, tinkering with, and reconfiguring technology from an empowered space that assumes these actions are both possible and desirable.

I also would warn against seeing hacker literacies as totally technical. As with the assumption that hackers are malicious, the assumption that hackers are solely solitary writers of code is also in need of a bit of corrective. That imagery is a far cry from how most people that engage in creative production with technology operate, and this is especially true in the case of computer programmers. From its origins, hacker culture was deeply communal, with a strong ethos of sharing and collaborating, of contributing both expertise and code to others. Within that culture are a range of practices, some more technical in nature, such as individual debugging of a compilation of computer code, and others more social in nature, such as advocating for the adoption of a new common technical standard and engaging in collaborative projects. The same is true for hacker literacies—some of the ways that people aim to reformulate sociotechnical spaces are more technical in nature while others are more social.

On Empowerment

As a final note in this more "definitional" section, I want to briefly address the usage of the word "empowerment," which is quite commonly used in educational contexts, especially by those advocating for critical perspectives. I have already used, and will continue to use, terms like "empowered digital practices" and "empowered mind-sets" in this chapter, and given that, I think it's important to be clear on what I mean when I say empowered. As Lankshear noted, "If people do not recognize and address the vague semantics and ambiguity of 'empowerment,' they may well fall for educational agendas they would otherwise have rejected on the grounds that they are in fact manipulative or oppressive" (1997, p. 64). He suggested the usage of a simple schema for clearly outlining what one means when using the term empowerment within a given context. For the purposes of talking about hacker literacies, the schema looks like this: users of digital participatory media (the subjects) are empowered in respect to the designs and formulations of those media (a particular aspect of the structuring of power) through engaging in hacker literacies that are based on an understanding of those media as changeable (a process) such that those media become reformulated to reflect the values of the user (the valued ends/outcome).

WHY BOTHER? EMERGING FORMS OF NEW MEDIA RISK

The example of synthesis I provide here is not just an academic exercise to see what happens when we remix theory; the practical stakes are high. Despite how important it is to not sound alarm bells when talking about digital culture at a time when traditional media and the government have developed a bad habit of making mountains out of molehills, such as in the case of overblown fears about online predators (Collier, 2011; Wolak, Finkelhor, Mitchell, & Ybarra, 2008), there are in fact substantive emerging forms of risk and media manipulation that we are going to have to face up to as a society.

Foremost in the mind of the public is the issue of privacy, a wide-ranging topic concerned with personal information posted online and its accessibility by various interested parties, whether they are other citizens, journalists, private companies, or governmental agencies. Emerging research is showing that users of online tools care about privacy issues, though not in ways that are evenly distributed among users (boyd & Hargittai, 2010)—a fact that has important implications in terms of who remains at risk. In more mainstream contexts, privacy issues are receiving deep scrutiny by the press, as evidenced by the *Wall Street Journal*'s series of reports on the subject, ominously titled "What They Know" (2010), displayed prominently for almost two years and counting in the technology section of the newspaper's website.

While much of the concern around privacy issues has focused on the role of companies in tracking online behavior and selling data to marketers, there is increasing scrutiny on the intersection of government and privacy issues as it relates to surveillance. With social media now established in their role as central tools in organizing, though not predicting the success of, public protest (Shirky, 2011), governments the world over have an increased stake in surveilling these technologies. Even in the United States, the Obama administration has proposed new laws that would give the government centralized "back-door" access to encrypted emails, peer-to-peer communication services such as Skype, and social network sites such as Facebook (Savage, 2010), a move that if successful would afford unprecedented governmental access to vast amounts of information with major implications for privacy and democracy.

Beyond privacy, many have begun to look at how the formulation and availability of certain technologies are norming sociality in new ways. Research has established that even when presented with the opportunity and ability to customize software according to their priorities, most people end up using the default settings (Mackay, 1991). This fact gives major power to the designers of technology in terms of how successful they will be in promoting certain types of behavior over others.

Research by the Pew Internet and American Life Project also hints at how the rise and decline of certain technologies correlates with changes in societal behaviors. A report about teen social-media habits (Lenhart, Purcell, Smith, & Zickuhr, 2010) documents how the number of teens blogging declined dramatically, by a full 50 percent, from 2006 to 2010. While not explicitly linked in the report, it is notable that during this same time period there was a major influx of teen users to Facebook from MySpace. That the decline in teen blogging correlates to a move to Facebook, which does not have a blogging feature, as contrasted to MySpace, which prominently displayed this functionality and had a strong blogging culture, is a fact not lost on many teen social-media watchers.

In a similar vein, emerging research on personalization of online spaces and tools is showing how an increased ability to deliver customized services might actually contribute to a balkanized Internet in which we're less likely to encounter views that challenge our own, a long-held, though contested, fear of many Internet researchers (Lessig, 2004; Sunstein, 2001). In his book *The Filter Bubble,* Pariser (2011) shared how the results displayed on Google are increasingly differentiated depending on what Google knows about you based on past behavior, to the point that we no longer have a common public experience of what results show up when a person searches for something as simple as "Egypt." He pointed to the fact that the current logic by which various websites personalize their user experiences, or even that they do, is increasingly non-transparent for those whom it affects the most: the user.

Finally, increased attention is being given to the possibilities and realities of exploitation of online activity. The increase in user-generated content online has coincided with the monetization of much of that content through what some call an "architecture of exploitation" (Petersen, 2008). Google Image Labeler, for example, engages people in an interactive matching game in which two people simultaneously look at the same image, with one person trying to get the other person to guess what the picture is of without using certain common keywords. In the process, enormous value is created for Google, whose image search is now that much more accurate. While the proposal that this is an exploitative practice is complicated by the fact that users get entertainment value in the process, these continuities between online labor, play, and value exchange merit scrutiny (Sholtz & Liu, 2010).

All of the examples are not here to serve as more fodder for a culture of fear around the Internet and technology. I personally believe that the flourishing of participatory culture that coincided with rise of the Internet is something we should be proud of as a society. At the same time, its development wasn't an accident: many people were very intentional about what they wanted from these technologies, and technology took shape accordingly. I point out these emerging forms of risk to highlight the reasons that the public needs to continue to engage with technology intentionally, and according to considered values, rather than assume that it is always being developed according to the public's best interests. These examples lay the groundwork needed to highlight what I see as new practices that acknowledge and are already actively responding to these types of issues, responses that form the basis of how we might understand hacker literacies.

HACKER LITERACIES IN CONTEXT

One of the central things that I'd like to convey in this chapter is not just the idea of what hacker literacies are, but also that this is a phenomenon well under way in current culture. In this section, I explore a number of examples of this so that various dimensions of hacker literacies can be made more transparent.

The great Facebook privacy debacle of 2010

Facebook has a well-documented history of making controversial, and some believe ham-handed, decisions when it comes to issues of privacy on its social network site (boyd & Hargittai, 2010). But the particular situation I'd like to talk about, referred to by some as "The Great Facebook Privacy Debacle of 2010" (Beale, 2010) resulted in what was arguably the greatest negative reaction up to that point among not only its users but also larger cultural, social, and political actors.

In late April of that year, Facebook announced at their annual F8 conference two new features: Instant Personalization and Social Plugins (McCarthy, 2010). Both of these changes to the popular site aimed to leverage a user's personal connections within Facebook to augment and "add value" to their usage of third-party websites.

The particularities of these features themselves are less important than the fact that both of them included new kinds of access to personal information not just for third-party websites but also for any interested party. A lack of clarity in terms of what user information was now available to whom in this process was the antecedent to an extended public backlash that included Facebook's user base, government actors including United States senators and regulators at the U.S. Federal Trade Commission, activist groups such as MoveOn.org and the American Civil Liberties Union, and a range of journalists from both technology-oriented and mainstream news sources.

In a study of the incident, I examined responses of 242 individuals to the situation in terms of how they evidenced hacker literacies. I applied a coding scheme based on the theoretical construct to 280 comments posted to mainstream (*New York Times, Washington Post*) and technology-focused (Mashable, Techcrunch) news sources on articles about Facebook's privacy changes (Santo, under review). The data contained a wide diversity of both the critical mind-sets present in hacker literacies as well as the empowered participatory practices that are expressions of those mind-sets.

Critical mind-sets

The critical mind-sets at play in the data largely fell into two categories: pointing to the effects of the new designs for users, and interpreting the values and intentions that drove those new designs.

In this first category, many pointed to ways that the new privacy settings had practical negative consequences for users, such as this individual: "By making a connection on FB, I'm invading that connection's privacy: revealing that connection's identity to the world, making the person behind that connection searchable" (fjpoblam, posting on Techcrunch.com). Beyond considering Facebook less useful and being disinclined to use it, this individual pointed to specific design implications that could result in personal and professional issues arising through the simple, and central, act of adding someone as a "friend" after the new privacy setting changes were implemented. This evidences a form of design thinking in which a person links the particular designs of a tool or space to the kinds of behaviors afforded or constrained and the implications this has for the user—a cornerstone of hacker literacies.

Those who fell into the second category of critical mind-sets, pointing to values and intentions behind the new designs, were more explicitly political in their commentary, such as this individual's implied comparison of Facebook to the fictional regime in the book *1984*: "They are not redefining privacy, they are debasing the language of privacy. George Orwell understood this principle completely: newspeak" (Anonymous, posting on Mashable.com). The statement is not just a clear indictment of what this person saw as the values inherent in Facebook's new designs, but acknowledgment that there in fact *were* values that were guiding those designs. This is no small thing, as technology is often easily seen as "value neutral," despite the old saying about what happens when you only have a hammer.

Empowered participatory practices

This interpretative space of critical mind-sets in which individuals "read" the "text" of the Facebook platform in order to uncover values and design implications can be seen as the basis for the wide range of empowered participatory responses to the situation. Three categories of advocacy and action showed up in the data I examined: advocating individual actions, voicing alternative designs, and advocating collective actions.

On the individual level, many felt that it was the responsibility of the user to respond to the situation accordingly, either by not posting certain things in their Facebook profiles if they wanted to keep them private, or by educating themselves about the contours of the new privacy policies. Others argued for personal deletion of Facebook accounts. Some of these calls were sarcastic responses to others complaining about the new policies and were of the "if you don't like it, why don't you leave" variety. Others, though, were from individuals who had essentially decided to boycott a service that no longer lined up with their values and intentions. All of these responses, at their core, were somewhat representative of libertarian notions of civic engagement, wherein the individual citizen, given freedom and choice, can determine her own destiny according to her values, and avoid things that are undesirable or create her own means of response to them.

A second category of advocacy and action was aimed at creating alternative models that Facebook might follow in order to become better aligned with what their users might want, such as this suggestion for how Facebook should reconfigure its privacy settings: "I'd like to see Facebook adopt a much more simple model:— Share with my Friends.—Share with Friends of my Friends.—Share with everybody. If you want to go crazy granular on settings under those buckets, great. But at least at a high level I can choose one of 3 things and feel mostly comfortable. That's enough for most users" (Chad Whitney, posting on Mashable.com).

Most common was the suggestion that Facebook should adopt an "opt-in" model when making changes to the kinds of information that can be shared. Rather than defaulting users into settings that made their information more rather than less public, a practice that Facebook has engaged in on numerous occasions (boyd & Hargittai, 2010), many suggested that Facebook make these possibilities available for people to choose to opt into if they so desired.

These sorts of design suggestions evidence a different notion of agency and understanding of the possibilities for reconfiguring sociotechnical spaces than those individuals who suggested that users educate themselves on the new policies or just leave Facebook. One can imagine these suggestions emerging from the experiences of individuals who had encountered a wide range of changes to Facebook prior to this one. They understood that Facebook was completely capable of implementing new designs, and via their suggestions these individuals in some respects positioned themselves as advisers to Facebook's architects, or as advocates exerting public pressure for specific policy decisions and self-regulation on the part of Facebook.

Finally, numerous individuals voiced the need for collective action to explicitly exert pressure on Facebook to change how it operated. Many of these had less implicit trust in Facebook's ability or desire to self-regulate than those who suggested alternative policies and designs. Common in this category were calls for governmental regulation, mass exodus from Facebook, and suggestions that users collectively join sites deemed more respectful of privacy. The individual below advocated for a group action that displayed a deep understanding of the underlying market logic on which Facebook operates: "We are taking the fight to Facebook. We know how the info game is played, so every week we're going to change a detail on our Facebook profiles en masse to throw off their marketing data" (Amy Stein, posting on Mashable.com).

The collective actions more often seemed to align with somewhat traditional notions of community organization and nodded to the use of online civil disobedience, to desires for regulation of powerful entities and to treating Facebook like a traditional utility such as electricity or telephones with all of the implications for consumer rights that come with those assumptions.

These varied responses, on the level of individual action, design recommendation, and collective action serve to complicate what hacker literacies can look like when enacted in practice. There is clearly not only one response here that qualifies as empowered. Rather, underlying the differences in these responses were a range of value systems, understandings of what it means to be empowered, and decisions about what an appropriate reaction to the situation was. At the core of each of them though is a notion that there is something that can be done in the face of a sociotechnical space that is misaligned with one's values, an idea central in distinguishing hacker literate practices as ones that are not only critical but also participatory.

New media as a means of change

On analyzing the data, a final unique property relating to hacker literacies became clear: the fluidity with which the technological tools and spaces moved back and forth from norming user behavior through their designs to being themselves the very means of changing those designs. I saw examples of people first understanding that Facebook was now norming their behavior in some way, but then saw others who used Facebook as an organizing tool to advocate for changes. In the example noted earlier of a woman who advocated large groups of people changing profile information to "throw off their marketing data," a link was shared to a page that had been set up on Facebook to coordinate these efforts. Others again shared more individualistic approaches to using Facebook as a means of resistance: "In my profile all my 'about me' fields now contain: 'As protest to Facebook's constant change in privacy rules, I have removed this field'" (Dude, posting on Techcrunch.com).

Facebook, though, was far from the only new media tool that individuals were employing to share, seek, or enact responsive strategies. Some people shared custom tools that had been created to make transparent what information was currently being shared, potentially inadvertently, by a Facebook user: "Lots of tools emerging now to turn the balance of power back to consumers. Here's ours, for FF and Chrome users who want to change settings to 'Friends Only' and keep them there—http://onebuttonrule.com/ Gets to *all* settings, works *automatically* to react to Facebook's changes" (Ginsu, posting on Mashable.com).

During the month that followed Facebook's F8 announcement, tools like this spread widely on the web. Reclaim Privacy, a tool recommended by a user commenting on Techcrunch, provided an open-source method of providing awareness of Facebook user-privacy settings. The designers of this tool were quite explicit in wanting to create a technical response to Facebook's changes that embodied the values they saw missing in Facebook itself:

> Our privacy policy is not long:
> - we **never see** your Facebook data
> - we **never share** your personal information
>
> Simple. After the scanner is downloaded from reclaimprivacy.org, it operates entirely between your own browser and Facebook. (ReclaimPrivacy.org. Retrieved May 2011)

At the time of this writing (December 2011), the Reclaim Privacy tool had been shared using Facebook's own "share page" feature more than 271,000 times.

Taken in a broader context, people's responses to Facebook's privacy changes in spring 2010 are notable for a number of reasons. Most significantly, they resulted in a shift in the way Facebook was formulated: in May 2010 Facebook introduced a "simplified" privacy interface (Zuckerberg, 2010). And while this response on Facebook's part can be problematized as one that in the process also removed the ability to restrict certain kinds of data from public view (boyd & Hargittai, 2010), the overall ecology that emerged as a result points to a culture that is characterized by both participation and criticality. Projects like Diaspora, an open-source decentralized social network, were supported by many in the technology world and elsewhere (Baio, 2010) who saw problems with Facebook's behavior and sought an alternative that respected their privacy. Others, like YourOpenBook.org, sought to promote awareness of the vast amounts of personal information Facebook made public through its changes by creating a site that allowed public Facebook status updates to be searched. The launch of Google+, a privacy-conscious social network created by the search giant, was seen by some as responding to many of the critiques people had of Facebook in terms of the ways it deals with privacy issues. Finally, a settlement between Facebook and the Federal Trade Commission in November 2011 required the company to be subject to a number of checks around privacy issues including regular privacy audits until 2031 as well as requiring many privacy changes to be opt-in by users, as opposed to imposing sharing by default (Sengupta, 2011). These and other examples of mobilization and response are all indicators that the kinds of critical and participatory mind-sets evidenced in the data were also found more broadly.

The Origin of the #Hashtag

Despite the case of the Facebook privacy debacle, an oppositional relationship between users and developers is not a prerequisite to hacker literacies, something well illustrated by the case of the hashtag on Twitter.

In August 2007, an open-web advocate named Chris Messina posted a proposal for how people might self-organize on the microblogging social network Twitter using "hashtags," pound signs followed by a distinct signature that were placed at the end of posts on twitter (Messina, 2007). By early 2010, this was a common social practice used by millions of Twitter users from around the world to participate in wide-ranging conversations relating to real-world events and to organize around important issues (Carvin, 2009; Gannes, 2010).

Hashtags gained positive public attention during the "Arab Spring" of 2011, when a series of revolutions, some successful, some less so, broke out across the Arab world. The posts associated with Hashtags became sources for mainstream news media, including #Jan25, the date when protests broke out across Egypt that eventually led to the downfall of the Mubarak regime, and #sidibouzid, which referred to the town in Tunisia where its equally successful protest movement started.

What is unique here aside from the incredible organizing power that hashtags have is that the hashtag itself was a "hack" of Twitter. Chris Messina didn't work for Twitter; he just saw a tool that wasn't meeting his needs and values, and he proposed a solution and started to use it. His understanding of both the technical dimensions of search and the social dimensions of the needs that people had on Twitter led to an innovation that had mass public appeal. This also leads back to the point that hacker literacies are implicitly sociotechnical in nature in that Messina's hack could not have been achieved solely through a technical understanding of Twitter's features, nor would he have been able to come up with this innovation if he were only attuned to social behaviors and needs and not to the technical formulation of the medium. Like the spaces it aims to affect, hacker literacies involve understandings and practices of both the technical and social variety.

While it is important to note that Messina did not have an oppositional relationship with Twitter (he merely saw that there was a way that it could be better aligned with his values around group organization), equally important is Twitter's response to this and other innovations that have emerged from its community: it embraced them. Part of why Twitter might have been more likely to respond in this way has to do with its comparatively pared-down design when placed next to a platform like Facebook, which has a much more robust and complex feature set. At the same time, Twitter's ability to adapt according to the values and innovations users bring to it points to a potentially supporting trend when it comes to hacker literacies: the iterative and responsive culture of "Web 2.0."

In general, the diverse ecology of the Internet has made web developers much more attuned to user experience and desires as a key factor in determining features. With a potential competitor a click away, participatory websites are often in "perpetual beta," an environment where untested features are regularly rolled out and users are treated as "co-developers" (O'Reilly, 2005). On a technical level, the features are relatively easy to change, and so on a social level, a culture of responsiveness to user desires has developed. At the same time, we cannot conflate wanting a better widget on the part of the user as wanting a participatory experience that embodies the values they want to live by, as so often more base desires for ease and function overshadow living according to more deeply held values.

If the case of Twitter and hashtags points to the cultural aspects of Web 2.0 that make it receptive to practices associated with hacker literacies, then the case of Facebook might point us to some of the challenges to hacker literacies that come up as a result of engineering culture. As Flanagan, Howe, and Nissenbaum (2008) note in "Embodying Values in Technology," the part of the academy that is most developed in engaging in systemic reflection about values is the humanities. They note that while computer science, design, and engineering programs can draw on lessons from those disciplines, these sorts of reflections are not central, and designers can often experience the limitations of their training. The case of Facebook's privacy practices itself was construed by some as resulting from engineers in that company who were "tone deaf" with regards to what users' values were, which alludes to this broader point about the limitations of technical culture's ability to reflect on values at play in designs.

We can look at Twitter, with its embrace of the hashtag as well as other user-generated practices that have affected the design of the platform as a case where the designers of a sociotechnical space actively valued the priorities of their users and responded to user innovation accordingly. The degree to which a "hacker-literate" individual such as Messina is able to reformulate a medium according to his values is not only dependent on the depth of his understanding and innovative nature of his actions, but also on the culture within and surrounding a given sociotechnical space and how that affects its technical makeup and social landscape.

"Grid unification" and teen protest in a virtual world

For the final case, I return to a previous life, one where I would stay late at work, after all my other colleagues had left for the day, to explore vast landscapes with people from around the world. Occasionally I would go skydiving into an active volcano with a young man wearing a Godzilla costume. If my boss stayed late too, we would sometimes get into snowball fights, no matter what time of year it was. I was working in the 3D, user-generated virtual world of Second Life, a space where the surreal was always possible, and if you could imagine it, you could build it—that is, if you had facility with the world's extensive 3D modeling and scripting tools. Alex Harbinger, one of the amazing people I had the fortune to meet in Second Life during my years working in this space, was a person with such skills.

Alex was not only talented at creating complex virtual objects and landscapes, but in the time I knew him, he also created an empire. Harbinger Industries was Alex's "in-world" business. It sold any variety of virtual goods including clothing for "avatars" (the physical character of Second Life residents) to wear, accessories such as virtual paintball guns and grappling hooks, and games that could be set up on virtual properties and played by groups of Second Life residents that congregated in these spaces. His goods were not just sold in the virtual shopping centers that could be found on the more commerce-oriented areas of the virtual world; eventually Alex himself set up a number of virtual islands (the largest unit of land available for purchase within Second Life) where he both set up shop and also rented space to other entrepreneurial residents. These "sims" (in-world parlance for islands) not only made Harbinger Industries into a sustainable business, they also became extremely popular areas where people would gather not just for commerce but also for socializing.

There are a couple of details that I haven't mentioned yet though: Alex accomplished all of this by the time he was 15 in what may have been the world's only teen-run economy. In Second Life, those between the ages of 13 and 17 did not have access to the adult-only "Main Grid." Instead, they were restricted to the "Teen Grid," a much smaller collection of "sims" with a decidedly *Lord of the Flies* feel. I was working as one of the few adults cleared for access to this space. As an educator at Global Kids, a New York–based nonprofit that focuses on international affairs and human-rights education, I was part of a program within our organization that aimed to leverage new media in innovative ways to achieve our mission, hence my involvement in the Teen Grid of Second Life. As an adult, I was restricted to the "sims" that my organization owned, never able to visit the "mainland" of the Teen Grid, but I interacted with many teens who turned out for a range of workshops, camps, and competitions that we ran over the years. It was in this context that I got to know Alex, and his political views about the issue of "grid unification."

While some of the Teen Grid population enjoyed having their own space within Second Life, others felt that the separation of the grids was a problem. The teen population and physical land-space of the grid was small, and many residents felt like it was a less dynamic space than it could have been. Many complained that the economy was depressed. More than any of these, there was a strong sentiment that next to the Main Grid where the adults were located, those on the Teen Grid were treated like second-class citizens, and were subject to a form of age discrimination.

This is where "grid unification" came in. The idea could be considered by some to be the first age-based civil-rights issue in a virtual world, and by others to be an unrealistic pipe-dream put forth by naïve young people who didn't understand the issues at play in designing complex online communities. In its essence, grid unification was about creating a common space between the main and teen grids where parents could hang out with their kids, where teens could engage in commerce with a much larger market, where adults could mentor teens, and where teens in turn could showcase their creativity for a larger world. The teen-only space of the Teen Grid would be maintained, and "mature" areas of the Main Grid would be off limits to teen residents. The idea was essentially to create a bridge that would "unify" the two grids of Second Life.

"Imagine a world free of segregation, a world without discrimination—A world that we live in? Not quite, but the goal is within our reach. Grid unification is the first step—one to remove unneeded censorship and age discrimination. A movement that benefits everybody." These are Alex's words, which preceded a public debate he held on Global Kids Island in early May 2007 (Harbinger, 2007). When I asked him about grid unification for this chapter, Alex told me that it wasn't his idea originally. "It was a communal thing—we didn't want to be the small 1 percent. We wanted to be part of the whole thing. The idea of unification was floating around, but nobody was really doing anything." Alex decided that something should be done, and in the process created a movement.

In a 20-page document titled "The Grid Unification Proposal" that circulated around the Teen Grid in mid-2007, Alex artfully outlined his vision for unification. It was a proposal aimed directly at Linden Lab, the company that owns and runs Second Life. It outlined what unification would look like, how potential legal and social issues would be mitigated, and included potential alterations and additions to the proposed policies that could be taken under consideration. He even included a Q&A section that addressed major questions that both adults and teens had raised about the idea of unification. Staff members at Linden Lab at the time reported to me that the document was influential during internal discussions regarding the issue, and was printed out and hung in the offices of those responsible for the Teen Grid.

More than that, the proposal was the articulation of a larger civic movement that had developed around the idea of unification. In early May 2007, following the initial release of the document, Alex organized hundreds of teens to participate in a non-violent protest walk called "The Walk for Intergrid Commerce." A version of the Grid Unification Proposal that was updated after the walk reported on it:

> After months of planning, Teen Grid residents organized and commenced a grid-wide walk to promote Grid Unification and cross-Grid commerce. The Walk took place on May 6th, 2007 officially starting at noon and ending near 1:30 PM. The walk consisted of hundreds of residents gathering to join in a non-violent walk across the Teen Grid.

What is so amazing about this story is not just that it is a powerful example of teen civic engagement, but it is that these teens couched their desires around the reformulation of a communications medium using the language of rights, discrimination, and censorship. Hacker literacies were implicit in their behaviors the entire time. To them, Second Life was not "just a game," a derisive jab commonly aimed at the virtual world, but a valid social and cultural space in which they could engage in acts of self-determination.

At the same time, they also held robust debate about the technical affordances of the medium, the potential social implications of varying governance policies and how the medium's current formulations were implicitly biased in certain ways. And they assumed that these were things that could be changed.

CONCLUSION

Beyond these examples, the broader world and current digital literacy movement both offer a lot to be hopeful for in terms of the development of hacker literacies. The rapid pace of technological change is beginning to make the malleability inherent in all technologies more transparent. Just as media watchdog groups and ombudsmen emerged as important voices in the broadcast media space, strong voices in mainstream media, academia, the blogosphere, and civil society are emerging to ask important questions about the ways that technology is formulated and how that affects society. More importantly, there are many burgeoning subcultures that youth are already involved in including the game modding, DIY, and "Maker" spaces that place a high value on tinkering with, customizing, and pushing back against existing designs to create what one wants.

Likewise, increased interest in digital literacies and design thinking within the education community will likely be a boon for the development of hacker literacies. More and more projects, especially those oriented towards Papert's Constructionist learning principles, are aiming to position youth as designers of technology using tools like Scratch (Resnick et al., 2009), Gamestar Mechanic (Salen, 2007), Mozilla's Hackasaurus, and many others. Projects like these have strong potential to develop fundamental building blocks of hacker literacies, and put young people in the role of creators and makers of their own technosocial world. As a society, we need to be prepared to let that happen.

With appropriate development, critical participation with popular new media tools can come to occupy a similar space within participatory culture as has been filled by critical voices in other mainstream concerns. In the domain of consumer apparel, a movement of fair-trade-oriented consumers ask where, how, and by whom something is made, and with those answers are then empowered to make choices that affect the lives of others who lie at the other end of the supply chain. That example, however, serves as cautionary as well, as we still live in a world where exploitative labor practices associated with clothing manufacturing are rampant. While I believe participatory culture cannot, by virtue of its many-to-many structure, be completely dominated by one player, interest, or type of interactive approach, without incorporating critical practices into participatory ones, without the development of hacker literacies, people may find themselves living in a digitally mediated culture dictated by interests other than their own.

ACKNOWLEDGMENTS

I want to express my deep gratitude to Michele Knobel, Jenna McWilliams, Joshua Danish, Henry Jenkins, James Paul Gee, Susan Herring, Kylie Peppler, and the editors of this volume, JuliAnna Ávila and Jessica Zacher Pandya, for providing valuable feedback on the ideas in and drafts of this chapter. And of course to Alex Harbinger, who for me embodied what a hacker-literate teen can look like.

NOTE

1. Those within the computer programming world apply the word "crackers" to those who use technological knowledge and skills for ill intent. Alternatively, these individuals are referred to as "black-hat hackers" in contrast to "white-hat hackers."

REFERENCES

Baio, A. (2010, September 22). Diaspora opens up. *Kickstarter Blog*. Retrieved from http://blog.kickstarter.com/post/1167759632/diaspora-opens-up

Beale, R. (2010, May 19). Chronology of the great Facebook privacy debacle of 2010. *Human Capitol League*. Retrieved from http://humancapitalleague.com/Home/5276

boyd, d., & Hargittai, E. (2010, August 2). Facebook privacy settings: Who cares? *First Monday, 15*(8). Retrieved from http://firstmonday.org/htbin/cgiwrap/bin/ojs/index.php/fm/article/view/3086/2589

Buckingham, D. (2003). *Media education: Literacy, learning and contemporary culture.* Cambridge, UK: Polity Press.

Carvin, A. (2009, June 19). In Iran, the revolution will be tagged. *NPR.org*. Retrieved from http://www.npr.org/templates/story/story.php?storyId=105679927

Collier, A. (2011). Sex offenders in social sites: Consider the facts. *ConnectSafely.org*. Retrieved from http://www.connectsafely.org/Safety-Advice-Articles/sex-offenders-in-social-sites-consider-the-facts.html

Flanagan, M., Howe, D., & Nissenbaum, H. (2008). Embodying values in technology: Theory and practice. In J. van den Hoven & J. Weckert (Eds.), *Information technology and moral philosophy*. New York: Cambridge University Press.

Gannes, L. (2010, April 30). The short and illustrious history of Twitter #Hashtags. Gigaom.com. Retrieved from http://gigaom.com/2010/04/30/the-short-and-illustrious-history-of-twitter-hashtags/

Gee, J. P. (2007). *Good video games and good learning: Collected essays on video games, learning, and literacy.* New York: Peter Lang.

Hannon, P. (2000). *Reflecting on literacy in education*. London: Routledge/Falmer.

Harbinger, A. (pseudonym) (2007, May 10). Grid unification debate. Global kids online leadership program blog. *olpglobalkids.org*. Retrieved from http://www.olpglobalkids.org/content/slteen-grid-unification-debate

Hobbs, R. (2006). *Reading the media: Media literacy in high school English*. New York: Teachers College Press.

Jenkins, H., Clinton, K., Purushotma, R., Robison, A., & Weigel, M. (2009). *Confronting the challenges of participatory culture: Media education for the 21st century*. John D. and Catherine T. MacArthur Foundation Reports on Digital Media and Learning. Cambridge, MA: MIT Press.

Lankshear, C. (1997). Literacy and empowerment. In *Changing literacies*. Bristol, UK: Open University Press.

Lankshear, C., & Knobel, M. (2006). *New literacies: Everyday practices and classroom learning*. UK: Open University Press.

Lankshear, C., & Knobel, M. (Eds.). (2007). *A new literacies sampler*. New York: Peter Lang.

Lenhart, A., Purcell, K., Smith, A., & Zickuhr, K. (2010). *Social media and young adults*. Pew Internet & American Life Project. Retrieved from http://www.pewInternet.org/Reports/2010/Social-Media-and-Young-Adults.aspx

Lessig, L. (2004, August 17). The balkanization of the Internet. *Lessig.org.* Retrieved from http://lessig.org/blog/2004/08/the_balkanization_of_the_inter.html

Mackay, W. (1991). *Triggers and barriers to customizing software.* Proceedings of the SIGCHI Conference on Human Factors in Computing Systems (New Orleans), pp. 153–160.

McCarthy, C. (2010, April 21). Facebook F8: One graph to rule them all. *CNET The Social.* Retrieved from http://news.cnet.com/8301–13577_3–20003053–36.html

Messina, C. (2007, August 25). Groups for Twitter; or a proposal for Twitter tag channels. Factory City. Retrieved from http://factoryjoe.com/blog/2007/08/25/groups-for-twitter-or-a-proposal-for-twitter-tag-channels/

National Association for Media Literacy Education. (2007, November). Core principles of media literacy education in the United States. Retrieved from http://namle.net/wp-content/uploads/2009/09/NAMLE-CPMLE-w-questions2.pdf

O'Reilly, T. (2005, September 30). What is Web 2.0? *oreillynet.com.* Retrieved from http://www.oreillynet.com/pub/a/oreilly/tim/news/2005/09/30/what-is-web-20.html?page=4

Papert, S. (1980). *Mindstorms: Children, computers, and powerful ideas.* New York: Basic Books.

Pariser, E. (2011). *The filter bubble: What the Internet is hiding from you.* New York: Penguin.

Petersen, S. M. (2008 March 3). *Loser generated content: From participation to exploitation. First Monday, 13*(3). Retrieved from http://www.uic.edu/htbin/cgiwrap/bin/ojs/index.php/fm/article/viewArticle/2141/1948

Reclaim Privacy (2010). Privacy Policy. Retrieved from http://www.reclaimprivacy.org

Resnick, M., Maloney, J., Monroy-Hernández, A., Rusk, N., Eastmond, E., Brennan, et al. (2009). Scratch: Programming for all. *Communications of the ACM, 52*(11), 60.

Rushkoff, D. (2011). *Program or be programmed: Ten commands for a digital age.* New York: O/R Books.

Salen, K. (2007). Gaming literacies: A game design study in action. *Journal of Educational Multimedia and Hypermedia, 16*(3).

Santo, R. (under review). *Towards hacker literacies: What Facebook's privacy snafus can teach us about empowered digital practices.*

Savage, C. (2010, September 27). U.S. tries to make it easier to wiretap the Internet. *New York Times.* Retrieved from http://www.nytimes.com/2010/09/27/us/27wiretap.html?pagewanted=all&_r=1&hp=

Sengupta, S. (2011, November 29). F.T.C. settles privacy issue at Facebook. *New York Times.* Retrieved from http://www.nytimes.com/2011/11/30/technology/facebook-agrees-to-ftc- settlement-on-privacy.html

Shirky, C. (2011, January/February). The political power of social media. *Foreign Policy.* Retrieved from http://www.foreignaffairs.com/articles/67038/clay-shirky/the-political-power-of-social-media

Scholz, T., & Liu, L. (2010). *From mobile playgrounds to sweatshop city.* SituatedTechnologies.net. Retrieved from http://www.situatedtechnologies.net/files/ST7MobilePlaygrounds_SweatshopCity.pdf

Sunstein, C. (2001). *Republic.com*. Princeton, NJ: Princeton University Press.

Wall Street Journal. (2010, November). What they know (Series of reports). Retrieved from http://online.wsj.com/public/page/what-they-know-digital-privacy.html

Wolak, J., Finkelhor, D., Mitchell, K., & Ybarra, M. (2008). Online "predators" and their victims: Myths, realities, and implications for prevention and treatment. *American Psychologist*, *63*(2), 111–128.

Zuckerberg, M. (2010, May 26). Making controls simple. *Facebook blog*. Retrieved from http://blog.facebook.com/blog.php?post=391922327130

So Now You Know. What Are You Going To Do about It?

MARGARET C. HAGOOD

Lankshear and Knobel (2008) offer a definition of digital literacies as "myriad social practices and conceptions of engaging in meaning making mediated by texts that are produced, received, distributed, exchanged, etc., via digital codification" (p. 5). It probably goes without saying, but digital literacies are part and parcel of 21st-century life. Just from general exposure to youth today, few would argue about the role that digital literacies play in the overall spectrum of literacy development, and that role continues to grow. Long-range studies have shown increases in youths' digital literacy habits in a relatively short time period. The Kaiser Family Foundation study *Generation M2: Media in the Lives of 8- to 18-Year-Olds* reports on the changes of this age group's digital literacy uses at three different periods. Youth between the ages of 8 and 18 have increased their daily media usage from 7:29 hours in 1999 to 8:33 hours in 2004 to 10:45 hours in 2009 with media including TV, music, computer, video, print, and movies (Rideout, Foehr, & Roberts, 2010). Across these three time periods, youth spent an average of 43 minutes daily on print-based texts in 1999 and 2004, and 38 minutes in 2009. With those averages, it's not uncommon to see youth plugged in with cell phones equipped with texting capabilities, cameras, and digital recorders; ereaders or tablets; or laptop computers—and rarely with a book in their hands. (Not to say that they aren't reading; they're reading differently.)

So it makes sense that literacy acquisition at the intersection of digital literacies is also part and parcel of the buzz of literacy initiatives concerned with impacting and positively affecting instruction that is not only relevant now but attends to the preparation of learners for life after graduation from high school (be it post-graduate studies or workforce). National organizations such as the International Reading Association (IRA) and the National Council for the Teachers of English (NCTE), and the Common Core State Standards (CCSS), noting the changes in youths' literacy practices and proclivities, have coupled teaching spoken, written, and visual dimensions of literacy, including print and nonprint texts, with uses of digital tools. For example, IRA and NCTE share a set of 12 standards for English/Language Arts that highlight the intersection of print, nonprint, and media in order develop students' reading, writing, listening, speaking, viewing, and designing of texts (International Reading Association, 1996). IRA's position statement on new literacies also focuses attention on the integration of ICTs (information and communications technologies) and on the development of critical thinking into literacy practices (International Reading Association, 2009). In addition, the CCSS standards recognize the relationship between digital tools and the development of print literacy (National Governors Association Center for Best Practices, 2010). In some senses, the coupling of print literacies and digital literacies isn't a newly formed venture. Since 1970, NCTE has actively created resolutions that explore the relationships between literacy, media, and technology to the benefit of students' literacy development (see http://www.ncte.org/positions/21stcenturyliteracy). But rather than set forth explicit standards related to media uses for the development of digital literacies, these documents embed these throughout the standards.

Standards also designate that literacy professionals should assume digital literacies as part of the literacy repertoire to be taught. IRA Standards for Reading Professionals, for example, which outline the standards by which many literacy educators are evaluated, state, "Traditional print, digital, and online reading and writing experiences that incorporate multiple genres, multiple perspectives, and media and communication technologies are necessary to prepare learners for literacy tasks of the 21st century" (Standard 2) (http://www.reading.org/General/Current Research/Standards/ProfessionalStandards2010/ProfessionalStandards2010_Standard2.aspx). And the CCSS website states that the standards "clearly communicate what is expected of students at each grade level. This will allow our teachers to be better equipped to know exactly what they need to help students learn and establish individualized benchmarks for them" (http://www.corestandards.org/the-standards). Furthermore, the CCSS (National Governors Association Center for Best Practices, 2010) gives teachers full rein for instruction with digital literacies, explaining,

While the Standards focus on what is most essential, they do not describe all that can or should be taught. A great deal is left to the discretion of teachers and curriculum developers. The aim of the Standards is to articulate the fundamentals, not to set out an exhaustive list. (p. 6)

Interestingly, despite all of the mandates to corral teachers and students into functioning via the same parameters and outcomes, teachers actually have a great deal of autonomy about how to address digital literacies. And while this autonomy might fit nicely with some teachers' backgrounds, expertise, and comfort levels to teach this subject matter, others may well feel at sea for a variety of reasons. Issues of teaching with and using digital literacies have been well documented in both reviews of technology uses and in teacher perception surveys (Hew & Brush, 2007; Hutchinson & Reinking, 2011). Several barriers to integration of technologies persist, including lack of resources and institutional support, the culture of the subject to be taught, teachers' attitudes and beliefs, teachers' knowledge and skills, and the lack of professional development and assessment. The majority of 1,441 teachers in grades K–12 surveyed by Hutchinson and Reinking (2011) viewed technology instruction as a component of ICTs related to the "know-how" of using digital tools (e.g., creating a word-processing document or PowerPoint presentation) rather than using the tools to develop digital literacies of the kind defined by Knobel and Lankshear at the opening of this Afterword.

So teachers have much leeway in their instructional approaches to teaching digital literacies, but obstacles still exist. Some research reports that teachers resist teaching with digital literacies, even as they are aware of the centrality of these literacies in students' lives. Alvermann (2011) found that teachers and teacher educators (of pre-service and in-service teachers) choose to exclude these forms of literacies in their instruction, mostly because they feel that students already have plenty of time with digital literacies outside of school. Other teachers call attention to the dissonance between instruction that addresses digital literacies and standardized assessments that measure functional literacies of reading and writing print text, explaining they can't justify spending valuable time (especially in "underperforming schools") teaching digital literacies when they aren't assessed on statewide high-stakes tests (Burke & Hammett, 2009; Hagood, Provost, Egelson, & Skinner, 2008). And still other teachers recognize the importance of teaching digital literacies, but see these literacies as technological supplements rather than central curricula to the literacy being taught (Hutchinson & Reinking, 2011).

To be sure, teachers consistently recognize the import of digital literacies in students' lives. Hutchinson and Reinking (2011) also found that although most of the K–12 teachers they surveyed (98 percent) have access to a computer and Internet at school or in their classroom (86 percent), two-thirds of them believed that technology needs to be integrated into instruction as supplemental—not central—to the curriculum. Many teachers are still unclear about the import of integration and instruction (and without standards that point to those issues, many teachers are stymied about how to utilize and teach digital literacies). Hence it seems that now the focus of digital tools has shifted from the intersection of digital literacies and students' literacy practices to the intersection of definitions of digital literacies and of instruction. How are digital literacies defined and taken up and taught as part of a global society (which the standards state as a goal of standards' mastery)? I believe, like Ertmer (2005), that forms of instruction with digital literacies stem from teacher belief systems. He succinctly said:

> The decision regarding whether and how to use technology for instruction rests on the shoulders of classroom teachers. If educators are to achieve fundamental, or second order, changes in classroom teaching practices, we need to examine teachers themselves and the beliefs they hold about teaching, learning, and technology. (p. 27)

Ertmer's directive rang in my ears as I read *Critical Digital Literacies as Social Praxis*. The ideas expressed throughout this text are exemplars for considering belief systems, the relationships, and the kinds of instruction necessary for literacy acquisition that accounts not only for digital literacies but also for the needed development of critical digital literacies. The chapters in this volume take seriously the portion of the Knobel and Lankshear's (2008) definition of digital literacies that includes "social practices and conceptions of engaging in meaning making." Connecting to this definition, the contributors to this volume add another key layer to the discussion of the development of digital literacies with their commitment to critical digital literacies. Critical digital literacies stem from critical literacy education and are concerned with teaching learners to identify and work within understandings of the relations between language and power.

The chapters in this volume illustrate how the variables connected to "social practices of engaging in meaning making" influence the design and implementation of developing critical digital literacies. These chapters also illustrate classroom practices for teachers who want to reconsider their belief systems about the differences between digital literacies and those infused with critical literacy; their instructional practices that will move beyond seeing digital literacy as technology tools, making digital literacies a central (rather than ancillary component) of the curriculum; and their comfort levels with moving from teaching with digital literacies to critical digital literacies.

For practitioners to move into the space of implementing critical digital literacies beyond digital literacies as ICTs, they may consider several areas related to teaching, learning, and technology that were explored throughout this text. These include the following:

1. Determining a working definition of digital literacies and critical digital literacies;
2. Creating connections between critical digital literacies and functional/foundational literacies;
3. Considering the changes in relationship identities needed between teachers and students who engage in critical digital literacies; and
4. Mapping out changes in instruction to reflect these ideas.

Such an exercise isn't intended for those who aren't interested in real changes in oneself, in relationships with students, and in instructional practices. As Merchant (2009) notes, reflections on critical practices including digital literacies "can have a destabilising effect in that it begins to make its users see the possibilities for different kinds of learning relationships, different kinds of interactions, and of course different genres and purposes for literacy" (p. 54). This text has pushed me to think about how shifts in my own instruction using critical digital literacies impact my own belief systems, relationships, and instruction.

The chapters in this volume push the envelope regarding what constitutes digital literacies instruction as a component of literacy curricula. Ultimately, the studies and theories described use digital literacies for raising and changing consciousness though a focus on the critical literacies of language and power. The focus on developing critical literacies of students as they engage with new media and digital tools takes the discussion of the inclusion of digital literacies in instruction one step further. Alvermann and Hinchman (2011) caution that "awareness is one thing; acting on that awareness is quite another" (p. 273). To engage in critical digital literacies is to move from awareness to action. These chapters set a path for others who would like to follow suit. The conditions are right. So, now you know. What are you going to do about it?

REFERENCES

Alvermann, D. E. (2011). Moving on, keeping pace: Youth's literate identities and multimodal digital texts. In S. Abrams & J. Rowsell (Eds.), *Rethinking identity and literacy education in the 21st century. National Society for the Study of Education Yearbook, 110*(1), 109–128.

Alvermann, D., & Hinchman, K. (2011). Afterword. In D. Alvermann & K. Hinchman (Eds.), *Reconceptualizing the literacies in adolescents' lives: Bridging the everyday/academic divide* (pp. 270–274). New York: Routledge.

Burke, A., & Hammett, R. (2009). *Assessing new literacies: Perspectives from the classroom.* New York: Peter Lang.

Ertmer, P. (2005). Teacher pedagogical beliefs: The final frontier in our quest for technology integration. *Educational Technology Research and Development, 53*(4), 25–39.

Lankshear, C., & Knobel, M. (2008). *Digital literacies: Concepts, policies,and practices.* New York: Peter Lang.

Hagood, M.C., Provost, M., Skinner, E., & Egelson, P. (2008). Teachers' and students' literacy performance in and engagement with new literacies strategies in underperforming middle schools. *Middle Grades Research Journal, 3,* 57–95.

Hew, K. F., & Brush, T. (2007). Integrating technology into K–12 teaching and learning: Current knowledge gaps and recommendations for future research. *Educational Technology, Research, and Development, 55*(3), 223–252. Retrieved from http://courses.ischool.berkeley.edu/i290-pm4e/f10/files/Hew-Brush.pdf

Hutchinson, A., & Reinking, D. (2011). Teachers' perceptions of integrating information and communication technologies into literacy instruction: A national survey in the United States. *Reading Research Quarterly, 46*(4), 312–333.

International Reading Association. (1996). *Standards for the English language arts.* Newark, DE: Author.

International Reading Association. (2009). *New literacies and 21st-century technologies: A position statement of the International Reading Association.* Newark, DE: Author.

International Reading Association. (2010). *IRA standards for reading professionals.* Newark, DE: Author.

Merchant, A. (2009). Literacy in virtual worlds. *Journal of Research in Reading, 32*(1), 38–56.

National Governors Association Center for Best Practices, Council of Chief State School Officers. (2010). *Common Core State Standards: The standards for English language arts and literacy in history, social studies, science, and technical subjects.* Washington, DC: Author. Retrieved from http://www.corestandards.org/the-standards

Rideout, V. J., Foehr, U. G., & Roberts, D. F. (2010, January). *Generation M2: Media in the lives of 8- to 18-year-olds.* Washington, DC: Kaiser Family Foundation. Retrieved from http://www.kff.org/entmedia/8010.cfm

Author Biographies

JULIANNA ÁVILA is an assistant professor in the Department of English at the University of North Carolina at Charlotte, where she teaches undergraduate and graduate courses in English Education. A former high school teacher and literacy coach, she received her PhD from the University of California at Berkeley and has published in *Theory Into Practice, Pedagogies,* and *Teachers College Record.* She is the recipient of the 2011 AERA Writing and Literacies Steve Cahir Award. Her current research focuses on the ways in which teacher education students gain knowledge of critical literacies using digital tools.

CANDANCE DOERR-STEVENS is a doctoral candidate in Critical Literacy and English Education from the Department of Curriculum and Instruction at the University of Minnesota. She has taught writing at the elementary, junior high, and college levels and currently teaches education courses for pre-service and practicing teachers. Her current research interests include the emergent literacy practices involved in digital writing, in particular the rhetorical affordances of online role-play and identity practices of digital media composition.

ANTERO GARCIA, incoming assistant professor in the English department at Colorado State University, received his PhD in Urban Schooling at the Graduate School of Education and Information Studies at the University of California, Los Angeles. His research focuses on the role of digital media and game play in English education and critical literacies. He taught English and ESL at a high school in South Central Los Angeles for seven years.

MARGARET C. HAGOOD is an associate professor at the College of Charleston. She teaches undergraduate and graduate courses in literacy, including foundational and new literacies. She does research on adolescents and adults' literacies related to pop culture and identities, and is the co-editor of the *Journal of Adolescent & Adult Literacy*.

GLYNDA HULL is Professor of Education in Language, Literacy, and Culture at the University of California, Berkeley, and Visiting Research Professor at New York University. Her research examines digital technologies and new literacies, after-school as a space for learning, and community/school/university partnerships.

CHARLES K. KINZER is Professor of Communication and Technology, and coordinator of the program in Communication, Computing, and Technology in Education at Teachers College, Columbia University. He received his PhD in Language and Literacy from the University of California, Berkeley. His research interests include new literacies, and opportunities within virtual worlds and games for educational research and practice; recent work has appeared in *Educational Technology Research and Development (ETR&D)*, *Reading Research and Instruction*, *Instructional Science*, and *Reading Research Quarterly*. Dr. Kinzer has received the Computers in Reading Research Award from the International Reading Association. His work has been funded by the IERI/NSF, the U.S. Dept. of Education, FIPSE, the Office of Special Education Projects, and the Robert Wood Johnson Foundation.

CYNTHIA LEWIS is Professor of Critical Literacy and English Education at the University of Minnesota, where she holds the Emma M. Berkmaier Professorship in Educational Leadership. Her current research focuses on the relationship between literacy practices, social identities, and learning in urban schools. Her books include *Literary Practices as Social Acts: Power, Status, and Cultural Norms in the Classroom* and *Reframing Sociocultural Research: Identity, Agency, and Power* (with Patricia Enciso and Elizabeth Moje). Both books were awarded the Edward Fry book Award from the National Reading Conference.

SARAH LOHNES WATULAK is an assistant professor in the Department of Educational Technology and Literacy, College of Education, Towson University, Maryland. She earned her EdD in Communication and Education from Teachers College, Columbia University. Dr. Lohnes Watulak's research, which primarily focuses on undergraduate students' new literacies and technology practices, has been published in the *British Journal of Educational Technology*, *Digital Culture & Education*, the *Journal of Language and Literacy Education*, *Innovate*, and *Educational Technology: The Magazine for Managers of Change in Education*.

ALTHEA SCOTT NIXON is a visiting assistant professor at the Rossier School of Education at the University of Southern California. Prior to joining Rossier, she was a two-year University of California Presidential Postdoctoral Fellow at the

Laboratory for Comparative Human Cognition at the University of California, San Diego, and she received her PhD in Education at the University of California, Los Angeles. Dr. Nixon's research focuses on the ways children and adolescents from culturally, linguistically, and ethnically diverse backgrounds draw on new media technologies in learning and play.

ARNE OLAV NYGARD is a lecturer at the Norwegian National Center for Reading Education and Research, University of Stavanger. He holds a master's degree in Literacy Studies from the University of Stavanger and is currently a PhD candidate. His field of research is the use of digital technologies for reading and writing in school. He has published about design in digital media, most recently in M. Engebretsen's 2010 *Skrift/bilde/lyd: analyseavsammensattetekster* (Script/Image/Sound: Analysis of Multimodal Texts). He is active in professional development for high school teachers in Norway.

JESSICA ZACHER PANDYA is an associate professor at California State University, Long Beach, in Teacher Education and Liberal Studies. At CSULB, she teaches courses on literacy and urban education to undergraduate pre-service teachers. In her last project, she investigated the ways that urban children, including second-language learners, experience high-stakes assessments and highly structured language-arts curricula in high-poverty schools. She recently published a book in the Teachers College Press Language & Literacy Series about this project, titled *Overtested: How High-Stakes Accountability Fails English Language Learners* (2011). She has published about children's literacy practices in journals such as *Research in the Teaching of English*, *Review of Research in Education*, *Language Arts*, *Educational Studies*, and *Pedagogies: An International Journal*. She is currently collaborating with teachers in an urban bilingual K–12 school to operate to create critical digital literacies projects.

DANA E. SALTER is a doctoral candidate in Curriculum and Instruction at McGill University in Canada where her research focuses on issues in literacy, inclusion and exclusion, teacher education and digital media, and learning in alternative high school education contexts. Salter is also the North American program manager for the Beyond the Bricks Project. Salter has been a literacy, writing, and digital media and learning teacher for 12 years and has taught and designed curricula for middle school through graduate school courses in these disciplines in several countries (United States, Canada, South Korea, Turkey). Her most recent writing (2010) has been published in *Cultural Studies of Science Education*.

RAFI SANTO is an educator, researcher, technologist, and activist. He is currently pursuing his PhD in the Learning Sciences at Indiana University, with research and professional interests focusing on the intersection of new media, educational design, interest-driven learning, and online participatory cultures with a particular eye towards how to leverage these areas to create greater equity and democratization in society. He has consulted with foundations, community groups, NGOs, and educators to think about how they can add value to their work through meaningful integration of digital media, and he has more than 10 years of experience in youth development and education. Prior to starting his doctoral work, Rafi was a senior program associate at the youth development organization Global Kids.

CASSANDRA SCHARBER is an assistant professor of Learning Technologies and co-director of the Learning Technologies Media Lab at the University of Minnesota. Her research explores the nexus of literacy, power, and the possibilities that technologies offer in aiding the transformation of teaching and learning. For the past four years, Scharber has served as the co-editor for the Digital Literacies column for the *Journal of Adolescent and Adult Literacy*.

STEPHANIE ANNE SCHMIER is an adjunct assistant professor in the Rossier School of Education at the University of Southern California and holds an EdD in Curriculum and Teaching from Teachers College, Columbia University. She is interested in how youth take up new digital technologies, the ways in which adolescents' digital literacy practices travel across in- and out-of-school spaces, and the meanings that they make of these practices across multiple contexts in their lives. A recipient of a National Academy of Education Adolescent Literacy Fellowship, she has published in the journals *E- Learning* and *Language Arts*.

ANNA SMITH is a teacher, teacher educator, and educational researcher in English Education at New York University. Her dissertation research examines the transcontextual writing development of urban adolescent males. Anna's recently published co-authored book, *Developing Writers: Teaching and Learning in the Digital Age*, is available through Open University Press. Her work can also be found at www.developingwriters.org.

JESSICA DOCKTER TIERNEY is a doctoral candidate in Critical Literacy and English Education at the University of Minnesota. Her research examines how literacy practices with media shape racial identities with a particular interest in how white students imagine themselves as allies in anti-racist and social justice work. Her co-authored publications include "Redefining Rigor: Critical Engagement, Digital Media, and the New English/Language Arts" in the *Journal of Adolescent and Adult Literacy*, and "Reading Literature in Secondary School: Disciplinary Discourses in Global Times" in *The Handbook on Research on Children's and Young Adult Literature*.

Colin Lankshear & Michele Knobel
*General Editor*s

New literacies emerge and evolve apace as people from all
walks of life engage with new technologies, shifting values
and institutional change, and increasingly assume 'postmodern' orientations toward their everyday worlds. Despite many
efforts to take account of such changes, educational institutions largely remain out of touch with the range of new
ways of making and sharing meanings that increasingly mediate and shape the lives of the young people they teach and
the futures they face. This series aims to explore some key
dimensions of the changes occurring within social practices
of literacy and the educational challenges they present,
with a view to informing educational practice in helpful
ways. It asks what are new literacies, how do they impact on
life in schools, homes, communities, workplaces, sites of
leisure, and other key settings of human cultural engagement, and what significance do new literacies have for how
people learn and how they understand and construct knowledge. It aims to challenge established and 'official' ways
of framing literacy, and to ask what it means for literacies
to be powerful, effective, and enabling under current and
foreseeable conditions. Collectively, the works in this series will help to reorient literacy debates and literacy
education agendas.
    For further information about the series and submitting
manuscripts, please contact:

        Michele Knobel & Colin Lankshear
        Montclair State University
        Dept. of Education and Human Services
        3173 University Hall
        Montclair, NJ 07043
        michele@coatepec.net

    To order other books in this series, please contact our
Customer Service Department at:
        (800) 770-LANG (within the U.S.)
        (212) 647-7706 (outside the U.S.)
        (212) 647-7707 FAX

Or browse online by series at:
        www.peterlang.com